GOOD ENGLISH MODELS

A READER

A READER

GOOD ENGLISH MODELS

Barbara Mayo-Wells, Statewide Programs
Jeanne McNett, Asian Division
Martha Shull, European Division
Robert Speckhard, European Division

The University of Maryland

Harper & Row, Publishers
London

Cambridge
Mexico City
New York
Philadelphia
San Francisco
São Paulo
Singapore
Sydney

Series Editor: Dr Martha S. Shull, University of Maryland,
European Division.

Designer: Geri Davis, Quadrata Inc.

Project Editor: Byron O. Bush.

First published 1988

Harper & Row Ltd
Middlesex House
34–42 Cleveland Street
LONDON
W1P 5FB

Library of Congress Cataloging-in-Publication Data
Shull, Martha S.
Good English models: a reader/by Martha S. Shull, Jeanne M. McNett, Barbara Mayo-Wells.
p. cm.—(The University of Maryland series on good English writing)
ISBN 0-06-317501-0
1. College readers. 2. English language—Rhetoric. I. McNett, Jeanne M. II. Mayo-Wells, Barbara. III. Title IV. Series.
PE1417.S456 1988
808′.0427—dc19 87–35158
CIP

British Library Cataloguing in Publication Data
Shull, Martha S.
Good English models: a reader.
1. English language—Composition and exercises
I. Title II. McNett, Jeanne M.
III. Mayo-Wells, Barbara
808′.042 PE1413

ISBN 0-06-317501-0

Typeset by Rowland Phototypesetting Limited, Bury St Edmunds, Suffolk.
Printed and bound by Richard Clay Ltd, Chichester.

ACKNOWLEDGMENTS AND SOURCES

p. xi — From SEYMOUR, AN INTRODUCTION by J. D. Salinger

p. 2 — From THE OLD CURIOSITY SHOP by Charles Dickens

p. 3 — From PEONIES AND PONIES by Harold Acton

pp. 11–13 — "Abraham Lincoln Is Assassinated." From THE BLUE AND THE GRAY ed. by Henry Steele Commager with permission of the author.

pp. 14–19 — "Death of Lincoln." From LINCOLN by Gore Vidal. Copyright © 1984 by Gore Vidal. Reprinted by permission of Random House, Inc.

pp. 19–21 — "Shame." From NIGGER: AN AUTOBIOGRAPHY by Dick Gregory with Robert Lipsyte. Copyright © 1964 by Dick Gregory Enterprises, Inc. Reprinted by permission of the publisher, E. P. Dutton, a division of NAL Penguin, Inc.

pp. 22–23 — "Little Red Riding Hood Revisited" by Russell Baker. From *The New York Times*, January 13, 1980. Copyright © 1980 by The New York Times Company. Reprinted by permission.

pp. 23–24 — "Little Red Riding Hood and the Wolf." From ROALD DAHL'S REVOLTING RHYMES by Roald Dahl. Copyright © 1982 by Roald Dahl. Reprinted by permission of Alfred A. Knopf, Inc.

pp. 25–28 — "Miss Brill." From THE SHORT STORIES OF KATHERINE MANSFIELD by Katherine Mansfield. Copyright © 1922 by Alfred A. Knopf, Inc. and renewed 1950 by John Middleton Murry. Reprinted by permission of Alfred A. Knopf, Inc.

pp. 29–32 — "Plantation Life." From NARRATIVE OF THE LIFE OF FREDERICK DOUGLASS (1845) by Frederick Douglass. Reprinted by permission of Random House, Inc.

pp. 40–41 — "Rite of Passage, Right to Pick Up the Tab" by Richard Cohen. From *The Washington Post*, October 11, 1986. Copyright © 1986, Washington Post Writers Group, reprinted with permission.

pp. 42–44 — "Why women get the jobs." From *The Economist*, August 23, 1986. Reprinted with permission from The Economist, London.

pp. 55–57 — "Grant and Lee: A Study in Contrasts" by Bruce Catton. From THE AMERICAN STORY ed. by Earl Schenck Miers 1956. Copyright U.S. Capital Historical Society, All Rights Reserved. Used with Permission.

pp. 59–60 — "Two Ways of Seeing a River." From LIFE ON THE MISSISSIPPI, 1883 by Mark Twain.

p. 63 "There's a certain Slant of Light," (258) by Emily Dickinson. Reprinted by permission of the publishers and the Trustees of Amherst College from THE POEMS OF EMILY DICKINSON, edited by Thomas H. Johnson, Cambridge, Mass.: The Belknap Press of Harvard University Press, Copyright 1951, © 1955, 1979, 1983 by The President and Fellows of Harvard College.

pp. 65–66 "Democracy" by E. B. White. From THE WILD FLAG (Houghton Mifflin); Copyright © 1943, 1971 E. B. White. Originally in *The New Yorker*, July 3, 1943.

pp. 66–71 "Reading, the Most Dangerous Game" by Harold Brodkey. *The New York Times*, November 24, 1985 (Book Review). Copyright © 1985 by Harold Brodkey. Reprinted by permission of International Creative Management.

p. 72 "Recreation" entry from the Oxford English Dictionary reproduced by permission of Oxford University Press.

p. 74 "What Is Freedom?" by Wayne W. Dyer. Reprinted by permission of the author.

p. 81 From RICHARD THE THIRD by William Shakespeare.
From PREFACE: COURTEOUS READER by Benjamin Franklin.

pp. 90–92 "Why I Quit Watching Television" by P. J. O'Rourke. From *Parade*, December 8, 1985. Reprinted with permission of the author.

pp. 92–99 "Is History a Guide to the Future." From PRACTICING HISTORY by Barbara Tuchman. Copyright © 1966 by Alma Tuchman, Lucy T. Eisenberg and Jessica Tuchman Matthews. Reprinted by permission of Alfred A. Knopf, Inc.

pp. 100–102 "38 Who Saw Murder Didn't Call the Police" by Martin Gansberg. From *The New York Times*, March 17, 1964. Copyright © 1987 by The New York Times Company. Reprinted by permission.

pp. 102–103 "I Hear People Screaming; Of course, I Pass Them By" by A. M. Rosenthal. From *The New York Times*, February 12, 1987. Copyright © 1987 by The New York Times Company. Reprinted by permission.

pp. 104–106 "Insert Flap 'A' and Throw Away." From THE MOST OF S. J. PERELMAN by S. J. Perelman. Copyright © 1930, 1931, 1933, 1935, 1936–1953, 1955, 1956, 1958. Renewed © 1986 by Adam and Abby Perelman. Reprinted by permission of SIMON & SCHUSTER, INC.

pp. 107–109 "On the Benefits of Being Eaten" by Roger Lewin. From *Science*, May 1, 1987: Vol. 236, pp. 519–520. Copyright © 1987 by the AAAS.

pp. 111–112 "Naming of Parts." From A MAP OF VERONA by Henry Reed. Reprinted with permission of Jonathan Cape.

pp. 118–120 "Thirteen Ways of Looking at a Blackbird." From THE COLLECTED POEMS OF WALLACE STEVENS by Wallace Stevens.

Copyright 1923 and renewed 1951 by Wallace Stevens. Reprinted by permission of Alfred A. Knopf, Inc.

pp. 120–128 "Thirteen Ways of Looking at the Masters." From HUGGING THE SHORE by John Updike. Copyright © 1980 by John Updike. Reprinted by permission of Alfred A. Knopf, Inc.

pp. 128–135 "Proxemics in the Arab World." From THE HIDDEN DIMENSION by Edward T. Hall. Copyright © 1966 by Edward T. Hall. Reprinted by permission of Doubleday, a division of Bantam, Doubleday, Dell Publishing Group, Inc.

pp. 139–141 "Leave the Trade Deficit Alone" by Herbert Stein. From *The Wall Street Journal*, March 17, 1987. Reprinted by permission of The Wall Street Journal.

pp. 154–158 "No Contest: A case against competition" by Alfie Kohn. From *The New Age Journal*, October, 1986. Adapted from NO CONTEST: A CASE AGAINST COMPETITION. Boston: Houghton Mifflin, 1986. Courtesy of the author.

pp. 158–163 "The Other Side of Islam" from *The Economist*, February 15, 1986. Copyright © 1986 The Economist, distributed by Special Features.

CONTENTS

- **Preface** xi

- **Chapter One: Description** 1–36

Student Essays: "A Mere Smell", "What's in a Name?", "Poverty in Saigon", "The Closing Hour" and "The Unluckiest Person".
Abraham Lincoln Is Assassinated, Henry Steele Commager; *Death of Lincoln*, Gore Vidal; *Shame*, Dick Gregory; *Little Red Riding Hood Revisited*; Russell Baker; *Little Red Riding Hood and the Wolf*, Roald Dahl; *Miss Brill*, Katherine Mansfield; *Plantation Life*, Frederick Douglass.
Student Essays: "Plywood" and "How to Change a Tire on the Autostrada".

- **Chapter Two: Comparison and Contrast** 37–62

Student Essay: "Coming to Terms"
Rite of Passage, Right to Pick Up the Tab, Richard Cohen; *Why Women Get the Jobs*, The Economist.
Student Essays: "My Granddaughter and I", "Attending College", "Yard and Garden", "Separatism or Integration?", "Buying Faucet Washers", "Cities of Contrast" and "The Family Vacation—Then and Now".
Grant and Lee: A Study in Contrasts, Bruce Catton; *Two Ways of Seeing a River*, Mark Twain.

- **Chapter Three: Definition** 63–80

Democracy, E. B. White; *Reading, the Most Dangerous Game*, Harold Brodkey; *What Is Freedom?*, Wayne W. Dyer.
Students Essays: "What Is A Wife?", "The Good Life", "Offense or Defense?" and "A Basic Trainee".

• Chapter Four: Cause and Effect 81–110

Student Essays: “Erik—Problem Child”, “Mirror, Mirror”, “Answer to Question 7”, “Not Time Enough” and “Trade In Time”.
Why I Quit Watching Television, P. J. O’Rourke; *Is History A Guide to the Future?*, Barbara Tuchman; *38 Who Saw Murder Didn’t Call the Police*, Martin Gansberg; *I Hear People Screaming; Of Course, I Pass Them By*, A. M. Rosenthal; *Insert Flap “A” and Throw Away*, S. J. Perelman: *On the Benefits of Being Eaten*, Roger Lewin.

• Chapter Five: Classification 111–136

Naming of Parts, Henry Reed.
Student Essays: “First Date Foods” and “Dogs I’ve Known”.
Thirteen Ways of Looking at a Blackbird, Wallace Stevens; *Thirteen Ways of Looking at the Masters*, John Updike; *Proxemics in the Arab World*, Edward T. Hall.

• Chapter Six: Making a Case 137–164

Leave the Trade Deficit Alone, Herbert Stein.
Student Essays: “The Misconceptions About Mental Patients”, “Its Time Had Come”, “My Worst Enemy”, “A Popular Misconception”, “How to Do the Telemark”, “High School Social Clubs” and “Let’s Abolish Television”.
No Contest, A Case Against Competition, Alfie Kohn; *The Other Side of Islam*, The Economist.

• Appendix: Case Study—A Student Example 165–170

Student Essay: “Human Greed”.

PREFACE

> If only you'd remember before ever you sit down to write that you've been a reader long before you were ever a writer. You simply fix that fact in your mind, then sit very still and ask yourself, as a reader, what piece of writing in all the world Buddy Glass would want to read if he had his heart's choice. The next step is terrible, but so simple I can hardly believe it as I write it. You just sit down shamelessly and write the thing yourself . . . Oh, dare to do it, Buddy. Trust your heart.
>
> J. D. Salinger,
> From *Seymour, An Introduction*

Over the past four decades, The University of Maryland, through its Asian and European Divisions, has been providing college classes to Americans stationed overseas. Through these classes, thousands of adult students have been able to further their education. Classes have been, and continue to be, held wherever there are students: in the most modern, up-to-date classrooms, in the basements of housing units, on shipboard, in tents in the field, in caves, and even in the backs of jeeps under combat conditions.

Over the years, the English faculty of The University of Maryland, European Division, has relied on a short pamphlet of student essays and practical writing tips gathered from students and instructors. The student essay examples from that pamphlet have proven invaluable in hundreds of classrooms in twenty-three countries for thousands of American adult students because the paragraphs and compositions were written in direct response to assignments similar to those which you may be asked to prepare in a beginning composition class.

The present volume, *Good English Models*, incorporates the practical advice and student essays from this pamphlet and adds a large number of professional compositions. The result is a wide-ranging selection of writing models. Together with the other volumes in the Maryland series, *Good English Models*, offers you a sure-fire means of improving your writing skills.

Not all the student essays included in *Good English Models* were handed in to the instructor in the finished condition printed here;* in fact, practically all of them went through at least one revision, and many of them, several. Nor were all the student paragraphs and compositions necessarily "A" papers; some good, solid "B" and even some "C" papers have been included.

Each text in the series is arranged in an orderly, step-by-step fashion so that you can keep up with the class by following the texts if you have to miss one or more sessions. In this respect, the series may be used as a self-help guide on how to write. The University of Maryland instructors have learned that students serious enough about education to take freshman composition after their working hours or on week-ends are motivated enough to keep up even if they must miss a class or two.

Good English Models is designed especially for those of you who are apprehensive and anxious about taking an English course, particularly if you have been away from school for a long time.

Many students approach writing essays with the same wariness that they might the pleasures of the dentist's chair. If you are one of these nervous students, use this practical, easy-to-follow text; you will soon realize that others have not only survived the rigors of a composition course but actually have learned a great deal about writing and have gone on to excel in other courses because of their newly learned skills.

As you read these selections in *Good English Models*, consider the following questions:

1. **Has the writer really thought about the subject?**
   Is there something distinctive and fresh in what is said or does the writer disappoint you by merely echoing everyday commonplaces?
2. **Has the writer demonstrated straight thinking?**
   Does a singleness of purpose shape the writing? Are the themes clearly and logically developed?
3. **Has the writer organized effectively?**
   Does the writer use relevant examples to illustrate and support main ideas? Are necessary transitions and introductions provided so that you, the reader, can move smoothly from idea to idea maintaining a coherent train of thought?
4. **Has the writer shown a concern for phrasing and word usage?**
   Are particular words appropriate, accurate, and expressive? Are sentences varied, concisely tailored, and vividly phrased?
5. **Finally, is the writing mechanically acceptable?**
   Do the spelling, punctuation, and sentence construction meet the standards of acceptable prose?

*See *Human Greed* in the Appendix.

When you write your own paragraphs and papers, return to these questions. An instructor reading your writing will also have them in mind. Good luck and have a great time!

Martha S. Shull
Series Editor

CHAPTER

• ONE •

Description

Once upon a time—isn't that the way all good stories begin?—there was a newly enrolled college freshman who, at the age of forty, was uncomfortably aware that he no longer belonged to the "younger generation," but despite this was determined not to waste any more time getting started with his college education.

In his first class, English 101, he was asked to write a placement essay on one of the following time-worn topics: the seashore in summer or experiences at the university union.

Now this particular freshman had never spent his summers walking the beach at Nag's Head or sailing off the Maine coast, nor had he ever been part of the student union scene, ogling girls, swilling beer, and discussing the chances of the local football team. So his mind was as blank as the paper before him. He raised his hand gingerly. Our hero was not about to hand over good money for a course only to give up on the first round. A little bit wiser to the ways of life and also a little more gutsy than his eighteen year old classmates, he asked: "What sort of essay is this we're writing, anyway?"

What the teacher wanted from these students was a simple descriptive essay. The first topic—the seashore in summer—lends itself well to **static description**, and the second subject—experiences in the university union

—allows scope for an essay developed by narration, one of the most common types of **dynamic description**.

Static Description •

What is static description and how does this differ from dynamic description? Turn for a moment to this description of a man by Charles Dickens, a master of descriptive writing.

> The child was closely followed by an elderly man of remarkably hard features and forbidding aspect; and so low in stature as to be quite a dwarf, though his head and face were large enough for the body of a giant. His black eyes were restless, sly, and cunning; his mouth and chin, bristly with the stubble of a coarse hard beard; and his complexion was one of that kind which never looks clean or wholesome. But what added most to the grotesque expression of his face, was a ghastly smile, which, appearing to be the mere result of habit and to have no connection with any mirthful or complacent feeling, constantly revealed the few discolored fangs that were yet scattered in his mouth, and gave him the aspect of a panting dog. His dress consisted of a large high-crowned hat, a worn dark suit, a pair of capacious shoes, and a dirty white neckerchief sufficiently limp and crumpled to disclose the greater portion of his wiry throat. Such hair as he had, was of a grizzled black, cut short and straight upon his temples, and hanging in a frowsy fringe about his ears. His hands, which were of a rough coarse grain, were very dirty; his fingernails were crooked, long, and yellow.
>
> Charles Dickens
> From *The Old Curiosity Shop*

You will note that this passage is purely descriptive. Nothing actually happens: no events occur; nobody runs; nobody picks a fight; nobody lets out a blood-curdling scream; nobody lobs a custard pie. In fact, there is *no* action. The writer simply describes.

The following passage also describes, but in contrast to Dickens' selection, Harold Acton leaves us with a "spirit of place," the feeling of having been *somewhere* rather than of having made a new acquaintance.

> In Elvira's garden only the cicadas were alive, their tireless neurasthenic rattle grinding away as if eternity belonged to them. Everything else had been baked or suffocated, paralysed or hypnotized by the heat: the rocks were like chunks of smouldering lava; the muscles of the trees inert and swollen, their twisted branches lolled leadenly on the dust-laden air, and the dry turf exuded a funereal incense of its own. Elvira felt she was in a graveyard. Tombs

surrounded her. But graveyards and tombs were usually cool, mossy places. Here there was no coolness even among the shadows.

Harold Acton
From *Peonies and Ponies*

Both passages create strong images. They appeal to our senses and force their subjects into our experience. In addition, both passages are crammed full of adjectives and adverbs—the "color" words of language that add flavor, sound, scent, vision and texture to the language to stir the reader's imagination. Not once, however, does anything happen, for these brief passages are static descriptions, painting word pictures much as a camera captures images. Static descriptions, in fact, are evocative, verbal, still lifes.

The question now for you, the student writer, is how to use the technique of static description in developing a topic. Can you explain an issue or argue a point by describing it? In other words, how may static description be used in the context of expository writing? Quite simply, you must state your **controlling idea**—the purpose for writing the paragraph or essay—in a topic sentence and then develop that idea by means of descriptive detail. Any expository writing is expository by virtue of the fact that it "exposes" a point; it becomes descriptive expository writing if the means of exposition is description.

1. Read the following paragraph to determine the point the student writer is trying to make.
2. List all the adjectives and adverbs that express the five senses.
3. What other adjectives or adverbs might you use that would sharpen the reader's response?

A Mere Smell

I have always been fascinated by the fact that a mere smell has the power to trigger my memory and evoke the past.

Last evening while my friends and I were dining at the local greasy spoon, a man seated at a nearby table lighted up a cigar. As my tablemates were shrieking in hygienic horror at the stench and imploring the owner to force this reprobate to smoke his filthy weed out of doors, the rich aroma of the cigar filled the cramped, dingy cafe and momentarily transported me to my childhood. As the plummy fragrance wafted from the glowing red-tipped cigar, I was little again, seated comfortably on my grandfather's generous lap, nodding off with the pleasant exhaustion that comes after a day's hard play in the sunshine, and listening to the rumble of deep authoritative voices arguing over cattle prices and chuckling over dirty stories. In my revery for a moment I could almost feel the rough edge of my grandfather's linen suit pocket and the slippery silk of his hankie. For a moment yesterday I breathed the heady fumes of the old gentleman's cigar, and the room reeked of security, stability, and contentment.

Dynamic Description •

The second type of description—dynamic description—relies just as much on pure descriptive detail as static description, but as its name suggests, uses movement or action to further the point. Here, the writer need not rely solely on adjectives and adverbs for "color," but also makes use of action words—verbs—for dynamic effect. Where static description may be likened to "verbal still lifes," dynamic description works much as a roving camera, capturing images by swinging this way and that. Once again, if the composition is an expository paragraph or essay, a topic sentence must be included to make a writer's point.

1. Read the following student paragraph and ask yourself whether it is dynamic or static?
2. Check your answer by listing the verbs that indicate action and motion or bring a sense of life to the description.

What's in a Name?

My basic training drill sergeant was not at all what I had expected. I had pictured a tall, burly, husky-built, deep-voiced male who would command that we live our lives for him during our eight-week stay. Instead, we were greeted by a short, cherubic-faced young woman with a pixie haircut who could have easily passed for a high school senior. Little did we know that this innocent looking teenager was all drill sergeant and more. It was almost as if she had something to prove and looking at her appearance—she did! Throughout the first few weeks, we learned to take this lady very seriously.

On one occasion when I was being "corrected" by this unobtrusive-looking person, she stood within inches of my face and had to look almost straight up at me. In my mind's eye the whole scene seemed comical; and I had to refrain from laughing out loud. Within minutes, however, she had put fear into my soul and I never again felt an urge to laugh at her. I realized by this incident that even though her size and facial features were against her, she excellently compensated for this lack of physical threat with her perfect attire, forceful manner, and self-confidence.

Our platoon spent many week-ends on the drill field and long nights in the latrine with our Kiwi polish and boots while other platoons relaxed and slept. All of the hard work paid off for us when we won the Platoon of the Week seven out of eight weeks. To this day, I still don't know if this was an honor or just that no less was expected by Drill Sergeant Esposito.

The student writer of the next paragraph is not content to tell us merely that "there is poverty in Saigon." He is aware that poverty is a general and very abstract word that needs to be fleshed out with details before it becomes vividly clear. Therefore, he provides us with illustrative details that create a specific, concrete glimpse of the overwhelming poverty in Saigon in the seventies.

Poverty in Saigon

While stationed in Saigon, I was overwhelmed by the poverty of the Vietnamese. The dress of most of them consisted of shabby-looking silk "pajamas" that always looked dirty, probably because these people lack detergents. They made their huts of straw, mud, and miscellaneous materials which they could scrounge. These huts were perched on stilts emerging from the water of the refuse-filled Saigon River; they were there because the area was close to downtown and the "real estate" cost nothing. As the "rich" American, I was constantly pursued by the beggars that crowded the streets of Saigon. Some were children barely able to walk; some were men and women who looked a hundred years old. They did not expect much, maybe five piasters (about six and one-half cents) to acquire a small bag of rice or a piece of bread in order to survive another day. As prevalent as the begging was the thieving. While relaxing at a sidewalk cafe, I made the mistake of turning my back to my purchases—a pair of hand-carved wooden statues. One of the ever-present opportunists deftly relieved me of my purchases. On numerous occasions, as I walked down the streets of Saigon, a sad-faced Vietnamese mother would approach me with a baby in her arms and beg me to take her child. They did not do this because they did not love their children; a child to a Vietnamese parent is sacred, cherished above all else. Rather, those mothers believed that I, an American, could provide better for their babies than they could.

1. What descriptive details work especially well to help you visualize the scene?
2. Do illustrative details like "I made the mistake of turning my back," recreate for you relevant incidents which this student has experienced? How many other examples can you find?
3. What else is the student attempting to do in addition to creating atmosphere and describing a slice of life?

In reading the following student paragraph look for the specific details that make a sociological comment.

The Closing Hour

The closing hour at an English pub is a scene of hurried activity. The pub, now heavy with pungent tobacco smoke, rouses itself for a final effort before the last bell. Laden with empty pint glasses, last-minute drinkers charge the bar. Familiar faces waft by, cutting and parrying for position. Ashtrays, overflowing from an evening of heavy use, are pushed aside to make room for an elbow or a glass. Familiar voices rise and fall. There's Dave, the cheerfully plump landlord, grinning and hopping from table to table, loaded down with good night cheer and empties. The first drinking-up bell is sounded, but ignored. A blonde tart's laughter ricochets across the pub from where she sits, ringed round by male companions. Even at the closing hour she remains in command. "I can't go home with all of you lads!" The man with the retired RAF face makes his last proud march to the bar, his moustache bristling. At a corner table, an equine

> lady drones on and on; her husband continues to nod mechanically, as he has been doing all evening. The barmaid winks. At the same moment the lights dim. A glass shatters like a wind chime. The last bell sounds and the exodus begins, slowly, unhurriedly, reluctantly—accompanied by giggles and sighs.

Each of the three preceding paragraphs illustrates the truth of the old axiom that beginning writers do best when they write about what they **know best**. The power of personal experience in the context of good expository writing should not ever be underestimated. This is crucial when writing an essay answer for an examination. Essay answers show the instructor what you, the student knows and what you have learned, as well as how well you can write. Any essay question that begins "describe, illustrate, show, delineate, relate, or explain" is asking for an expository description.

THE TOPIC SENTENCE

A well-phrased statement of intention and direction is a vital first step in all writing. This first step is often accomplished by the use of a **topic sentence**. Notice that each of the three preceding student paragraphs contains a topic sentence:

1. My basic training drill sergeant was not at all what I had expected.
2. While stationed in Saigon, I was overwhelmed by the poverty of the Vietnamese.
3. The closing hour at an English pub is a scene of hurried activity.

Each of these topic sentences is a compressed statement that clues the reader into what the writer wants to say about the subject.

THE CONTROLLING IDEA

Note that each of the three sentences contains a kernel of words which are particularly important in stating the writer's intentions:

1. "not at all what I had expected"—an unexpected, untypical sergeant.
2. "overwhelmed by the poverty of the Vietnamese"—not just the poverty in Saigon.
3. "the closing hour at an English pub"—not the pub activity at other times of the day.

Such a kernel of words is termed the **controlling idea**: that idea which controls what goes into the paragraph and what does not go into it. Other terms commonly used for this "kernel of words" are the limiting idea or the narrowing idea.

POINT OF VIEW

In an essay or paragraph, **point of view** indicates the writer's attitude, angle, approach or response to the subject matter. When a writer creates an effective topic sentence, his or her point of view enters that topic sentence through the controlling idea.

Look at the three topic sentences on p. 6 and note that each defines the subject matter of the article, for example *poverty*. The topic sentence also indicates the student writer's point of view and expresses the controlling or narrowing idea, e.g. *the poverty in Saigon is overwhelming*. "Overwhelming" at once expresses the point of view and is the key word in this writer's controlling idea.

BLOCKING-OUT PATTERN

In planning your essay, try working with a three-column **blocking-out pattern** on a piece of scratch paper. In the first column, write in a possible subject. In the second column, write in a word or phrase reflecting your attitude, response, angle, approach, etc. Having settled on the word or group of words which best states your point of view, in the third column write a few specific details which support and clarify your point of view. More details will occur to you as you work out the blocking-out pattern.

SUBJECT MATTER	CONTROLLING IDEA	DESCRIPTIVE DETAILS
poverty of Vietnamese	overwhelming poverty in Saigon	dirty, shabby pajamas straw and mud huts begging in streets

CHOICE OF SUBJECT

Choose a subject about which you can write with some authority and personal knowledge. In most instances writers do best with subjects derived from their own genuine interests or first-hand observations. For example, as an American, you are acquainted with your country and fellow Americans. Some of our customs and institutions, attitudes, living patterns, hopes, fears, strengths, weaknesses, and goals may be easy for you to write about since you know them well. Of course, in a single paragraph or short composition you will need to limit your subject sharply. Read "The Closing Hour" again and note how that student chose to write about one small aspect of the subject in detail rather than cover the entire topic superficially.

Warm-up Exercises

To learn how to develop specific and concrete examples of your own, try the two following "warm-up exercises."

EXERCISE 1

a. *Adjectives*—on a piece of paper, write down specific adjectives for these general adjectives:

   red (scarlet, vermilion, maroon, etc.)

blue	tired	good
damaged	bad	nice

b. *Adverbs of manner*—similarly write down specific adverbs for the following:

   fast (quickly, speedily, hurriedly, etc.)

carefully	softly	hungrily
well	slowly	happily

c. *Verbs and verb forms*—list some specific verbs and verb forms for the following:

   walk (stroll, amble, stride, etc.)

get	go	write
talk	come	break

EXERCISE 2

a. On a scratch pad, compose some specific and concrete incidents which effectively illustrate general and abstract terms. For example, "She slipped her hand about Tommy's waist, and then, when he turned to smile at her, she gave his belt a gentle tug." Try to come up with at least three examples.

b. If you are having trouble creating your own examples, read through the three student compositions again. Write down the illustrative examples you find. Now, try your hand at rewriting three of those.

c. Compose illustrative examples for such general and abstract terms as: phoney behavior, discrimination, blind loyalty, negligence. If you find you are having problems in developing illustrative details for a general term, read how one student handled the general term, *greed* in the Appendix, pp. 165–170.

Narration •

Narration means telling a story and is the natural outgrowth of writing an experiential static or dynamic expository description. Expository narration means telling a story with a point.

Naturally, there has to be some sort of order to the narration or it will misfire. The writer needs to marshall the details so that, once combined, they make the point of the story clear and bring the writing to a logical conclusion. The controlling idea, or topic sentence, is the thread that ties the whole sequence of details together. All details must focus upon the controlling idea in order that the piece appears unified. In theory, anyone who can write a grocery list (an essay outline) and organize a shopping trip (the arrangement of that outline) can write a simple narration, especially if it's done with a little imagination.

Warm-up Exercises

EXERCISE 1

a. Using a personal experience, try your hand at writing a dynamic description that makes a social comment.

b. Try composing an illustrative incident for a general or abstract term such as phoney behavior, discrimination, blind loyalty, and negligence.

EXERCISE 2

a. How does this student develop the controlling idea in the following essay?

b. What dynamic details does the student use to create a sense of action?

c. The student uses details to create static description in this essay as well as dynamic. Which ones are they?

The Unluckiest Person

A freak accident with one of the world's unluckiest people on a bitterly cold, damp night in November is an experience I'll never forget. Frost had formed on the dead grass and shimmered in the brilliant moonlight like millions of diamonds carelessly strewn about the North Georgia countryside. The hour was late and the neighborhood lay quiet. In the distance I could hear the familiar sounds of Amos Ledbetter's prize-winning coon dog howling at the new moon in a feeble attempt to rid the sky of its omniscient presence. My wife, Jackie, and I were returning home from The Dugout, Bartow County's only respectable country honky-tonk, when suddenly, without warning a speeding Ford pick-up ran a stop sign. Brakes squealed as skidding tires unsuccessfully bit at the slippery pavement. The deathly quiet of the moment was shattered by the sound of colliding vehicles. Otha Void Smeltzer had crashed upon the scene! His antiquated excuse for a truck had just plowed headlong into my shiny new Buick Skylark.

Otha was the first to manage an exit from the tangled mess that he had just caused. His dirty jeans, well worn flannel shirt, and cheap western boots gave him the appearance of a down-on-his-luck field hand. As he meandered up to survey the damage, the two vehicles were steaming from their damaged radiators and hissing at one another like two angry alley cats. As he scratched his balding head, he strolled over to my wife's window and sheepishly peeked inside. "Are you folks OK in there?" he asks. "I've been meanin' to have those brakes fixed for some time now. I just ain't got around to it yet." Again he asked, his curiosity at its peak by now, "Are you folks sure you're OK? How come you ain't answered my question?" As I sat behind the wheel, the sudden confusion of the moment began to fade and I thankfully realized that no one was seriously injured, only a bit shaken up. "Yeah, we're both fine. Is anybody in your truck hurt?" I responded. "Nah," he answered, "It's just me and the dog, and we're OK too."

He walked over to his truck bumper, calmly sat down, and with his face buried in his hands, suddenly started sobbing. I quickly jumped out of the car and asked him why he's crying and if there is anything I can do to help. His answer sounded like something out of the soap opera, Days of our Lives. "I just lost my job today," he said. "Every year about this time they lay a bunch of us off 'cause business slacks off around the holidays. They'll hire us back as soon as they can, they always do. But that ain't all—my wife left me last week after fifteen years of marriage; my unwed teenage daughter is pregnant again; the truck ain't insured; and my driver's license got pulled last month 'cause the cops caught me drinkin' and drivin'." Any anger that I might have had suddenly subsided as I watched this wretched soul pouring out his trials and tribulations. I knew instinctively that this person must constantly stumble through life with an ever-present, threatening black cloud over his head. He was by far the unluckiest person that I'd ever met.

The seven selections that follow are essentially descriptive in form and illustrate much of what has been discussed about narration so far.

The first, a selection from Henry Steele Commager's two volume history of the Civil War, *The Blue and the Gray*, is an example of the use of primary source material. The famous twentieth century American historian, Henry Steel Commager, quotes from an account of Lincoln's death, as written by Gideon Wells in his diary, to form a narrative memoir by a witness of the event.

The second selection, Gore Vidal's description of the day Lincoln died, is a fictional narration. Note how it compliments the selection from *The Blue and the Gray*.

Dick Gregory's "Shame" is also a kind of descriptive narrative memoir. Just as letters, diaries and journals provide the reader with a view of another era or the sense of a personal experience, so do memoirs.

The two professionally written essays, one by Russell Baker, the other by Roald Dahl, also use descriptive techniques but of a different nature.

Katherine Mansfield's "Miss Brill" develops the character of a single person while the selection from the writings of Frederick Douglass gives a feeling for an entire group of people, the slave community on a large plantation that existed before the Civil War. Important, too, is his use of description to make a social commentary on slavery and community.

ABRAHAM LINCOLN IS ASSASSINATED

Lincoln had gone to Richmond the day after the Confederates had evacuated it—calling, while there, on Mrs. Pickett—and then had returned to Washington in time to make a memorable address on reconstruction. On the evening of April 14 he went to Ford's Theater to see Laura Keene in an English comedy, Our American Cousin. *John Wilkes Booth, brother of the more famous Edwin Booth, had concocted a plot to assassinate all the principal officers of the government; a Southern sympathizer, he thought that this might undo the work of the Union armies and save the South. Entering Lincoln's box he sent a ball through the President's head; then leaped to the stage, shouting,* "Sic semper tyrannis!" *and made good his escape.*

The moving story of Lincoln's death is told by the sorrowing Gideon Wells in an excerpt from his diary.

I had retired to bed about half past-ten on the evening of the 14th of April, and was just getting asleep when Mrs. Welles, my wife, said some one was at our door. Sitting up in bed, I heard a voice twice call to John, my son, whose sleeping-room was on the second floor directly over the front entrance. I arose at once and raised a window, when my messenger, James Smith, called to me that Mr. Lincoln, the President, had been shot, and said Secretary Seward and his son, Assistant Secretary Frederick Seward, were assassinated. James was much alarmed and excited. I told him his story was very incoherent and improbable, that he was associating men who were not together and liable to attack at the same time. "Where," I inquired, "was the President when shot?" James said he was at Ford's Theatre on 10th Street. "Well," said I, "Secretary Seward is an invalid in bed in his house yonder on 15th Street." James said he had been there, stopped in at the house to make inquiry before alarming me.

I immediately dressed myself, and, against the earnest remonstrance and appeals of my wife, went directly to Mr. Seward's, whose residence was on the east side of the square, mine being on the north. James accompanied me. As we were crossing 15th Street, I saw four or five men in earnest consultation, standing under the lamp on the corner by St. John's Church. Before I had got half across the street, the lamp was suddenly extinguished and the knot of persons rapidly dispersed. For a moment, and but a moment I was disconcerted to find myself in darkness, but recollecting that it was late and about time for the moon to rise, I proceeded on, not having lost five steps, merely making a pause without stopping. Hurrying forward into 15th Street, I found it pretty full of people, especially so near the residence of Secretary Seward, where there were many soldiers as well as citizens already gathered.

Entering the house, I found the lower hall and office full of persons, and among them most of the foreign legations, all anxiously inquiring what truth there was in the horrible rumors afloat. I replied that my object was to ascertain the facts. Proceeding through the hall to the stairs, I found one, and I think two, of the servants there holding the crowd in check. The servants were frightened and appeared relieved to see me. I hastily asked what truth there was in the story that an assassin or assassins had entered the house and assaulted the Secretary. They said it was true, and that Mr. Frederick was also badly injured. They wished me to go up, but no others. . . . As I entered, I met Miss Fanny Seward, with whom I exchanged a single word, and proceeded to the foot of the bed. Dr. Verdi and, I think, two others were there. The bed was saturated with blood. The Secretary was lying on his back, the upper part of his head covered by a cloth, which extended down over his eyes. His mouth was open, the lower jaw dropping down. I exchanged a few whispered words with Dr. V. Secretary Stanton, who came after but almost simultaneously with me, made inquiries in a louder tone till admonished by a word from one of the physicians. We almost immediately withdrew and went into the adjoining front room, where lay Frederick Seward. His eyes were open but he did not move them, nor a limb, nor did he speak. Doctor White, who was in attendance, told me he was unconscious and more dangerously injured than his father.

As we descended the stairs, I asked Stanton what he had heard in regard to the President that was reliable. He said the President was shot at Ford's Theatre, that he had seen a man who was present and witnessed the occurrence. I said I would go immediately to the White House. Stanton told me the President was not there but was at the theatre. "Then," said I, "let us go immediately there." . . .

The President had been carried across the street from the theatre, to the house of a Mr. Peterson. We entered by ascending a flight of steps above the basement and passing through a long hall to the rear, where the President lay extended on a bed, breathing heavily. Several surgeons were present, at least six, I should think more. Among them I was glad to observe Dr. Hall, who, however, soon left. I inquired of Dr. H., as I entered, the true condition of the President. He replied the President was dead to all intents, although he might live three hours or perhaps longer.

The giant sufferer lay extended diagonally across the bed, which was not long enough for him. He had been stripped of his clothes. His large arms, which were occasionally exposed, were of a size which one would scarce have expected from his spare appearance. His slow, full respiration lifted the clothes with each breath that he took. His features were calm and striking. I had never seen them appear to better advantage than for the first hour, perhaps, that I was there. After that, his right eye began to swell and that part of his face became discolored.

Senator Sumner was there, I think, when I entered. If not he came in soon after, as did Speaker Colfax. Mr. Secretary McCulloch, and the other members of the Cabinet, with the exception of Mr. Seward. A double guard was stationed at the door and on the sidewalk, to repress the crowd, which was of course highly excited and anxious. The room was small and overcrowded. The surgeons and members of the Cabinet were as many as should have been in the room, but there were many more, and the hall and other rooms in the front or main house were full. One of these rooms was occupied by Mrs. Lincoln and her attendants, with Miss Harris. Mr. Dixon and Mrs. Kinney came to her about twelve o'clock. About once an hour Mrs. Lincoln would repair to the bedside of her dying husband and with lamentation and tears remain until overcome by emotion.

(April 15.) A door which opened upon a porch or gallery, and also the windows, were kept open for fresh air. The night was dark, cloudy, and damp, and about six it began to rain. I remained in the room until then without sitting or leaving it, when, there being a vacant chair which some one left at the foot of the bed, I occupied it for nearly two hours, listening to the heavy groans, and witnessing the wasting of life of the good and great man who was expiring before me.

About 6 A.M. I experienced a feeling of faintness and for the first time after entering the room a little past eleven, I left it and the house, and took a short walk in the open air. It was a dark and gloomy morning, and rain set in before I returned to the house, some fifteen minutes [later]. Large groups of people were gathered every few rods, all anxious and solicitous. Some one or more from each group stepped forward as I passed, to inquire into the condition of the President, and to ask if there was no hope. Intense grief was on every countenance when I replied that the President could survive but a short time. The colored people especially—and there were at this time more of them, perhaps, than of whites—were overwhelmed with grief. . . .

A little before seven, I went into the room where the dying President was rapidly drawing near the closing moments. His wife soon after made her last visit to him. The death-struggle had begun. Robert, his son, stood with several others at the head of the bed. He bore himself well, but on two occasions gave way to overpowering grief and sobbed aloud, turning his head and leaning on the shoulder of Senator Sumner. The respiration of the President became suspended at intervals, and at last entirely ceased at twenty-two minutes past seven. . . .

I went after breakfast to the Executive Mansion. There was a cheerless cold rain and everything seemed gloomy. On the Avenue in front of the White House were several hundred colored people, mostly women and children, weeping and wailing their loss. This crowd did not appear to diminish through the whole of that cold, wet day; they seemed not to know what was to be their fate since their great benefactor was dead, and their hopeless grief affected me more than almost anything else, though strong and brave men wept when I met them.

Henry Steele Commager
From *The Blue and the Gray*

DEATH OF LINCOLN

The afternoon was clear and bright; and the spring flowers were already beginning to blossom, helter-skelter, where the military encampments had been at the foot of Washington's monument and in the grounds of the Smithsonian Institution, recently razed by fire. A cavalry detachment accompanied the carriage. Earlier that day, Lincoln and Stanton had argued, yet again, about protection. Lincoln thought that now, with the war over, he was of less interest to the assassin. Stanton said that now, more than ever, he was in danger. Lamon would have agreed; but he was in Richmond. Nevertheless, just before Lamon had gone South, he warned the President to stay away from the theater or any public place where his presence had been advertised in advance.

"Perhaps," Lincoln said, as the carriage swung down the less-peopled side of Pennsylvania Avenue, "we might stay at home tonight."

"But it's Laura Keene's last night; and she is counting on us." Mary frowned. "I cannot get over General Grant's rudeness. Yesterday he was coming with us, and today he is not."

"I suppose it is Mrs. Grant, wanting to get home to her children." The carriage paused as a line of ambulances passed in front of them. When Lincoln was recognized, the wounded cheered him. He removed his hat and held it in his hand until the last ambulance had passed.

Mary was concerned with Mrs. Grant. "I suspect that she does not dare to face me after the scene that she made at City Point. I have never seen anyone so out of control. She is an ambitious little thing. So is he, for that matter. I was watching from the window when he walked back to Willard's this morning. There was an enormous crowd all around him, as if he were you."

"Well, he isn't me but he *is* General Grant, Mother, and that's something very special."

The carriage proceeded down a side street toward the Navy Yard. "He is running for president. I can tell. I can always tell."

"So you can. So you can. And he's welcome to it. We've had our crack at it. So if he wants to take over, let him."

"Four years," said Mary. "When I was young that sounded like forever. Now it is nothing. Four weeks. Four days. Time rushes past us like the snowflake on the river."

"When it's all over," said Lincoln, "I want to go west. I want to see California and the Pacific Ocean."

"Well, *I* want to go to Europe. I must see Paris . . ."

"Certainly, a lot of Paris has already come your way, Molly. Fact, Paris clings to your person from shoes to hats."

"Oh, Father! I buy so little now. Keckley makes everything, anyway. Where will we live?"

"Springfield. Where else? I'll practise some law with Herndon . . ."

"If you do, I will divorce you." Mary was indignant. "Father, how could you live in Springfield now? Much less practise law with Billy."

"What else am I to do? I'll be sixty-one years old. I'll have to do something to make a living. So that means the law . . ."

"In Chicago then." Mary had already envisaged a fine new house on the lake-front, where palaces were now beginning to rise.

"If we can afford it. Well, today I refuse to be worried about anything." Although gaunt, Lincoln's face was like that of a man who had just been let out of prison. "I have not been so happy in many years."

"Don't say that!" Mary was suddenly alarmed. She had heard him say these exact words once before; with ominous result.

"Why not? It is true."

"Because . . . the last time you said those same words was just before Eddie died."

Lincoln looked at her a moment, then he looked at the Capitol on its hill to their left. "I feel so personally—complete," he said, "now that the new lid is on. And I also feel so relieved that Congress has left town, and the place is empty."

After dinner that evening, Mary went to change her clothes for the theater while Lincoln sat in the upstairs oval parlor and gossiped with the new governor and the new senator from Illinois; he also treated them to a reading from Petroleum V. Nasby. Then Noah Brooks announced the Speaker of the House, Mr. Colfax, a man who never ceased smiling no matter what the occasion. "Sir, I must know"—he smiled radiantly, teeth yellow as maize—"if you intend to call a special session of the Congress in order to consider Mr. Stanton's proposals for reconstruction."

If Lincoln was taken aback by the reference to Stanton's supposedly private memorandum, he made no sign. "No, I shall not call a special session. After the superhuman labors of the last session, I believe Congress deserves its rest."

Colfax beamed his disappointment. "In that case, I shall make my long-deferred trip to the west."

Lincoln spoke with some interest of Colfax's proposed tour of the mountain states. Then Lincoln was reminded that when Senator Sumner was recently in Richmond, he had purloined the gavel of the speaker of the Confederate Congress. "Sumner is threatening to give it to Stanton. But I want you to have it, as proper custodian for this particular spoil of war."

Colfax's delight was hyenaish. "I should like nothing better."

"Well, you tell Sumner I said you're to have it."

Mary swept into the room; splendidly turned out for the theater. She was unanimously complimented.

"I think," said Brooks, looking at his watch, "that it is time to go."

"All in all," said Lincoln, collecting Mary's arm, "I would rather not go. But as the widow said to the preacher . . ."

"Oh, Father, not that one!" Bickering amiably, they proceeded downstairs to the waiting carriage, which contained the daughter of Senator Harris of New York and her fiancé, Major Rathbone, the best company that Hay could find at such short notice.

As Lincoln got into the carriage, he said to Crook, "Goodbye." Then an old friend from Chicago appeared in the driveway, waving his hat. "I'm sorry, Isaac, we're going to the theater. Come see me tomorrow morning." Accompanied by one officer from the Metropolitan Police, the carriage pulled out into the avenue.

A long row of carriages blocked the entire east side of Tenth Street, except for the main entrance to the brightly illuminated theater where Mr. Ford's young brother was waiting. The play had already begun.

As young Mr. Ford led the presidential party up the stairs to the dress circle, where a box had been prepared for them at stage-left, the sharp-eyed actors onstage recognized the President and they began to interpolate lines of dialogue. A heavy play on the word "draught" was being made, which allowed the irrepressible Laura Keene to look up at the Presidential box and exclaim, "The draft has been suspended!" Then she shook her head vigorously until her much-admired ringlets threatened to detach themselves from her cap.

Thus cued, the audience began to cheer the President and General Grant. But it was only the President who showed himself, for a moment, in the box. Then Lincoln sat back in a large rocking chair; and a curtain screened him from the audience.

At ten o'clock, mounted and armed, Booth, Herold and Payne were in the street. At a gesture from Booth, David and Payne set out for Seward's house, while Booth rode up the back alley to Ford's Theater, where a stagehand helped him tie up his bay mare. Booth then walked around to the front of the theater, and entered the lobby. He waved at the doorkeeper. "I hope you don't want me to buy a ticket?"

The man said, no; and continued to count ticket receipts, while several cronies stared at Booth until the doorkeeper introduced them to the youngest star, who asked for a chew of tobacco. Then, as Booth made his way up the stairs to the dress circle, he saw that there was an empty chair to the presidential box. The policeman was not at his post. This was an unexpected bit of good luck.

In the half-light from the proscenium arch, Booth opened the door and stepped inside the vestibule to the box. The President was only a few feet in front of him, silhouetted by calcium light. To the President's right sat Mrs. Lincoln and to their right a young couple occupied a sofa.

As the audience laughed, Booth removed from his right-hand pocket a brass derringer; and from his left-hand pocket a long, highly sharpened dagger.

Mary had been resting her elbow, casually, on Lincoln's forearm; but then, aware that this was a most unladylike thing to do, she sat up straight and whispered into Lincoln's ear, "What will Miss Harris think of my lolling up against you like this?"

Lincoln murmured, "Why, Mother, she won't think anything about it."

At that moment, from a distance of five feet, Booth fired a single shot into the back of the President's head. Without a sound, Lincoln leaned back in the chair; and his head slumped to the left until it was stopped by the wooden partition. Mary turned not to Booth but to her husband, while in the wings, an actor stared, wide-eyed, at the box. He had seen everything.

Major Rathbone threw himself upon Booth, who promptly drove his dagger straight at the young man's heart. But Rathbone's arm deflected the blade. Miss Harris shrieked, as Booth shoved past her and jumped onto the railing of the box. Then, with the sort of athletic gesture that had so delighted his admirers in this same theater, he leapt the twelve feet from box to stage. But, as on several other occasions when Booth's effects proved to be more athletic and improvised than dramatic and calculated, he had not taken into account the silken bunting that decorated the front of the box. The spur of one boot got entangled in the silk, causing him to fall, off-balance, to the stage, where a bone in his ankle snapped.

Rathbone shouted from the box, "Stop that man!" Booth shouted something unintelligible at the audience; and hurried off stage.

In the box, Mary now stood, screaming. Miss Harris tried to comfort her. Laura Keene herself came; and she held the unconscious President's head in her lap until a doctor arrived to examine the wound. The bullet had gone into the back of Lincoln's head above the left ear and then downward to the right, stopping just below the right eye.

At the White House, Hay and Robert Lincoln were sitting comfortably in the upstairs parlor, drinking whiskey, when the new doorkeeper, Tom Pendel, broke in on them. "The President's been shot!"

As Hay hurried after Robert to the waiting carriage, he had a dreamlike sense that he had already lived through this moment before. Pendel was hysterical. "Mr. Seward's been murdered, too. The whole Cabinet's been murdered!"

"Who?" asked the stunned Robert as they drove through the crowd that had begun to fill up Tenth Street. "Who has done this?"

"Rebels?" Hay could not think.

In the small bedroom of a cabbage-scented boardinghouse, the Ancient lay at an angle on a bed that was, needless to say, too short for him. This is the last time, Hay thought inanely, that he will be so inconvenienced.

Lincoln lay on his back, breathing heavily, as a doctor tried with cotton to staunch the ooze of blood from the shattered skull. Lincoln's right eye was swollen shut; and the skin of the right cheek was turning black. Hay noted that the long bare arms on the coverlet were surprisingly muscular. Lately, he had tended to think of the Ancient as mere skin and bone. In the next room, he could hear the sobbing of Mrs. Lincoln. In the bedroom itself, he could hear, as well as witness, the sobbing of Senator Sumner, posed like a widow at the head of the bed. Where was his bodyguard? wondered Hay, who had never despised Sumner more than now. In a corner sat Welles, old and frowzy beneath his wig.

Members of the Cabinet came and went. Only Stanton remained; in total charge. When Robert asked, "Is there any hope at all?" Stanton had answered for the doctor, "There is none. He will simply sink. The brain is destroyed. The wound is mortal." Then Stanton turned to an aide. "Telegraph the news to General Grant in Philadelphia. He is to return immediately. But with a full complement of guards." To another, he said, "Go to the Chief Justice. Tell him what has happened. We will need him to swear in the new president."

An official from the State Department arrived to report: "A man broke into the Old Club House. The servant says he sounded like a dyed-in-the-wool rebel. He went upstairs and stabbed Mr. Seward, but that iron contraption on his jaw saved him. He's not hurt at all. But Fred Seward's head is broken; he is unconscious."

"I was with both of them less than an hour ago," said Stanton, bemused. "The man escaped?"

"Yes, sir."

Mary Lincoln entered the room. "Oh, Robert!" she cried. "What is to happen to us?" She looked down at her husband. "Father, speak to us! You can't die like this, not now. It is unthinkable. Robert, fetch Taddie! He'll speak to Taddie. He won't let himself die if Taddie's here."

Robert looked at Stanton, who shook his head. Then Mary gave a great shriek and threw herself on Lincoln's body. "Don't leave us!"

"Get that woman out of here," said Stanton, suddenly brutal to a lady whom he had for so long done his best to charm. He need never charm her again, thought Hay. "Don't let her back in."

Sumner and the man from the State Department led Mary out of the room, just as the Vice-President made his awkward entrance.

"Sir," said Stanton, suddenly deferential. "I wish you to remain under constant guard—the soldiers that I just assigned to you are at the Kirkwood House—until we know who the enemy is. I am sure that they meant to kill you, too."

"He . . . will die?" Johnson stared with wonder at the figure on the bed.

"Yes, sir. I have already made the necessary preparations. Mr. Chase has been notified. When the time arrives, he will come to your hotel, and administer the oath of office."

"We have been struck," said Johnson, with no great emphasis or—for him—grandiloquent flourish, "a mighty blow."

"Yes, sir. But *he* is lucky. He will belong to the ages, while we are obliged to live on in the wreckage."

As night became morning, Stanton sat next to Robert, beside the bed. Stanton's right hand, in which he still held his hat, supported his left elbow.

Shortly after seven o'clock Abraham Lincoln took a deep breath; exhaled it slowly; and died. Like an automaton, Stanton raised his right arm high in the air; then, precisely, he set his hat squarely on his head and then, as precisely, he removed it. He got to his feet. "The Cabinet will now meet," he said, "to discuss the notification and the swearing-in of President Johnson, and the orderly continuance of this government."

Mary was led into the room. Moaning softly, she lay across the still body; then, finally, of her own accord, she stood up, dry-eyed from so much weeping and said, to no one in particular, "Oh, my God! And I have given my husband to die." Robert led her from the room.

Hay stared at the Ancient, who seemed to be smiling, as the doctor tied a cloth under the chin to keep the mouth from falling ajar. He looked exactly as if his own death had just reminded him of a story. But then Hay realized that never again would the Ancient be reminded of a story. He had become what others would be reminded of.

Gore Vidal
From *Lincoln*

Dick Gregory, a popular satirist, is also well-known for his involvement in modern social movements. He is active in the civil rights movement and is presently also well-known for his interest and humorous commentaries on contemporary American politics and political issues. During the sixties, Dick Gregory spoke out fearlessly against the Vietnam Conflict and has continued to protest whatever he views as morally and socially destructive behavior on the part of Americans. The selection, "Shame," comes from his autobiography, *Nigger*, published in 1964, and employs the technique of narrating a personal incident to illustrate an abstract concept—shame—and to give this abstract word both personal and specific meaning.

SHAME

I never learned hate at home, or shame. I had to go to school for that. I was about seven years old when I got my first big lesson. I was in love with a little girl named Helene Tucker, a light-complexioned little girl with pigtails and nice manners. She was always clean and she was smart in school. I think I went to school then mostly to look at her. I brushed my hair and even got me a little old handkerchief. It was a lady's handkerchief, but I didn't want Helene to see me wipe my nose on my hand. The pipes were frozen again, there was no water in the house, but I washed my socks and shirt every night. I'd get a pot, and go over to Mister Ben's grocery store, and stick my pot down into his soda machine. Scoop out some chopped ice. By evening the ice melted to water for washing. I got sick a lot that winter because the fire would go out at night before the clothes were dry. In the morning I'd put them on, wet or dry, because they were the only clothes I had.

Everybody's got a Helene Tucker, a symbol of everything you want. I loved her for her goodness, her cleanness, her popularity. She'd walk down my street and my brothers and sisters would yell, "Here comes Helene," and I'd rub my tennis sneakers on the back of my pants and wish my hair wasn't so nappy and the white folks' shirt fit me better. I'd run out on the street. If I knew my place and didn't come too close, she'd wink at me and say hello. That was a good feeling. Sometimes I'd follow her all the way home, and shovel the snow off her walk and try to make friends with her Momma and her aunts. I'd drop money on her stoop late at night on my way back from shining shoes in the taverns. And she had a Daddy, and he had a good job. He was a paper hanger.

I guess I would have gotten over Helene by summertime, but

something happened in that classroom that made her face hang in front of me for the next twenty-two years. When I played the drums in high school it was for Helene and when I broke track records in college it was for Helene and when I started standing behind microphones and heard applause I wished Helene could hear it, too. It wasn't until I was twenty-nine years old and married and making money that I finally got her out of my system. Helene was sitting in that classroom when I learned to be ashamed of myself.

It was on a Thursday. I was sitting in the back of the room, in a seat with a chalk circle drawn around it. The idiot's seat, the trouble-maker's seat.

The teacher thought I was stupid. Couldn't spell, couldn't read, couldn't do arithmetic. Just stupid. Teachers were never interested in finding out that you couldn't concentrate because you were so hungry, because you hadn't had any breakfast. All you could think about was noontime, would it ever come? Maybe you could sneak into the cloak-room and steal a bite of some kid's lunch out of a coat pocket. A bite of something. Paste. You can't really make a meal of paste, or put it on bread for a sandwich, but sometimes I'd scoop a few spoonfuls out of the paste jar in the back of the room. Pregnant people get strange tastes. I was pregnant with poverty. Pregnant with dirt and pregnant with smells that made people turn away, pregnant with cold and pregnant with shoes that were never bought for me, pregnant with five other people in my bed and no Daddy in the next room, and pregnant with hunger. Paste doesn't taste too bad when you're hungry.

The teacher thought I was a troublemaker. All she saw from the front of the room was a little black boy who squirmed in his idiot's seat and made noises and poked the kids around him. I guess she couldn't see a kid who made noises because he wanted someone to know he was there.

It was on a Thursday, the day before the Negro payday. The eagle always flew on Friday. The teacher was asking each student how much his father would give to the Community Chest. On Friday night, each kid would get the money from his father, and on Monday he would bring it to the school. I decided I was going to buy me a Daddy right then. I had money in my pocket from shining shoes and selling papers, and whatever Helene Tucker pledged for her Daddy I was going to top it. And I'd hand the money right in. I wasn't going to wait until Monday to buy me a Daddy.

I was shaking, scared to death. The teacher opened her book and started calling out names alphabetically.

"Helene Tucker?"

"My daddy said he'd give two dollars and fifty cents."

"That's very nice, Helene. Very, very nice indeed."

That made me feel pretty good. It wouldn't take too much to top that. I had almost three dollars in dimes and quarters in my pocket, I stuck my hand in my pocket and held onto the money, waiting for her to call my name. But the teacher closed her book after she called everybody else in the class.

I stood up and raised my hand.

"What is it now?"

"You forgot me."

She turned toward the blackboard. "I don't have time to be playing with you, Richard."

"My Daddy said he'd . . ."

"Sit down, Richard, you're disturbing the class."

"My Daddy said he'd give . . . fifteen dollars."

She turned around and looked mad. "We are collecting this money for you and your kind, Richard Gregory. If your Daddy can give fifteen dollars you have no business being on relief."

"I got it right now, I got it right now, my Daddy gave it to me to turn in today, my Daddy said . . ."

"And furthermore," she said, looking right at me, her nostrils getting big and her lips getting thin and her eyes opening wide, "we know you don't have a Daddy."

Helene Tucker turned around, her eyes full of tears. She felt sorry for me. Then I couldn't see her too well because I was crying, too.

"Sit down, Richard."

And I always thought the teacher kind of liked me. She always picked me to wash the blackboard on Friday, after school. That was a big thrill, it made me feel important. If I didn't wash it, come Monday the school might not function right.

"Where are you going, Richard?"

I walked out of school that day, and for a long time I didn't go back very often. There was shame there.

Now there was shame everywhere. It seemed like the whole world had been inside that classroom, everyone had heard what the teacher had said, everyone had turned around and felt sorry for me. There was shame in going to the Worthy Boys Annual Christmas Dinner for you and your kind, because everybody knew what a worthy boy was. Why couldn't they just call it the Boys Annual Dinner; why'd they have to give it a name? There was shame in wearing the brown and orange and white plaid mackinaw the welfare gave to three thousand boys. Why'd it have to be the same for everybody so when you walked down the street the people could see you were on relief? It was a nice warm mackinaw and it had a hood, and my Momma beat me and called me a little rat when she found out I stuffed it in the bottom of a pail full of garbage way over on Cottage Street. There was shame in running over to Mister Ben's at the end of the day and asking for his rotten peaches, there was shame in asking Mrs. Simmons for a spoonful of sugar, there was shame in running out to meet the relief truck. I hated that truck, full of food for you and your kind. I ran into the house and hid when it came. And then I started to sneak through alleys, to take the long way home so the people going into White's Eat Shop wouldn't see me. Yeah, the whole world heard the teacher that day, we all know you don't have a Daddy.

Dick Gregory
From *Nigger*

Russell Baker, the popular and widely read columnist, comments humorously and pointedly on various aspects of American society, American mores, and contemporary moral issues. His columns in the *New York Times* are printed regularly in newspapers throughout the United States. In the following version of an old fairy tale, Russell Baker uses illustrative detail to remark on today's values.

The companion piece is a poem by Roald Dahl who is better known as a children's writer than as a writer of poetry for adults. All parents of children still in the read aloud stage know Roald Dahl as the author of the children's classic, *Charlie and the Chocolate Factory*. The poem illustrates through the use of humorous details precisely the sort of approach that this chapter is attempting to teach in the medium of prose.

LITTLE RED RIDING HOOD REVISITED

In an effort to make the classics accessible to contemporary readers, I am translating them into the modern American language. Here is the translation of "Little Red Riding Hood":

Once upon a point in time, a small person named Little Red Riding Hood initiated plans for the preparation, delivery and transportation of foodstuffs to her grandmother, a senior citizen residing at a place of residence in a forest of indeterminate dimension.

In the process of implementing this program, her incursion into the forest was in midtransportation process when it attained interface with an alleged perpetrator. This individual, a wolf, made inquiry as to the whereabouts of Little Red Riding Hood's goal as well as inferring that he was desirous of ascertaining the contents of Little Red Riding Hood's foodstuffs basket, and all that.

"It would be inappropriate to lie to me," the wolf said, displaying his huge jaw capability. Sensing that he was a mass of repressed hostility intertwined with acute alienation, she indicated.

"I see you indicating," the wolf said, "but what I don't see is whatever it is you're indicating at, you dig?"

Little Red Riding Hood indicated more fully, making one thing perfectly clear—to wit, that it was to her grandmother's residence and with a consignment of foodstuffs that her mission consisted of taking her to and with.

At this point in time, the wolf moderated his rhetoric and proceeded to grandmother's residence. The elderly person was then subjected to the disadvantages of total consumption and transferred to residence in the perpetrator's stomach.

"That will raise the old woman's consciousness," the wolf said to himself. He was not a bad wolf, but only a victim of an oppressive society, a society that not only denied wolves' rights, but actually boasted of its capacity for keeping the wolf from the door. An interior malaise made itself manifest inside the wolf.

"Is that the national malaise I sense within my digestive tract?" wondered the wolf. "Or is it the old person seeking to retaliate for her consumption by telling wolf jokes to my duodenum?" It was time to make a judgment. The time was now, the hour had struck, the body lupine cried out for decision. The wolf was up to the challenge. He took two stomach powders right away and got into bed.

The wolf had adopted the abdominal-distress recovery posture when Little Red Riding Hood achieved his presence.

"Grandmother," she said, "your ocular implements are of an extraordinary order of magnitude."

"The purpose of this enlarged viewing capability," said the wolf, "is to enable your image to register a more precise impression upon my sight systems."

"In reference to your ears," said Little Red Riding Hood, "it is noted with the deepest respect that far from being underprivileged, their elongation and enlargement appear to qualify you for unparalleled distinction."

"I hear you loud and clear, kid," said the wolf, "but what about these new choppers?"

"If it is not appropriate," said Little Red Riding Hood, "it might be observed that with your new miracle masticating products you may even be able to chew taffy again."

This observation was followed by the adoption of an aggressive posture on the part of the wolf and the assertion that it was also possible for him, due to the high efficiency ratio of his jaw, to consume little persons, plus, as he stated, his firm determination to do so at once without delay and with all due process and propriety, notwithstanding the fact that the ingestion of one entire grandmother had already provided twice his daily recommended cholesterol intake.

There ensued flight by Little Red Riding Hood accompanied by pursuit in respect to the wolf and a subsequent intervention on the part of a third party, heretofore unnoted in the record.

Due to the firmness of the intervention, the wolf's stomach underwent ax-assisted aperture with the result that Red Riding Hood's grandmother was enabled to be removed with only minor discomfort.

The wolf's indigestion was immediately alleviated with such effectiveness that he signed a contract with the intervening third party to perform with grandmother in a television commercial demonstrating the swiftness of this dramatic relief for stomach discontent.

"I'm going to be on television," cried grandmother.

And they all joined her happily in crying, "What a phenomena!"

Russell Baker
From *New York Times*, January 13, 1980

LITTLE RED RIDING HOOD AND THE WOLF

As soon as Wolf began to feel
That he would like a decent meal,
He went and knocked on Grandma's door.
When Grandma opened it, she saw
The sharp white teeth, the horrid grin,
And Wolfie said, "May I come in?"
Poor Grandmamma was terrified,

"He's going to eat me up!" she cried.
And she was absolutely right.
He ate her up in one big bite.
But Grandmamma was small and tough,
And Wolfie wailed, "That's not enough!
I haven't yet begun to feel
That I have had a decent meal!"
He ran around the kitchen yelping,
"I've *got* to have a second helping!"
Then added with a frightful leer,
"I'm therefore going to wait right here
Till Little Miss Red Riding Hood
Comes home from walking in the wood."
He quickly put on Grandma's clothes,
(Of course he hadn't eaten those).
He dressed himself in coat and hat.
He put on shoes and after that
He even brushed and curled his hair,
Then sat himself in Grandma's chair.
In came the little girl in red.
She stopped. She stared. And then she said,

"What great big ears you have, Grandma."
"All the better to hear you with," the Wolf replied.
"What great big eyes you have, Grandma,"
said Little Red Riding Hood.
"All the better to see you with," the Wolf replied.

He sat there watching her and smiled.
He thought, "I'm going to eat this child.
Compared with her old Grandmamma
She's going to taste like caviar."

Then Little Red Riding Hood said, *"But Grandma,*
what a lovely great big furry coat you have on."

"That's wrong," cried Wolf, "Have you forgot
To tell me what BIG TEETH I've got?
Ah well, no matter what you say,
I'm going to eat you anyway."
The small girl smiles. One eyelid flickers.
She whips a pistol from her knickers.
She aims it at the creature's head
And *bang bang bang*, she shoots him dead.
A few weeks later, in the wood,
I came across Miss Riding Hood.
But what a change! No cloak of red,
No silly hood upon her head.
She said, "Hello, and do please note
My lovely furry wolfskin coat."

Roald Dahl
From *Roald Dahl's Revolting Rhymes*

Katherine Mansfield (1888–1923) published this very short story, "Miss Brill" in a collection of her short stories, *Jardins Publiques* in 1922. Katherine Mansfield was born and grew up in New Zealand, but lived most of her adult life in London. When you read this story, look for ways the writer uses both static and dynamic detail to develop character, setting, and mood.

Just as Katherine Mansfield gives the reader a literary photograph of Miss Brill, both physically and spiritually, Frederick Douglass creates for his readers and for posterity a close look at a plantation slave community in the American South before the Civil War. Narrative description is employed here to illustrate a community and a social system.

Frederick Douglass (1817–1895) is famous as a lecturer and writer whose autobiography, *Narrative of the Life of Frederick Douglass* (1845), was important in the abolitionist movement and remains today a vivid and compelling memoir as well as a marvelous primary source for information about the slave world and the antebellum American South. Frederick Douglass was an escaped slave who lectured tirelessly with the abolitionists and who rallied black soldiers to fight for the Union. After the Civil War, he became a prominent newspaper publisher, a United States marshal, and eventually the consul-general to the Republic of Haiti.

MISS BRILL

Although it was so brilliantly fine—the blue sky powdered with gold and great spots of light like white wine splashed over the Jardins Publiques—Miss Brill was glad that she had decided on her fur. The air was motionless, but when you opened your mouth there was just a faint chill, like a chill from a glass of iced water before you sip, and now and again a leaf came drifting—from nowhere, from the sky. Miss Brill put up her hand and touched her fur. Dear little thing! It was nice to feel it again. She had taken it out of its box that afternoon, shaken out the moth powder, given it a good brush, and rubbed the life back into the dim little eyes. "What has been happening to me?" said the sad little eyes. Oh, how sweet it was to see them snap at her again from the red eiderdown! . . . But the nose which was of some black composition, wasn't at all firm. It must have had a knock, somehow. Never mind—a little dab of black sealing-wax when the time came—when it was absolutely necessary . . . Little rogue! Yes, she really felt like that about it. Little rogue biting its tail just by her left ear. She could have taken it off and laid it on her lap and stroked it. She felt a tingling in her hands and arms, but that came from walking, she supposed. And when she breathed, something light and sad—no, not sad, exactly—something gentle seemed to move in her bosom.

There were a number of people out this afternoon, far more than last Sunday. And the band sounded louder and gayer. That was because the Season had begun. For although the band played all the year round on Sundays, out of season it was never the same. It was like some one playing with only the family to listen; it didn't care how it played if there weren't any strangers present. Wasn't the conductor wearing a new coat, too? She was sure it was new. He scraped with his foot and flapped his arms like a rooster about to crow, and the bandsmen sitting in the green rotunda blew out their cheeks and glared at the music. Now there came a little "flutey" bit—very pretty! —a little chain of bright drops. She was sure it would be repeated. It was; she lifted her head and smiled.

Only two people shared her "special" seat: a fine old man in a velvet coat, his hands clasped over a huge carved walking-stick, and a big old woman, sitting upright, with a roll of knitting on her embroidered apron. They did not speak. This was disappointing, for Miss Brill always looked forward to the conversation. She had become really quite expert, she thought, at listening as though she didn't listen, at sitting in other people's lives just for a minute while they talked round her.

She glanced, sideways, at the old couple. Perhaps they would go soon. Last Sunday, too, hadn't been as interesting as usual. An Englishman and his wife, he wearing a dreadful Panama hat and she button boots. And she'd gone on the whole time about how she ought to wear spectacles; she knew she needed them, but that it was no good getting any; they'd be sure to break and they'd never keep on. And he'd been so patient. He'd suggested everything—gold rims, the kind that curve round your ears, little pads inside the bridge. No, nothing would please her. "They'll always be sliding down my nose!" Miss Brill had wanted to shake her.

The old people sat on the bench, still as statues. Never mind, there was always the crowd to watch. To and fro, in front of the flower beds and the band rotunda, the couples and groups paraded, stopped to talk, to greet, to buy a handful of flowers from the old beggar who had his tray fixed to the railings. Little children ran among them, swooping and laughing; little boys with big white silk bows under their chins, little girls, little French dolls, dressed up in velvet and lace. And sometimes a tiny staggerer came suddenly rocking into the open from under the trees, stopped, stared, as suddenly sat down "flop," until its small high-stepping mother, like a young hen, rushed scolding to its rescue. Other people sat on the benches and green chairs, but they were nearly always the same, Sunday after Sunday, and—Miss Brill had often noticed—there was something funny about nearly all of them. They were odd, silent, nearly all old, and from the way they stared they looked as though they'd just come from dark little rooms or even—even cupboards!

Behind the rotunda the slender trees with yellow leaves down drooping, and through them just a line of sea, and beyond the blue sky with gold-veined clouds.

Tum-tum-tum tiddle-um! tiddle-um! tum tiddley-um tum ta! blew the band.

Two young girls in red came by and two young soldiers in blue met them, and they laughed and paired and went off arm-in-arm. Two peasant women with funny straw hats passed, gravely, leading beautiful smoke-colored donkeys. A cold, pale nun hurried by. A beautiful woman came along and dropped her bunch of violets, and a little boy ran after to hand them to her, and she took them and threw them away as if they'd been poisoned. Dear me! Miss Brill didn't know whether to admire that or not! And now an ermine toque and a gentleman in gray met just in front of her. He was tall, stiff, dignified, and she was wearing the ermine toque she'd bought when her hair was yellow. Now everything, her hair, her face, even her eyes, was the same color as the shabby ermine, and her hand, in its cleaned glove, lifted to dab her lips, was a tiny yellowish paw. Oh, she was so pleased to see him—delighted! She rather thought they were going to meet that afternoon. She described where she'd been—everywhere, here, there, along by the sea. The day was so charming—didn't he agree? And wouldn't he, perhaps? . . . But he shook his head, lighted a cigarette, slowly breathed a great deep puff into her face, and, even while she was still talking and laughing, flicked the match away and walked on. The ermine toque was alone; she smiled more brightly than ever. But even the band seemed to know what she was feeling and played more softly, played tenderly, and the drum beat, "The Brute! The Brute!" over and over. What would she do? What was going to happen now? But as Miss Brill wondered, the ermine toque turned, raised her hand as though she'd seen some one else, much nicer, just over there, and pattered away. And the band changed again and played more quickly, more gayly than ever, and the old couple on Miss Brill's seat got up and marched away, and such a funny old man with long whiskers hobbled along in time to the music and was nearly knocked over by four girls walking abreast.

Oh, how fascinating it was! How she enjoyed it! How she loved sitting here, watching it all! It was like a play. It was exactly like a play. Who could believe the sky at the back wasn't painted? But it wasn't till a little brown dog trotted on solemn and then slowly trotted off, like a little "theater" dog, a little dog that had been drugged, that Miss Brill discovered what it was that made it so exciting. They were all on stage. They weren't only the audience, not only looking on; they were acting. Even she had a part and came every Sunday. No doubt somebody would have noticed if she hadn't been there; she was part of the performance after all. How strange she'd never thought of it like that before! And yet it explained why she made such a point of starting from home at just the same time each week—so as not to be late for the performance—and it also explained why she had quite a queer, shy feeling at telling her English pupils how she spent her Sunday afternoons. No wonder! Miss Brill nearly laughed out loud. She was on the stage. She thought of the old invalid gentleman to whom she read the newspaper four afternoons a week while he slept in the garden. She had got quite used to the frail head on the cotton pillow, the hollowed eyes, the open mouth and the high pinched nose. If he'd been dead she mightn't have noticed for weeks; she wouldn't have minded. But suddenly he knew he was having the paper read to him by an actress! "An actress!" The old head lifted; two points of light quivered in the old eyes. "An actress—are ye?" And Miss Brill smoothed the newspaper as though it were the manuscript of her part and said gently: "Yes, I have been an actress for a long time."

The band had been having a rest. Now they started again. And what they played was warm, sunny, yet there was just a faint chill—a something, what was it?—not sadness—no, not sadness—a something that made you want to sing. The tune lifted, lifted, the light shone; and it seemed to Miss Brill that in another moment all of them, all the whole company, would begin singing. The young ones, the laughing ones who were moving together, they would begin, and the men's voices, very resolute and brave, would join them. And then she too, she too, and the others on the benches—they would come in with a kind of accompaniment—something low, that scarcely rose or fell, something so beautiful—moving . . . And Miss Brill's eyes filled with tears and she looked smiling at all the other members of the company. Yes, we understand, we understand, she thought—though what they understood she didn't know.

Just at that moment a boy and girl came and sat down where the old couple had been. They were beautifully dressed; they were in love. The hero and heroine, of course, just arrived from his father's yacht. And still soundlessly singing, still with that trembling smile, Miss Brill prepared to listen.

"No, not now," said the girl. "Not here, I can't."

"But why? Because of that stupid old thing at the end there?" asked the boy. "Why does she come here at all—who wants her? Why doesn't she keep her silly old mug at home?"

"It's her fu-fur which is so funny," giggled the girl. "It's exactly like a fried whiting."

"Ah, be off with you!" said the boy in an angry whisper. Then: "Tell me, ma petite chère—"

"No, not here," said the girl. "Not *yet*."

On her way home she usually bought a slice of honeycake at the baker's. It was her Sunday treat. Sometimes there was an almond in her slice, sometimes not. It made a great difference. If there was an almond it was like carrying home a tiny present—a surprise—something that might very well not have been there. She hurried on the almond Sundays and struck the match for the kettle in quite a dashing way.

But today she passed the baker's by, climbed the stairs, went into the little dark room—her room like a cupboard—and sat down on the red eiderdown. She sat there for a long time. The box that the fur came out of was on the bed. She unclasped the necklet quickly; quickly, without looking, laid it inside. But when she put the lid on she thought she heard something crying.

Katherine Mansfield
From *Miss Brill*

PLANTATION LIFE

My master's family consisted of two sons, Andrew and Richard; one daughter, Lucretia, and her husband, Captain Thomas Auld. They lived in one house, upon the home plantation of Colonel Edward Lloyd. My master was Colonel Lloyd's clerk and superintendent. He was what might be called the overseer of the overseers. I spent two years of childhood on this plantation in my old master's family. . . . As I received my first impressions of slavery on this plantation, I will give some description of it, and of slavery as it there existed. The plantation is about twelve miles north of Easton, in Talbot county, and is situated on the border of Miles River. The principal products raised upon it were tobacco, corn, and wheat. These were raised in great abundance; so that, with the products of this and the other farms belonging to him, he was able to keep in almost constant employment a large sloop, in carrying them to market at Baltimore. This sloop was named Sally Lloyd, in honor of one of the colonel's daughters. My master's son-in-law, Captain Auld, was master of the vessel; she was otherwise manned by the colonel's own slaves. Their names were Peter, Isaac, Rich, and Jake. These were esteemed very highly by the other slaves, and looked upon as the privileged ones of the plantation; for it was no small affair, in the eyes of the slaves, to be allowed to see Baltimore.

Colonel Lloyd kept from three to four hundred slaves on his home plantation, and owned a large number more on the neighboring farms belonging to him. The names of the farms nearest to the home plantation were Wye Town and New Design. "Wye Town" was under the overseership of a man named Noah Willis. New Design was under the overseership of a Mr. Townsend. The overseers of these, and all the rest of the farms, numbering over twenty, received advice and direction from the managers of the home plantation. This was the great business place. It was the seat of government for the whole twenty farms. All disputes among the overseers were settled here. If a slave was convicted of any high misdemeanor, became unmanageable, or evinced a determination to run away, he was brought immediately here, severely whipped, put on board the sloop, carried to Baltimore, and sold to Austin Woolfolk, or some other slave-trader, as a warning to the slaves remaining.

Here, too, the slaves of all the other farms received their monthly allowance of food, and their yearly clothing. The men and women slaves received, as their monthly allowance of food, eight pounds of pork, or its equivalent in fish, and one bushel of corn meal. Their yearly clothing consisted of two coarse linen shirts, one pair of linen trousers, like the shirts, one jacket, one pair of trousers for winter, made of coarse negro cloth, one pair of stockings, and one pair of shoes; the whole of which could not have cost more than seven dollars. The allowance of the slave children was given to their mothers, or the old women having the care of them. The children unable to work in the field had neither shoes, stockings, jackets, nor trousers, given to them; their clothing consisted of two coarse linen shirts per year. When these failed them, they went naked until the next allowance-day. Children from seven to ten years old, of both sexes, almost naked, might be seen at all seasons of the year.

There were no beds given the slaves, unless one coarse blanket be considered such, and none but the men and women had these. This, however, is not considered a very great privation. They find less difficulty from the want of beds, than from the want of time to sleep; for when their day's work in the field is done, the most of them having their washing, mending, and cooking to do, and having few or none of the ordinary facilities for doing either of these, very many of their sleeping hours are consumed in preparing for the field the coming day; and when this is done, old and young, male and female, married and single, drop down side by side, on one common bed,—the cold, damp floor,—each covering himself or herself with their miserable blankets; and here they sleep till they are summoned to the field by the driver's horn. At the sound of this, all must rise, and be off to the field. There must be no halting; every one must be at his or her post; and woe betides them who hear not this morning summons to the field; for if they are not awakened by the sense of hearing, they are by the sense of feeling: no age nor sex finds any favor. Mr. Severe, the overseer, used to stand by the door of the quarter, armed with a large hickory stick and heavy cowskin, ready to whip any one who was so unfortunate as not to hear, or, from any other cause, was prevented from being ready to start for the field at the sound of the horn.

Mr. Severe was rightly named: he was a cruel man. I have seen him whip a woman, causing the blood to run half an hour at the time; and this, too, in the midst of her crying children, pleading for their mother's release. He seemed to take pleasure in manifesting his fiendish barbarity. Added to his cruelty, he was a profane swearer. It was enough to chill the blood and stiffen the hair of an ordinary man to hear him talk. Scarce a sentence escaped him but that was commenced or concluded by some horrid oath. The field was the place to witness his cruelty and profanity. His presence made it both the field of blood and of blasphemy. From the rising till the going down of the sun, he was cursing, raving, cutting, and slashing among the slaves of the field, in the most frightful manner. His career was short. He died very soon after I went to Colonel Lloyd's; and he died as he lived, uttering, with his dying groans, bitter curses and horrid oaths. His death was regarded by the slaves as the result of a merciful providence.

Mr. Severe's place was filled by a Mr. Hopkins. He was a very different man. He was less cruel, less profane, and made less noise, than Mr. Severe. His course was characterized by no extraordinary demonstrations of cruelty. He whipped, but seemed to take no pleasure in it. He was called by the slaves a good overseer.

The home plantation of Colonel Lloyd wore the appearance of a country village. All the mechanical operations for all the farms were performed here. The shoemaking and mending, the blacksmithing, cartwrighting, coopering, weaving, and grain-grinding, were all performed by the slaves on the home plantation. The whole place wore a business-like aspect very unlike the neighboring farms. The number of houses, too, conspired to give it advantage over the neighboring farms. It was called by the slaves the *Great House Farm*. Few privileges were esteemed higher, by the slaves of the out-farms, than that of being selected to do errands at the Great House Farm. It was associated in their minds with greatness. A representative could not be prouder of his election to a seat in the American Congress, than a slave on one of the out-farms would be of his election to do errands at the Great House Farm. They regarded it as evidence of great confidence reposed in them by their overseers; and it was on this account, as well as a constant desire to be out of the field from under the driver's lash, that they esteemed it a high privilege, one worth careful living for. He was called the smartest and most trusty fellow, who had this honor conferred upon him the most frequently. The competitors for this office sought as diligently to please their overseers, as the office-seekers in the political parties seek to please and deceive the people. The same traits of character might be seen in Colonel Lloyd's slaves, as are seen in the slaves of the political parties.

The slaves selected to go to the Great House Farm, for the monthly allowance for themselves and their fellow-slaves, were peculiarly enthusiastic. While on their way, they would make the dense old woods, for miles around, reverberate with their wild songs, revealing at once the highest joy and the deepest sadness. They would compose and sing as they went along, consulting neither time nor tune. The thought that came up, came out—if not in the word, in the sound;—and as frequently in the one as in the other. They would sometimes sing the most pathetic sentiment in the most rapturous tone, and the most rapturous sentiment in the most pathetic tone. Into all of their songs they would manage to weave something of the Great House Farm. Especially would they do this, when leaving home. They would then sing most exultingly the following words:—

> I am going away to the Great House Farm!
> O, yea! O, yea! O!

This they would sing, as a chorus, to words which to many would seem unmeaning jargon, but which, nevertheless, were full of meaning to themselves. I have sometimes thought that the mere hearing of those songs would do more to impress some minds with the horrible character of slavery, than the reading of whole volumes of philosophy on the subject could do.

I did not, when a slave, understand the deep meaning of those rude and apparently incoherent songs. I was myself within the circle; so that I neither saw nor heard as those without might see and hear. They told a tale of woe which was then altogether beyond my feeble comprehension; they were tones loud, long, and deep; they breathed the prayer and complaint of souls boiling over with the bitterest anguish. Every tone was a testimony against slavery, and a prayer to God for deliverance from chains. The hearing of those wild notes always depressed my spirit, and filled me with ineffable sadness. I have frequently found myself in tears while hearing them. The mere recurrence of those songs, even now, afflicts me; and while I am writing these lines, an expression of feeling has already found its way down my cheek. To those songs I trace my first glimmering conception of the dehumanizing character of slavery. I can never get rid of that conception. Those songs still follow me, to deepen my hatred of slavery, and quicken my sympathies for my brethren in bonds. If any one wishes to be impressed with the soul-killing effects of slavery, let him go to Colonel Lloyd's plantation, and, on allowance-day, place himself in the deep pine woods, and there let him, in silence, analyze the sounds that shall pass through the chambers of his soul,—and if he is not thus impressed, it will only be because "there is no flesh in his obdurate heart."

I have often been utterly astonished, since I came to the north, to find persons who could speak of the singing, among slaves, as evidence of their contentment and happiness. It is impossible to conceive of a greater mistake. Slaves sing most when they are most unhappy. The songs of the slave represent the sorrows of his heart; and he is relieved by them, only as an aching heart is relieved by its tears. At least, such is my experience. I have often sung to drown my sorrow, but seldom to express my happiness. Crying for joy, and singing for joy, were alike uncommon to me while in the jaws of slavery. The singing of a man cast away upon a desolate island might be as appropriately considered as evidence of contentment and happiness, as the singing of a slave; the songs of the one and of the other are prompted by the same emotion.

Frederick Douglass
From *Narrative of the Life of Frederick Douglass*

EXERCISE 3

a. Think of a familiar "character" and describe that person much as Katherine Mansfield presents Miss Brill.

b. Use any community of which you have been or are a part—your high school clique, your family, a sports team, or your church group—and describe that microcosm of which you are a part as a reflection of the world as a whole.

Process Analysis •

A common form of dynamic description is known as **process analysis**, perhaps best described as the art of writing readable instructions that explain "how to do" something. The principle of understanding the subject matter ("Write about what you know about") is as important in this variation of dynamic description as in any of the other forms. Clear and logical organization is crucial.

You need only briefly consider the difficulties in teaching a squirming five year old how to tie shoelaces to understand the need for accuracy, clarity, simplicity, and directness in the process of description. For anyone who has ever attempted to put together a bicycle on Christmas Eve, the indispensability of simple and readable instructions need not be belabored.

Similarly, anyone who has ever asked directions and gotten the response "Go down the road a piece and turn left at the mailbox—the one on this side of Mr. Jenkins' old house, the one that used to belong to old man Thompson. See, after he passed away, Mr. Jenkins bought the place. When you leave the main road, turn along the curve where the Simpson kid was killed just last year. He was always a one for drinking, ever since he was a kid. His father's no better. You'll see the house you're looking for right there, not too far from the road to the right. Can't miss it . . ."

From this illustration, it is easy to understand the frustration one feels from poorly illustrated and sloppily organized directions. The following essay is one student's attempt not to frustrate the reader, but to explain clearly how plywood is made.

Plywood

Plywood is a construction material composed of thin sheets of wood glued together. The process of making plywood involves three major stages: peeling the thin layers of wood from the log, gluing the layers together, and pressing the sheets in large hydraulic presses.

Peeling the thin layers of wood from the log is done by a huge lathe. Logs, with the bark removed, are placed in the lathe, which turns them against a long, razor-sharp knife. As the thin, continuous layers of wood are peeled from the log, they slide onto conveyor tables. At this point the layers of wood are inspected for defects, sorted into needed lengths and widths, and graded. Then, to reduce the amount of moisture in the layers, they are put through automatic dryers.

The next major stage in making plywood is gluing together the dried layers of wood. Each layer, as it is placed on another, is turned so that the grain is at right angles with the layer below it. Then the layers are glued together. Each layer, or ply, may be as thin as 1/100 of an inch or as thick as 1/2 inch. Any number of plies may be glued together.

The final stage is pressing the plywood to set the glue. The plywood is put in large hydraulic presses, where heat and pressure are applied. As the plywood comes from the presses, it is sanded and trimmed to specified lengths and widths, depending on the use it will be put to. The finished plywood sheets are now ready to be shipped to the dealer or consumer.

Plywood has become enormously popular construction material for airplanes, houses, furniture, boats, and hundreds of other items. Because of the cross-laying of the plies, plywood is very strong, and it is relatively lightweight.

> The waterproof glue used in some plywood is so strong that the plywood will stand up under repeated changes of boiling and drying and continuous exposure to salt water.

This following "how-to-do-it" student essay is obviously the result of direct experience.

How to Change a Tire on the Autostrada

> As I was driving along the autostrada between Florence and Bologna a week ago, I had the opportunity to test the instructions on how to change a tire that the US government so very obligingly attaches to the inside of the trunk lid on every government vehicle. Fortunately, I had been able to pull the car safely off the road much as I had been taught nearly a lifetime ago in driver's education. The instructions told me forcibly that I was to apply the emergency brake first before jacking up the car to remove the wheel. After ten minutes of frustration and two broken fingernails, I managed to jack up the car. The directions then insisted that a piece of equipment called a lug wrench would be found in the trunk and with that I could unscrew and remove the lugs preparatory to removing the tire from the wheel. The spare tire and the lug wrench were purported to have the trunk as their official home of residence.
>
> In searching for the lug wrench, a creature with which I was unfamiliar and not sure that I would recognize even when it was at home in the trunk, I located two cans of oil—one opened and one unopened, several different grimy rags, a bag of decomposing trash patiently awaiting the proper disposal, someone's smelly running clothes and shoes, and a case of empty soda bottles. Finally, hot and dirty, I located an item that I felt sure must be a lug wrench. Hanging on to the lug wrench for dear life and exerting every pound of pressure in my frame, I managed to remove the lugs and pull the tire from the wheel.
>
> Then it was a matter of once more to the trunk to search for the tire boasted about in the directions. The directions assured the reader that the spare tire was in the spare-tire well. There was a well in this vehicle, but it sported paper towels, a chamois, and windex. There was no tire.
>
> By this time I was hot, sweaty, and miserable. Faced with this dilemma, I threw away my lifelong attachment to Betty Friedan. I walked to the edge of the road, hitched my skirt appealingly above my knee, and listened to the glorious sound of salvation—the squealing tires of a Fiat belonging to an Italian male who in driving past me as if he were in the Indy 500 had just turned on a dime to rescue me. To complete my confession, I must add that upon the arrival of this knight in shining Fiat, I burst into tears. I may never fit into the motor pool gang again, but I have learned how to change a tire on the autostrada.

Warm-up Exercises

EXERCISE 1

a. As you read these two "how to" essays, list those points where you don't quite understand the process being described.

b. Try to fit either one of the two process analysis student essays into a blocking out pattern. If you cannot, where would you make changes in the essay?

EXERCISE 2

a. Pick a familiar task involving many steps and try to explain in detail how to accomplish the task or activity. It can be as simple as how to teach a child to tie his shoes or how to change a ribbon on a typewriter.

b. Write an essay giving specific directions to a familiar place. You might want to try your hand at a humorous "you can't get there from here" type of description.

Cross-curricular Essay Questions

One very important reason students take composition courses is to prepare them to write well-organized and readable answers to essay questions in other college courses. The following are typical questions that might warrant the use of descriptive writing techniques.

1. How is creeping urbanism changing the local scene of the American small town.
2. Describe the importance of education in the growth and development of a four to five year old.
3. Describe a neurotic personality explaining in some detail the coping patterns that others use to handle the subject's neuroses.
4. Discuss the kinetic theory of liquids and solids, describing what occurs during evaporation and melting.
5. Discuss with specific, pertinent details the following statement: "American agriculture is highly dependent on the products of the chemical and petrochemical industries."
6. Describe the qualities of a good manager within the context of both a large or small establishment.
7. Use Frederick Douglass' essay on plantation life as source material for a description of the effects of slavery on both the white and black inhabitants of the American South, pre-Civil War.

CHAPTER

• TWO •

Comparison and Contrast

When a young man first describes his true love to his parents, he tries to tell them what she's really *like*. A wise and tactful son will comment, "Well, she's actually a lot like you, Mom."

Everyday we hear that men are attracted to women like their mothers, and women to men like their fathers. Just as frequently, we remark that a child is exactly like his or her mother, father, favorite cousin or even like a not-so-popular member of the family, especially if the child is behaving in a fashion of which we don't approve. The operative word in this context is, of course, *like*. Events, things, or people who are in some ways like other events, things or people can be explained and understood via the medium of comparison. Such a simple and widely used technique may also be an important asset in essay writing.

Comparison •

As writers, we often focus on similarities. The quality of two or more things being alike in some recognizable and significant manner is the essence of the comparison technique in prose and the simile or the metaphor in poetry. To write a comparison paragraph in an essay, or to compose a metaphor in a line of poetry, requires a knowledge of the "likenesses" or shared aspects of the subjects being discussed.

The writer starts with the basic premise that can easily be explained in mathematical terms: A is like B in x number of ways. After this first premise is expressed, the writer goes on to expand upon the similarities to show how or why these likenesses exist. The author then moves to a conclusion that says why the similarity between the two subjects is worth commenting upon. Even when these three premises have been fulfilled, the whole success of the essay or paragraph ultimately depends upon the writer's choice of subject matter.

If a writer compares apples and peaches and the only point of similarity is their both being fruits, the reader's response will probably be "so what?" Whenever someone comments on a child's being "rosy-cheeked," the comparison, even when apt, is stale and unimaginative. Even Shakespeare's "Shall I compare thee to a summer's day?"[1] has, after three centuries of repetition, lost some of its freshness as a comparison. The writer needs to select two concepts that are alike in such a way that the writer is making a genuinely interesting or striking comparison, thus jogging the reader into thinking about the subject from a new perspective or reconsidering an old comparison in a new way.

The subject matter need not be necessarily serious or scholarly. For instance, a student writing on desserts for the local weekly used comparison techniques to enliven her article.

> Virtually unheard of by yesterday's American shopper, today the kiwi sits in the supermarket fruit and vegetable section almost as unremarkable as the orange or apple. This three inch, furry-skinned, egg-shaped tropical fruit has a unique taste that combines the flavor of the banana with the strawberry and serves much the same purpose in garnishing a frozen dessert as parsley with a roast beef platter.

Even though comparisons emphasize similarities and frequently seem to have a positive connotation, the comparison does not necessarily have to be positive. For example, one student wrote:

> My sister Beatrice favors my Aunt Ella in matters of money. Both of them wince when spending a quarter for a cup of coffee and positively weep to pay for lunch.

In spite of not being particularly flattering to either Beatrice or Aunt Ella, the structure still remains a comparison because it tells in what way these two women are alike.

---

[1]William Shakespeare, "Sonnet XVIII."

Likewise, by the use of an unusual comparison, the following student essay was developed and it received an "A."

Coming to Terms

Losing my job was for me in many ways like learning that I had a terminal illness. First, I thought that I could beat the system and get another, better job immediately. "I'll have a job within two weeks," I said to myself, my wife and my friends. When I didn't find a better job within a month, I became angry with my friends and neighbors who were still employed, angry with my wife who had found a job to tide us over until I could get another position, and resentful of a society in which this could happen to a hard-working adult male. My anger was not too unlike the anger that the cancer patient feels after he or she has given up the first enthusiastic determination that he or she will "beat this illness." Like my hostility towards management, the cancer patient's hostility towards those who are well becomes a wild cry of "Why me and not them?" I began to ask myself, "What right do all those other people have to be employed when I'm without a job?"

I hated staying home all day. I was bored, frustrated, and felt demeaned by cleaning, cooking, and baby-sitting—all of which I also discovered that I wasn't too skillful at doing. I became increasingly resentful of the demands placed upon me that I had always thought of as "women's work." Finally, I became depressed and resigned to failure as so many cancer patients do to the "inevitable" that I drank heavily and sat around watching television all day. I tried to numb myself much as a cancer patient frequently longs to take the easy way out with an overdose.

Fortunately, I went to a job counselor before I lost my wife, my family, and my sanity over losing my job. Like the dying patient, I still have dark periods of resentment, apathy, even fear. I have come to respect, however, the role of the hand that rocks the cradle and scrubs the sink. In so doing, I have put a new value on my wife and on myself. I have learned to appreciate the value of what I do and try to accomplish rather than judging all jobs by the money they bring in. Like the patient in the cancer clinic, I, too, have learned to treasure today and let tomorrow take care of itself when it comes. The cancer of self-hatred and regret seems to be healing itself as I start on the road to retraining myself. Unlike the patient with whom I have been comparing myself, I hope to live to see my long-term goals succeed. My prognosis is good.

Warm-up Exercises

EXERCISE 1

a. What details does the writer employ to tell how he felt about losing his job at the age of forty?

b. How does the writer show that he came to terms with his personal disaster?

Contrast •

Much as the comparison structure depends on similarities as its key, the contrast structure makes its essential point by revealing the differences between two subjects, usually two subjects that are generally seen to be similar or related. Woe to the daughter who when she is asked what her boyfriend is like, replies rashly, "Well, he's nothing like you, Dad." A negative contrast has been established—lover boy is nothing like good old Dad. If this undiplomatic response is further buttressed with an adoring, "He's the most marvelous man in the whole world," then the contrast has been even further extended by implication.

Contrast and comparison structures require that the writer indicate likenesses and differences, but they do not always require the repeated use of signals; such as like, as, different from, similar to, etc. The concept of contrast and comparison can be implied, and often is. A skillful writer uses both words that alert the reader to a contrast or comparison together with sentences that cleverly imply contrast or comparison.

The following editorial "Rite of Passage, Right to Pick up the Tab," depends heavily on contrast by implication as does the essay, "Why Women Get the Jobs."

RITE OF PASSAGE, RIGHT TO PICK UP THE TAB

Washington—Years ago, my family gathered on Cape Cod for a weekend. We met at one of those resort restaurants where the menu is written on a blackboard held by a chummy waiter, and we had a wonderful time. With dinner concluded, the waiter brought the check and set it down in the middle of the table. That's when it happened. My father did not reach for the check.

In fact, my father did nothing. Conversation continued. I waited and waited and, finally, it dawned on me. Me! I was supposed to pick up the check. After hundreds of restaurant meals with my parents, after a lifetime of always thinking of my father as the one with the bucks, it had all changed. I reached for the check and whipped out my American Express card. My view of myself was suddenly altered. With a stroke of the pen, I was suddenly an adult.

Some people mark off their life in years, others in events. I am one of the latter and I think of some events as rites of passage. For instance, I did not become a young man at a particular age like 13. It was later, when a kid strolled into the store where I worked and called me "Mister." I turned around to see who he was calling. He repeated it several times—"Mister, mister"—looking straight at me. The realization hit like a punch: Me! He was talking to me.

There have been other milestones and I remember them all well. One occurred when I noticed that policemen seemed to be getting younger, not to mention smaller. Another came when I suddenly realized that I was older than every football player I knew. Instead of being big men, they were merely big kids. With that milestone went the fantasy that sometime, maybe, I too could be a player—maybe not a football player, but certainly a baseball player.

I had a good eye as a kid—not much power, but a keen eye—and I always thought I could play the game. One day I realized that I couldn't. Without having ever reached the hill, I was over it.

For some people, the ultimate milestone comes with the death of a parent and the realization that you have moved up a notch. As long as your parents live, you stay in some way a kid. At the very least, there remains at least one person whose love is unconditional.

I count other, less serious, milestones. I remember the day when I had a ferocious argument with my son and realized that I could no longer bully him. He was too big and the days when I could just pick him up and take him to his room/isolation cell were over. I needed to persuade, to reason. He was suddenly, rapidly, older. The other conclusion was inescapable: So was I.

One day you go to your friends' weddings. One day you celebrate the birth of their kids. One day you see one of their kids driving and one day they have kids of their own. One day you meet at parties and then at funerals. It all happens in one day. Take my word for it.

I never thought I would ever fall asleep in front of the television set as my friends' fathers did. I never thought I would have trouble sleeping. I remember my parents and their friends talking about insomnia like they were members of a different species. Not able to sleep? How ridiculous. It was all I did once. It was what I once did best.

I thought that I would never eat a food that did not agree with me. Now I meet them all the time. I thought I would never stop playing basketball and never go to the beach and not swim. I spent all of August at the beach and never went into the ocean once.

I thought I would never appreciate opera, but now the pathos, the schmaltz and, especially the combination of voice and music, appeal to me. The deaths of Mimi and Tosca move me. They die in my home as often as I can manage it.

I thought I would never prefer to stay home instead of going to a party, but now I find myself passing them up. I used to think that people who watch birds were weird, but this summer I found myself watching them and maybe I'll get a book on the subject.

I yearn for a religious conviction I never thought I would want, exult in my heritage anyway, feel close to ancestors long gone and echo my father in arguments with my son. I still lose.

One day I made a good toast. One day I handled a head waiter. One day I bought a house. One day—what a day!—I became a father and not too long after that I picked up the check for my own. I thought then and there it was a rite of passage for me. Not until I got older did I realize that it was one for him too. Another milestone.

Richard Cohen
From *The Washington Post*, October 11–12, 1986

WHY WOMEN GET THE JOBS

Throughout the industrial world, women have been finding jobs faster than men have been losing them. This quiet social revolution has done more than any number of feminist tracts to transform the way men regard women, and the way women regard themselves. Although women initially went into a narrow range of familiar part-time jobs, the next decade is going to see more of them emerge as employers, entrepreneurs, bankers and politicians. Many others will move into a wider range of higher positions than their mothers' generation could have hoped for. Their prospective success should make everybody more optimistic about economic growth.

Women have long found it easy to pick up work when economies boom. They are now doing so fast even in hard times. Since 1979 some 73% of the extra jobs created in the United States have been taken by women. In the other six largest OECD economies, which have been much less successful at building new jobs, women's employment has risen by 7% while men's has fallen by 2%. In a few countries, almost as many women as men now go out to work.

The flexible half of mankind

Women owe their advance partly to the changing demands of the market. In the 1970s, they were carried along by the boom in public-sector employment. In many countries, working for the state has become almost a women's preserve: in Scandinavia, seven out of ten public-sector workers are women. In the private sector, women have benefited from the spread of part-time jobs. In most industrial countries, at least four out of five part-timers are women. In Belgium, Denmark, West Germany and Britain, over 90% are. The growing service industries are the main employers of part-timers. Many women now perform for pay the services which they provide for free at home—cooking, cleaning, nursing, looking after children.

What women—especially married women—want from their jobs has meshed much better with the demands of most employers than what men want. Even with the equal-pay legislation that most industrial countries have now adopted, women often have the big advantage of being cheaper to employ than men, particularly if they work part-time and therefore qualify for fewer expensive fringe benefits. They are less likely to join trade unions than men, and to play an active part in union affairs when they do. They are more likely to work for pleasure, as well as for cash. They do not have the unmarketable arrogance of many men who still assume that the skills acquired in their early 20s will earn them their living in their 50s. Men expect a full-time job, a life-long career. Women are used to the idea of career breaks, retraining and flexible hours. Because most women stop work when their first child is born, more women than men change occupations at some point during their working lives.

This jobs revolution is still far from complete. It has barely begun in most third-world countries, where women work longer hours than their menfolk—and than their sisters in the West—but virtually none of them works for pay. In some industrial countries, the proportion of women in paid work has only recently overtaken the levels reached in the heyday of the industrial revolution (in Victorian Britain, for example, women were 30% of the workforce—almost all of them unmarried or poor, or both). And the huge increase in the number of jobs for women since 1970 has so far done little to widen the range of things they do. Most women in OECD countries are still in only a handful of occupations, usually unskilled or semi-skilled. Because women still do different jobs from men, it has been easier for employers to pay women less. In the next ten years this will change, as women move into a wider variety of jobs where "equal pay for equal work" will be an unquestioned truth.

At the bottom of the market, change will be forced on employers by demography. Their other source of cheap, flexible labour—the young, will dwindle: in Britain, the number of 15- to 19-year-olds in 1994 will be 28% less than in 1984. Married women will provide the main source of new workers. But women will also be in demand for other reasons, because they are becoming better educated. In several countries, more than half the secondary-school students are now girls. Education is likely to be at an increasing premium in the job market, and some British evidence suggests that staying on at school improves girls' employment prospects more than boys'. Women are still a minority of university students (except, significantly, in the United States), but the proportion everywhere is rising.

These newly educated women are choosing from a wider range of careers. Some of them swell the growing ranks of women entrepreneurs: women now own a quarter of all American small businesses, a third of all Canadian, a fifth of all French. The women graduates of the 1960s went into relatively few occupations—often, teaching. The graduates of the 1970s have chosen medicine, the law, banking, insurance. In Britain, 47% of medical-school graduates are now women. Over the past ten years, the proportion of women members of the Chartered Insurance Institute has risen from 4% to 14%, and of solicitors from 6% to 17%. In America, the proportion of executive, administrative and managerial jobs filled by women nearly doubled between 1970 and 1985. The more women move into professional jobs, the more they will prosper—and not just in the short term, before they have children. Well-educated women are more likely to go back to work after the birth of their children, and to go back more quickly, than those who leave school young and with few qualifications.

Dowries come with PhDs

The advantages of more education do not stop just with the job market. Women doing interesting, "real" jobs will command more social capital than their less qualified sisters. In that most rational of markets, the marriage market, men will increasingly come to realise that a wife with a good job brings not only the social pleasures of a second circle of friends, and a second set of work-related interests, but also the financial security of a second income. Thrifty bachelors should consider the extraordinary bargain presented by the West's new bride price: a woman who marries at 30, and who earns an average of £20,000 a year for the remaining 30 years of her career, provides her household with as much gross annual income as would a capital sum of £307,000 invested at 5% a year and used up over those 30 years. That is some dowry.

Employers who seize the chance to recruit women into high-powered jobs should flourish. Some have grasped that already. Last year women accounted for 28% of the graduates hired by General Electric, and 37% of those taken on in the United States by IBM. Not surprisingly, it is the fastest-growing industries that feel most comfortable with women in their senior ranks: the information industry (including public relations, computer services and the press), financial services, tourism, design. The parts of the economy where women are rarest—upper and middle management in medium-sized and larger companies, especially in manufacturing—are generally those now entering into relative decline.

Remember what peasants did for postwar industry. The economies that grew fastest in the 1950s and 1960s were usually those that switched most workers from under-productive farms to expanding factories. Well-educated women, as they become one-half of university graduates, will do for the 1985–2010 post-industrial economies what those suddenly more productive peasants did for the 1950–75 factory boom. Just think what will happen to companies that double the pool of talent at the top.

From *The Economist*,
August 23, 1986

The following student essay is a rebuttal of many popular feminist articles. It contrasts what the writer found to be true in her own way of life with what some women find is generally the case in twentieth century America.

My Granddaughter and I

My granddaughter and I share a common birthday. This year I turned sixty-nine as my youngest grandchild turned nineteen. We also both announced momentous life decisions at our shared family birthday party: she, to drop out of college "to find herself," and I, to enroll in college "to find out more about myself." My granddaughter has chosen to clerk in a hardware store. When asked why she chose this over college, she has insisted, "I want to learn about real life." I, too, have answered when queried about my decision to go to college that I hope to learn more about real life. The difference between my granddaughter and me is that she is confident that she will succeed and I am hesitant about my decision and apprehensive of my ability to succeed in college at my age.

My choice to go to college now was not a rejection of my past life choices, but simply a new direction for my life to take. Unlike Ms Friedan whom we are reading in class, I never considered my bringing up a family or providing a clean and attractive home for my husband and children solely as "the full routine of housework." My memories of those years are of work, pleasure and sorrow, much as any vocation provides. There was nothing meaningless about scrubbing down a bedroom or boiling and bleaching bed linens because a child brought home worms from camp nor was there anything frivolous or boring about sitting up three nights running with a child who had the croup.

Perhaps because I am middle-class, midwestern and middle-aged, I do not understand Ms Friedan's description of the typical American housewife's life as that of leisured passivity. Bringing up three children in the depression and the war years was neither leisurely nor routine. I never felt that my home was a kind of "comfortable concentration camp" nor that my identification with my husband's and children's successes and failures was a kind of personal suicide. I am as proud to be Mrs. Smith, Janey's mother, and Myra Smith as I am to be a member of my community, a Democrat and an American. I am all of these and would not want to be less.

My granddaughter has as much right to clerk in a hardware store as her grandfather in a hay and feed store; I, too, have the right to marry, rear a family, and go to college. If my granddaughter finds the routine of her chosen job dull, boring or even a kind of "concentration camp," she is free to choose again.

EXERCISE 2

a. Using the blocking out pattern from Chapter One, list the contrasts, explicit and implicit, that this student used to develop her controlling idea.

b. Do you think this essay has weak points in its development? What are they?

c. Does the subjectivity of this essay limit its effect on you? List some examples.

A late blooming college student wrote the following comparison of college versus high school life.

Attending College

Attending college more than twenty years after completing high school is a stimulating experience for me and contrasts in several ways with my high school days. For one thing, in high school the relationship between teacher and students, as I perceived it, was one of parent to child. I saw the teacher as the authority and the authoritarian possessor of knowledge and administrator of discipline. She imparted her knowledge with assurance and confidence, and I was expected to absorb and memorize this information, and, subsequently, recall it when exam time came.

There was no talking out in class without first raising a hand and being recognized. Most of the students were the same age as I and, since I attended a neighborhood school, came from similar social and economic backgrounds. We were also involved with each other in activities outside the classroom, but even though I knew most of my classmates, I was reluctant to speak out in class, as

I feared making a mistake and being judged "stupid" by my peers. The emphasis was on making good grades, and I felt pressured to excel.

By contrast, a different atmosphere prevails in my college classes today. The teachers invite class participation; along with the other students, I am invited to express my views and opinions. A free exchange of ideas exists, demonstrating an adult-to-adult relationship within the class. An atmosphere of openness prevails, and we can speak without waiting to be called on first. Individuals from a diversified range of occupations, age groups, and economic and intellectual levels make up the classes. Even though I know the other students only during class hours and have no contact or involvement with them between sessions, and in spite of the fact that many of my classmates are young enough to be my own children, I feel accepted by them without regard to the age difference. I feel at ease about speaking out and am not fearful of being judged. In fact, I am often listened to and my opinions are always respected.

The biggest difference for me is in the attitude I take to class. Although I enjoyed high school, I went basically because it was required and expected of me in order to be prepared for the future. Today I go because I choose to—it is something I want to do. My college classes are stimulating and challenging, opening new doors and broadening my life experiences. Perhaps I will decide to apply my studies toward a new job or career; but, at present, that is not my motive for attending. I just enjoy learning.

EXERCISE 3

a. What specific element of contrast does this student use?

b. Do you see any problems with this student's paragraph structure? How would you paragraph the piece?

c. Try revising this essay by creating first a blocking-out pattern that incorporates all the contrast elements as well as any telling descriptive details.

Combining Comparison and Contrast •

Surprisingly enough, the whole concept of **comparison and contrast** techniques of composition is remarkably simple and straight-forward. There is nothing esoteric or erudite about a writing technique that employs the thinking and speaking patterns used in conversations and thought from childhood on.

The only time that complications arise for the writer is when he or she decides to combine both comparison and contrast in the same essay. Since this is a very common pattern in essay examination questions, the combined technique is an important one to master. Don't lose any sleep anticipating insurmountable difficulties combining comparison and contrast. It is much like learning to play the piano. First one learns to play the treble keys with the right hand and then the bass keys with the left. After some concerted effort, the budding pianist can get both hands playing simultaneously. From then on, it is just a matter of practice.

The same concept holds true with writing. One simply has to make an effort to organize those items about subject A that are being compared with similar items about subject B and to keep those contrasting comments about A and B in parallel format, too. A writer needs organization, preplanning, and outlining to make smooth contrasts and comparisons effective; otherwise, the essay has a tendency to wander from point to point, sometimes even leaving out telling points.

FLEXIBILITY

Essentially, there are two patterns which can be seen in the following diagrams.

PATTERN 1		
SECTION I:	comparisons A–B 1. 2. 3.	contrasts A–B 1. 2. 3.
SECTION II:	contrasts A–B 1. 2. 3.	comparisons A–B 1. 2. 3.

PATTERN 2	
SECTION I:	comparison 1 A–B contrast 1 A–B
SECTION II:	comparison 2 A–B contrast 2 A–B
SECTION III:	comparison 3 A–B contrast 3 A–B

Perhaps the most interesting aspect of the comparison-contrast technique is its **flexibility**—the different effects that a writer can create simply by organizing and re-organizing the points that he or she wishes to make. In other words, a writer must decide during the process of drafting the essay whether to make a full frontal assault on the reader or whether to delay the attack and, instead, creep up from the rear.

If the writer plans to spring the major point of the comparison or contrast – the one that really clinches the argument – upon the unsuspecting reader scarcely before the reader has had time to absorb the introduction, the reader, reeling from the impact, cannot fail to be impressed by the essay. Alternatively, the writer may opt to graduate the impact of his argument by placing the least important point of the comparison or contrast first and working up to the most significant immediately before the conclusion. Then the conclusion becomes the burst of fire that conquers the reader completely.

Make short outlines of the following student essays to see how the two writers handled their essay structures.

Yard and Garden

To an American that little patch of land surrounding his house means one thing, but to an Englishman it means quite another. The American typically calls it a yard but the Englishman calls it a garden. However, the difference is more than just the name. The American arranges his shrubs and flowers around the grassy area which becomes his badminton court or croquet field. The Englishman places the grassy areas in his garden behind, in front of, in-between, and around those selected spots where he plants his flowers and shrubs. The Englishman takes care to give his shrubs and flowers the central positions he thinks they deserve; the patches of grass that he landscapes into his garden are there to highlight his darlings. As the weekend approaches, the American usually feels irritated because the chore of cutting the grass or trimming the shrubs must be completed before he proceeds to his weekend hobbies. In contrast, the Englishman looks toward the weekend with pleasure because the care of his garden is his hobby, and he feels irritated if something he considers a chore interrupts him. The tools each uses reflect the different attitudes. The American chooses various powered tools that will aid him in completing the job as soon as possible; the Englishman selects hand tools that can be used patiently and slowly to produce just the right effect. Even the purpose of that piece of land has different meanings for each. The American sees his yard as a functional area, a place for living, for playing, and at times an outright nuisance. The Englishman sees in his garden an instrument for self-expression, something to be nurtured, caressed, and then proudly exhibited in all its beauty.

Separatism or Integration?

Both Booker T. Washington and Martin Luther King are giants in American history who dedicated their lives to black betterment and racial harmony. Both were products of the South; both were Afro-Americans; both were effective spokesmen for their race during their respective periods of leadership. The influences these two men have exerted on black and white life in America is astronomical. Yet their individual methods were quite different.

Both men stressed cooperation as a keystone in building positive race relations. Washington espoused his philosophy in a classic analogy—"We can be as separate in all things as the fingers on one hand"—for which he has been widely rebuked by blacks then and now. In that statement Washington implied that the road of social separation between blacks and whites was a beneficial one to Negro betterment and American progress as a whole. Tuskegee Institute of Alabama is a highly regarded testimonial to Washington's practicality. For years, as the major black institute for higher learning, it graduated educators, architects, engineers, and other practically oriented black students.

In contrast to Mr. Washington, Dr. King was opposed to racial separation in any form. His rise to prominence began with his dogged attacks on Southern segregation policies. Utilizing the concepts of universal love and civil disobedience to attain his goals, he won worldwide acclaim as a crusader for peace after the fashion of Christ and Ghandi. Like them, he became the center of much turmoil, for he campaigned aggressively against racial hatred and injustice. Unlike Booker T. Washington, Dr. King believed that as long as black America and white America were separate, there would never be a true American democracy.

Both "Yard and Garden" and "Separatism or Integration?" are chiefly developed by contrasts. But note the different patterns of contrast they employ. In "Yard and Garden," we find this pattern.

Point A: ____________ American
Point A: ____________ Englishman
Point B: ____________ American
Point B: ____________ Englishman
Point C: ____________ American
Point C: ____________ Englishman
Point D: ____________ American
Point D: ____________ Englishman

In "Separatism or Integration?" after an opening paragraph listing how King and Washington were similar, we find this pattern:

Racial Philosophy of Booker T. Washington in paragraph two:
Point A: ____________
Point B: ____________
Point C: ____________

Racial Philosophy of Martin Luther King in paragraph three:
Point A: ____________
Point B: ____________
Point C: ____________

Warm-up Exercises

EXERCISE 4

a. In the philosophies of "Yard and Garden," what are the detailed points of contrast between Americans and Englishmen? Write a four or five word summary of each of these points.

b. How would you phrase the points of contrast between the racial philosophies of Washington and King?

c. Indicate the sub-parts of "Yard and Garden" and of "Separatism or Integration?"

Buying Faucet Washers

Since the English and Americans share a common language, it is easy to assume there will always be clear communication between a Brit and a Yank. One Saturday morning I found out differently as I stood outside Pearce's Hardware Store, intent on buying two faucet washers. Pushing the door open, I stepped inside and back into the nineteenth century. Gone was the sterility of hardware stores from my youth—places like Honest Jack's, with row after row of neatly stacked, pre-packaged goods. Instead, I was assaulted with a wealth of smells emanating from open hoppers of nails and screws quietly rusting away and the sharp tang of paint, varnish, and kerosene all clamoring for my attention. Picking my way past piled up goods, I moved to the counter and caught the attention of Mr. Pearce himself. "I'd like two faucet washers," I said. "Two what?" Mr. Pearce asked questioningly. My mind froze! For the next ten minutes I tried to explain the object I wanted. Finally, one old man who had dealt with Yanks during the war explained to Mr. Pearce that I wanted to buy water tap washers. Embarrassed, I bought two different sizes and hurried home muttering "water tap washers" the whole way.

After reading "Buying Faucet Washers," look at "Yard and Garden" and "Separatism or Integration?" again to test the following assertions:

1. Contrasts are most interesting when through them the reader becomes aware of differences not noticed before.
2. Fresh contrasts reveal unfamiliar differences in subjects supposedly alike or, in reality, much alike.
3. It is usually not rewarding to contrast the obviously different.
4. Fresh comparisons reveal unsuspected similarities in subjects.
5. By explaining what a subject essentially is and is not, paragraphs developed by contrast, comparison, or comparison-contrast may also be said to *define*.
6. Paragraphs developed by contrast, comparison, or comparison-contrast may employ all or some of the basic means of development already

studied in how to write essays developed by descriptive and illustrative details.

EXERCISE 5

a. Consider how the three student writers gave coherence to their paragraphs by means of logical ordering and transitions. List the translations and transitional phrases that the students used to give order to their essays.

b. Reread the three student essays and make a list of the descriptive or illustrative details that give life and individuality to each essay.

LONGER BLOCKING-OUT PATTERNS

The paragraphs you write for the comparison-contrast essay will almost certainly be longer than those you wrote earlier since you are trying to explain more now than you were before. It will be helpful for you to think of the paragraphs you are currently writing as transitional. They are steps in the process of learning to write compositions of five or six hundred words. Writing an essay with many distinct parts requires control. If the piece is to be clear and coherent, the parts must be well arranged. Blocking-out can help you think through a subject before you write as well as give order to what you write.

Although you may find that a blocking-out pattern is sufficient, a simple working outline will carry your writing a step further and help prepare you for longer compositions. Working with the student essay, "Cities of Contrast," try both the blocking-out schema and a simple outline.

Cities of Contrast

The cities of Athens and Rhodes are geographically separated by less than 300 miles, inhabited by the same nationalities, and frequented by countless tourists each year; however, comparisons end here.

I have resided in a suburb of Athens for more than seven years now and, believe me, the city's charm quickly diminishes with day-to-day life. Driving in downtown Athens is a chaotic experience, complete with congested streets, obnoxious drivers, dangerous intersections, and constantly blaring horns. During peak rush hour, one can find oneself caught in a traffic jam and unable to move in any direction for an hour or more. One of the contributing factors to the frightening traffic situation is the poor road conditions. The streets have poorly marked traffic lanes, are dotted with potholes, and are interspersed with uncontrolled intersections. Just to reach one's destination safely, without suffering a headache from the noise and overpowering exhaust fumes, is a minor accomplishment. Also, the shops in downtown Athens are so commercialized a person is disgusted by the offensive vendors constantly trying to force their wares on everyone who strolls by. The goods are usually of inferior quality, overpriced, and guaranteed only until the customer steps from the shop. Even if one manages to find a respectable merchant with quality merchandise, the mobs of people pushing and shoving are usually enough to deter any inclination to shop and barter prices. As is often the case, Athens is a reflection of her inhabitants. The people are distrusting, aloof, and representative of the big city syndrome—"each man for himself." Every week many women fall victim to purse-snatching, while apathetic witnesses stand by without offering any assistance. Additionally, several years ago Athenians would take time to converse, even if one's Greek wasn't fluent; however, today the majority of the inhabitants avoid superfluous conversations altogether.

On the other hand, Rhodes combines a refreshing touch of the old and new to create a tranquil atmosphere. Her streets are crowded during the peak of tourism, but surprisingly, the traffic flows unimpeded with a conspicuous absence of blaring horns. The motorists are courteous, adhere to posted speed limits, and stop for pedestrians. The streets have clearly defined lanes of traffic, are free of potholes, and have prominently displayed traffic signs or signal lights at every intersection. The combination of well designed roads and organized traffic flow makes driving in Rhodes a pleasant experience. The bazaars of the old city are a delightful carry-over from the days of Ottoman rule and overflow with quality merchandise of every type imaginable. One can purchase souvenirs ranging from the finest imported oriental silks to the island's specialty, umbrellas. The vendors are jovial and quick to assist one in comparing wares and prices with neighboring merchants. Without a doubt, the most positive influence on life in Rhodes is her friendly and warm residents. The locals go about their daily routine with a carefree attitude and stand ready to offer assistance to anyone in need. For instance, I was lost during one of my excursions in the old Turkish sector and a Greek couple invited me into their home. We drank tea, exchanged pleasantries, and discussed the routes by which I could reach my destination. I was genuinely amazed at how trusting and kind they were to me, a complete stranger. After experiencing life in both cities, I am convinced Rhodes is the place for me.

A blocking-out pattern for "Cities of Contrast" might look like this one:

SUBJECT MATTER	POINT OF VIEW AND CONTROLLING IDEA	DETAILED MATERIALS OF DEVELOPMENT
contrasting Athens and Rhodes	pro-Rhodes Rhodes is a better place to visit and live	1. traffic 2. condition of roads 3. shops 4. people

EXERCISE 6

a. Fill out points of the preceding blocking-out pattern with additional words or phrases. These will be the materials for a simple working outline. Following the bare bones outline given below, develop a specific outline for "Cities of Contrast."

OUTLINE SCHEMA

I. Topic Sentence or Thesis Statement:
II. Elements of Contrast:
    A.
    B.
    C. etc.
III. Conclusion:

b. Decide on the key statement or controlling idea that you propose to develop. This need not be, nor should be, lengthy or detailed.

c. Read the following two essays and make short working outlines from them.

As you read this student's paper, consider how it could be outlined following the Outline Schema above.

The Family Vacation—Then and Now

Twenty years ago, a family vacation was a carefree, relaxed time when the entire family could get away from day-to-day life and enjoy themselves for a short period. It was also a chance for the kids in our family to get out from under the watchful eyes of Mom and Dad for awhile. Mom and Dad always seemed too engrossed in relaxing to pay much attention to what we were doing.

The atmosphere surrounding our entire vacation seemed to be relaxed and easygoing. Preparations consisted of packing a change of clothes or two for everyone and some food to tide us over until we reached our deserted lake where we usually spent our vacation. Once there, Mom and Dad did not seem concerned that there was no entertainment director around to ensure that we enjoyed ourselves. Instead, they seemed to think that we were doing a pretty good job without any help. The lack of adult supervision was a part of the fun of our vacation. It was much more fun to be able to swim or climb a tree without an adult standing around giving instructions on how it should be done.

Today a family vacation is a well organized, businesslike trip to a commercial vacation resort where Moms and Dads leave the kids under the care of paid entertainment directors while they participate in planned adult activities. From beginning to end, the modern family vacation is more work than play. Many months are spent just planning a vacation. A suitable site has to be selected from the many well publicized "vacationlands." After selecting the site, the next problem is coming up with enough money to finance a couple of weeks at such a place. Then, fitting the vacation into the family's schedule is quite a problem. It seems that every member of the family is involved in some sort of outside activity that conflicts with Dad's time off from work. Dad himself is involved in golf, bowling or some other sport which is having a tournament at that time. Mom is involved in charity work which will suffer if she is away at that particular time. The kids' Little League baseball, Scouts, and the like also have to be taken into consideration. Some outside activity usually forces the family to take its vacation at other than the most suitable time.

Finally, the site is selected and the date set. As departure time nears, planning and organizing become even more hectic. In addition to an almost complete wardrobe for everyone, all the small items so necessary to "enjoying" a modern vacation, such as swimming vests, umbrellas, and transistor radios, have to be rounded up and packed away. When this is done, the family is finally ready to set out on a much needed vacation.

Upon arriving at the beach which has been selected for this year's vacation, the kids are turned over to the entertainment director for two weeks of planned activity. Supervised swimming, boating, and dancing are provided from morning until night. Mom and Dad also have a tight schedule of planned activities. There are golf lessons in the morning, tennis or swimming in the afternoon, and also dancing in the evening. After two long weeks of this planned entertainment, the family is in desperate need of an "old-fashioned" vacation of rest and relaxation. They wearily pack for the long trip back, resolving to spend a quiet, relaxing vacation next year—at home.

Now, compare your outline with the practice outline done by a previous student.

Practice Outline

Thesis Statement: In the last twenty years, the once carefree, relaxed family vacation has been replaced by a hectic, tiring annual excursion to commercial resorts.

I. Twenty years ago, our family vacations just sort of happened.
- A. There was little or no pre-vacation planning.
- B. The preparations prior to departure were minimal.
- C. There were no blueprints for enjoying ourselves.

II. Today, a great deal of time, money and effort go into a vacation that is not at all relaxing.
- A. There is, first of all, a great amount of pre-vacation planning.
  1. Suggestions for a suitable site have to be mulled over.
  2. Enough money to finance the vacation has to be found.
  3. The vacation itself has to be fitted into a tight family schedule of activities.
- B. The preparations prior to departure are complicated.
- C. The vacation time itself is tightly scheduled and the "enjoyment" organized.

Conclusion: (Draw your own conclusion to reflect why the comparison or contrast between these two subjects is worth commenting upon.)

Bruce Catton (1899–1978), a Pulitzer Prize winner for historical journalism, is best remembered for his works on the Civil War. "Grant and Lee: A Study in Contrasts," which is actually a chapter of his book, *The American Story*, is an especially fine example of a carefully constructed comparison-contrast essay.

When reading this essay, notice how the contrast and comparison structural pattern is carefully developed.

GRANT AND LEE: A STUDY IN CONTRASTS

1 When Ulysses S. Grant and Robert E. Lee met in the parlor of a modest house at Appomattox Court House, Virginia, on April 9, 1865, to work out the terms for the surrender of Lee's Army of Northern Virginia, a great chapter in American life came to a close, and a great new chapter began.

2 These men were bringing the Civil War to its virtual finish. To be sure, other armies had yet to surrender, and for a few days the fugitive Confederate government would struggle desperately and vainly, trying to find some way to go on living now that its chief support was gone. But in effect it was all over when Grant and Lee signed the papers. And the little room where they wrote out the terms was the scene of one of the poignant, dramatic contrasts in American History.

3 They were two strong men these oddly different generals, and they represented the strengths of two conflicting currents that, through them, had come into final collision.

4 Back of Robert E. Lee was the notion that the old aristocratic concept might somehow survive and be dominant in American life.

5 Lee was tidewater Virginia, and in his background were family, culture, and tradition . . . the age of chivalry transplanted to a New World which was making its own legends and its own myths. He embodied a way of life that had come down through the age of knighthood and the English country squire. America was a land that was beginning all over again, dedicated to nothing much more complicated than the rather hazy belief that all men had equal rights and should have an equal chance in the world. In such a land Lee stood for the feeling that it was somehow of advantage to human society to have a pronounced inequality in the social structure. There should be a leisure class, backed by ownership of land; in turn, society itself should be keyed to the land as the chief source of wealth and influence. It would bring forth (according to this ideal) a class of men with a strong sense of obligation to the community; men who lived not to gain advantage for themselves, but to meet the solemn obligations which had been laid on them by the very fact that they were privileged. From them the country would get its leadership; to them it could look for the higher values—of thought, of conduct, or personal deportment—to give it strength and virtue.

6 Lee embodied the noblest elements of this aristocratic ideal. Through him, the landed nobility justified itself. For four years, the Southern states had fought a desperate war to uphold the ideals for which Lee stood. In the end, it almost seemed as if the Confederacy fought for Lee; as if he himself was the Confederacy . . . the best thing that the way of life for which the Confederacy stood could ever have to offer. He had passed into legend before Appomattox. Thousands of tired, underfed, poorly clothed Confederate soldiers, long since past

the simple enthusiasm of the early days of the struggle, somehow considered Lee the symbol of everything for which they had been willing to die. But they could not quite put this feeling into words. If the Lost Cause, sanctified by so much heroism and so many deaths, had a living justification, its justification was General Lee.

7 Grant, the son of a tanner on the Western frontier, was everything Lee was not. He had come up the hard way and embodied nothing in particular except the eternal toughness and sinewy fiber of the men who grew up beyond the mountains. He was one of a body of men who owed reverence and obeisance to no one, who were self-reliant to a fault, who cared hardly anything for the past but who had a sharp eye for the future.

8 These frontier men were the precise opposites of the tidewater aristocrats. Back of them, in the great surge that had taken people over the Alleghenies and into the opening Western country, there was a deep, implicit dissatisfaction with a past that had settled into grooves. They stood for democracy, not from any reasoned conclusion about the proper ordering of human society, but simply because they had grown up in the middle of democracy and knew how it worked. Their society might have privileges, but they would be privileges each man had won for himself. Forms and patterns meant nothing. No man was born to anything, except perhaps to a chance to show how far he could rise. Life was competition.

9 Yet along with this feeling had come a deep sense of belonging to a national community. The Westerner who developed a farm, opened a shop, or set up in business as a trader could hope to prosper only as his own community prospered—and his community ran from the Atlantic to the Pacific and from Canada down to Mexico. If the land was settled, with towns and highways and accessible markets, he could better himself. He saw his fate in terms of the nation's own destiny. As its horizons expanded, so did his. He had, in other words, an acute dollars-and-cents stake in the continued growth and development of his country.

10 And that, perhaps, is where the contrast between Grant and Lee becomes most striking. The Virginia aristocrat, inevitably, saw himself in relation to his own region. He lived in a static society which could endure almost anything except change. Instinctively, his first loyalty would go to the locality in which that society existed. He would fight to the limit of endurance to defend it, because in defending it he was defending everything that gave his own life its deepest meaning.

11 The Westerner, on the other hand, would fight with an equal tenacity for the broader concept of society. He fought so because everything he lived by was tied to growth, expansion, and a constantly widening horizon. What he lived by would survive or fall with the nation itself. He could not possibly stand by unmoved in the face of an attempt to destroy the Union. He would combat it with everything he had, because he could only see it as an effort to cut the ground out from under his feet.

12 So Grant and Lee were in complete contrast, representing two

diametrically opposed elements in American life. Grant was the modern man emerging; beyond him, ready to come on the stage, was the great age of steel and machinery, of crowded cities and a restless burgeoning vitality. Lee might have ridden down from the old age of chivalry, lance in hand, silken banner fluttering over his head. Each man was the perfect champion of his cause, drawing both his strengths and his weaknesses from the people he led.

13 Yet it was not all contrast, after all. Different as they were—in background, in personality, in underlying aspiration—these two great soldiers had much in common. Under everything else, they were marvelous fighters. Furthermore, their fighting qualities were really very much alike.

14 Each man had, to begin with, the great virtue of utter tenacity and fidelity. Grant fought his way down the Mississippi Valley in spite of acute personal discouragement and profound military handicaps. Lee hung on in the trenches at Petersburg after hope itself had died. In each man there was an indomitable quality . . . the born fighter's refusal to give up as long as he can still remain on his feet and lift his two fists.

15 Daring and resourcefulness they had, too: the ability to think faster and move faster than the enemy. These were the qualities which gave Lee the dazzling campaigns of Second Manassas and Chancellorsville and won Vicksburg for Grant.

16 Lastly, and perhaps greatest of all, there was the ability, at the end, to turn quickly from war to peace once the fighting was over. Out of the way these two men behaved at Appomattox came the possibility of a peace of reconciliation. It was a possibility not wholly realized, in the years to come, but which did, in the end, help the two sections to become one nation again . . . after a war whose bitterness might have seemed to make such a reunion wholly impossible. No part of either man's life became him more than the part he played in their brief meeting in the McLean house at Appomattox. Their behavior there put all succeeding generations of Americans in their debt. Two great Americans, Grant and Lee—very different, yet under everything very much alike. Their encounter at Appomattox was one of the great moments of American history.

Bruce Catton
From *The American Story*

If you were to diagram Catton's chapter, paragraph by paragraph, it might look something like this:

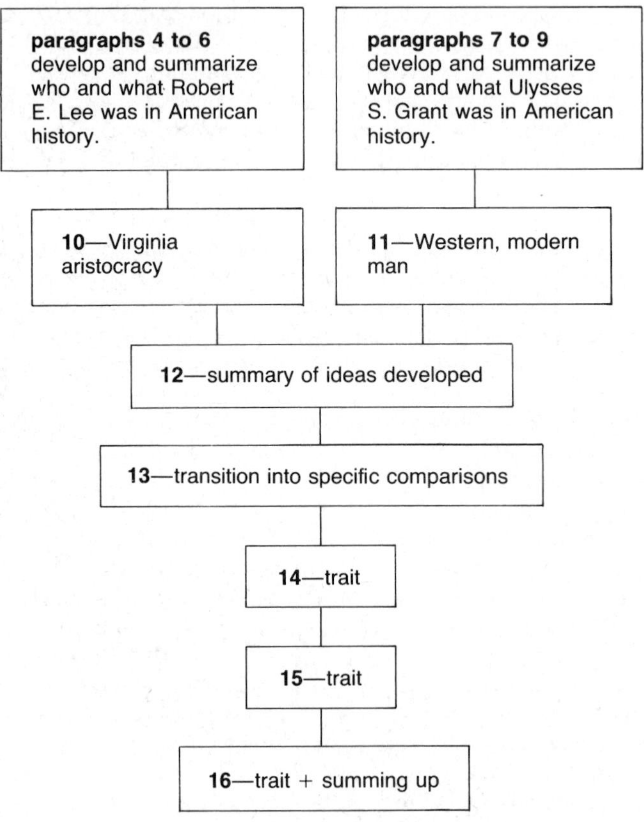

After having examined this essay with its funneling type of contrast and comparison structure, see if you can apply this format to other essays that follow. Perhaps you can also use this structure in writing your own compositions.

The next selection, usually referred to as "Two Ways of Seeing a River," is actually a portion from *Life on the Mississippi* by Mark Twain, published in 1883. Mark Twain, the famous American nineteenth century humorist, is remembered for his classic novel, *Adventures of Huckleberry Finn*, and beloved for his children's favorite, *Tom Sawyer*. Probably no single essay is more popular with readers than "Two Ways of Seeing a River" nor more valuable for the student who wishes to examine the skillful use of comparison-contrast techniques.

TWO WAYS OF SEEING A RIVER

Now when I had mastered the language of this water and had come to know every trifling feature that bordered the great river as familiarly as I knew the letters of the alphabet, I had made a valuable acquisition. But I had lost something, too. I had lost something which could never be restored to me while I lived. All the grace, the beauty, the poetry, had gone out of the majestic river! I still kept in mind a certain wonderful sunset which I witnessed when steam-boating was new to me. A broad expanse of the river was turned to blood; in the middle distance the red hue brightened into gold, through which a solitary log came floating, black and conspicuous; in one place a long, slanting mark lay sparkling upon the water; in another the surface was broken by boiling, tumbling rings that were as many-tinted as an opal; where the ruddy flush was faintest was a smooth spot that was covered with graceful circles and radiating lines, ever so delicately traced; the shore on our left was densely wooded, and the somber shadow that fell from this forest was broken in one place by a long, ruffled trail that shone like silver; and high above the forest wall a clean-stemmed dead tree waved a single leafy bough that glowed like a flame in the unobstructed splendor that was flowing from the sun. There were graceful curves, reflected images, woody heights, soft distances, and over the whole scene, far and near, the dissolving lights drifted steadily, enriching it every passing moment with new marvels of coloring.

I stood like one bewitched. I drank it in, in a speechless rapture. The world was new to me and I had never seen anything like this at home. But as I have said, a day came when I began to cease from noting the glories and the charms which the moon and the sun and the twilight wrought upon the river's face; another day came when I ceased altogether to note them. Then, if that sunset scene had been repeated, I should have looked upon it without rapture and should have commented upon it inwardly after this fashion: "This sun means that we are going to have wind to-morrow; that floating log means that the river is rising, small thanks to it; that slanting mark on the water refers to a bluff reef which is going to kill somebody's steamboat one of these nights, if it keeps on stretching out like that; those tumbling 'boils' show a dissolving bar and a changing channel there; the lines and circles in the slick water over yonder are a warning that that troublesome place is shoaling up dangerously; that silver streak in the shadow of the forest is the 'break' from a new snag and he has located himself in the very best place he could have found to fish for steamboats; that tall dead tree, with a single living branch, is not going to last long, and then how is a body ever going to get through this blind place at night without the friendly old landmark?"

No, the romance and beauty were all gone from the river. All the value any feature of it had for me now was the amount of usefulness it could furnish toward compassing the safe piloting of a steamboat. Since those days, I have pitied doctors from my heart. What does the lovely flush in a beauty's cheek mean to a doctor but a "break" that ripples above some deadly disease? Are not all her visible charms sown thick with what are to him the signs and symbols of hidden decay? Does he ever see her beauty at all, or doesn't he simply view her professionally and comment upon her unwholesome condition all to himself? And doesn't he sometimes wonder whether he has gained most or lost most by learning his trade?

Mark Twain
From *Life on the Mississippi*

Cross-curricular Essay Questions

Although the comparison-contrast type of question is especially common in the disciplines of history, psychology, sociology, political science, and literature, you can see from the sample questions that follow, that the sciences also employ these kinds of questions.

1. Contrast and compare the use of executive powers during the administrations of Thomas Jefferson, Andrew Jackson, and Abraham Lincoln. (American History)
2. Contrast and compare the differences in interpretations and the uses to which these interpretations are put for the thirteenth, fourteenth, and fifteenth amendments to the Constitution. (Political Science)
3. Define the elegy as a poetic form. Then contrast and compare the uses and developments in the elegy in the works of Milton, Tennyson, and Whitman. (Literature)
4. Contrast and compare the Czarist attitude toward foreigners and the attitude of the present regime. (Russian Studies)
5. Select two management theories and contrast and compare them. Comment on the differences in the cultural approaches of two different countries towards the role of business and management. (Management Studies)
6. Compare and contrast the small town and its sociological structure before 1877 and afterwards. Also comment in detail on the contrasts and similarities between the small towns of different sections of the United States. (Sociology)
7. Choose any two types of aberrant behavior and contrast and compare the theories dealing with child development that may account in part for these patterns of behavior and how to handle them. (Psychology)
8. Contrast and compare the early ideas of atomic structure with modern ones. Explain in detail the experiment by which Rutherford and co-workers established the modern idea of atomic structure. Discuss the structure of the atomic nucleus and explain how its component parts are held together despite mutual repulsion. (Physics)
9. Compare and contrast three scientific ideas on the origin of the

universe. Include in this account various types of evidence which support, or might support, after further research any of these theories. (Biology)

10. "By means of the chemical industry we have made American agriculture highly productive. However, we may have made as many problems as we have solved." Discuss this quotation by comparing and contrasting the effects of chemicals on modern agriculture with the pre-chemical agriculture of the last century. (Chemistry)

11. In what ways were the systems of Ptolemy and Copernicus similar? In what ways did they differ? (Astronomy)

12. Discuss the advantages and disadvantages of the two main ideas of optical telescopes. What are the three powers of a telescope? Why are radio telescopes so large? (Physics)

Practice Essay

Pick a subject familiar enough to you that you can compare and contrast it thoroughly or try your hand at using a subject that you are currently studying. Decide on the key statement or controlling idea that you propose to develop. This should not be, nor need to be, lengthy or detailed.
Fill out points of the blocking-out pattern with a word, words or phrases. These will form the basis for your working outline.
Make a short working outline from your blocking-out pattern before you actually start writing your essay.

CHAPTER
• THREE •

Definition

There's a certain Slant of Light,
Winter Afternoons—
That oppresses, like the Heft
Of Cathedral Tunes—

Heavenly Hurt, it gives us—
We can find no scar,
But internal difference,
Where the Meanings, are—

Emily Dickinson

"What is it?" "What's its purpose?" "What's its function?" These are three of the many common questions we ask and are asked daily, questions which seek definition of an unknown in our world. That unknown may be concrete and tangible, such as a chair, or abstract and exceedingly difficult to pin down to a precise, agreed-upon meaning, such as beauty, goodness, and freedom.

• Simple Definition

There are several types of definition we want to examine here for their possible usefulness in our writing: the simple definition, the stipulative definition, the operational definition and the lexical definition. The first type, the **simple definition**, may be nothing more than a dictionary definition we use to make sure that our readers understand our terms. Simple definitions help the writer when the terms we use are not in our reader's vocabulary and when the terms themselves may be understood quite differently by different members of our audience.

Take the term *equity*. To a general audience, equity will probably mean fairness. Yet to a banker, this very term may be understood as describing the difference between a property's market value and the claim, such as a mortgage, held against it. To a securities broker, equity is the excess of securities over a debit balance in a margin account. And what if one reader is a stock investor? To such a person, equity describes the ownership interests of shareholders in a corporation—stocks as opposed to bonds. If you use such a term as equity in one of its narrower meanings, you may want to add a simple definition to ensure that your readers understand the term in the same way you use it.

Good simple definitions meet two criteria:

(1) they are exclusive; that is, they apply only to the term being defined; and

(2) they are true.

At times, a good synonym is all we may need for a simple definition.

> Equity-based interests, those of stockholders, often conflict with management interests in multi-national companies.

Usually, though, a simple definition will require a bit more. These more complex definitions fit a logical model:

TERM	= CLASS	+ DISTINGUISHING CHARACTERISTICS
fairy tale	a story	about mysterious pranks and supernatural spirits
fez	a hat	shaped like a truncated cone and worn by men in some Middle Eastern countries
arbitrage profits	profits which result from price differences	of the same commodity in different markets

We find a wonderful example of a simple definition given in context in Lewis Carroll's *Through the Looking Glass*. Alice and Humpty Dumpty are finishing up their conversation on un-birthday presents:

> "I don't know what you mean by 'glory,'" Alice said.
> Humpty Dumpty smiled contemptuously. "Of course you don't—till I tell you. I meant 'there's a nice knock-down argument for you!'"
> "But 'glory' doesn't mean 'a nice knock-down argument,'" Alice objected.
> "When *I* use a word," Humpty Dumpty said, in rather a scornful tone, "it means just what I choose it to mean—neither more nor less."
> "The question is," said Alice, "whether you *can* make words mean so many different things."
> "The question is," said Humpty Dumpty, "which is to be master—that's all."

Humpty Dumpty's definition of *glory* certainly meets the first of the definition criteria, since it is exclusive. Does it meet the second criterion? Is it true?

1. Contrast Humpty Dumpty's definition of *glory* with a dictionary definition. Use a new edition standard dictionary.
2. Write definitions for the following terms, using the classification-distinguishing characteristics model.

tomato	tea pot
book	charity
pencil	trust

• Stipulative Definition

A **stipulative definition** is one in which the writer goes beyond a general definition and specifies a certain additional meaning for the term, usually based on the writer's own experience. E. B. White's short essay "Democracy" illustrates stipulative definition well.

DEMOCRACY
by E. B. White

We received a letter from the Writers' War Board the other day asking for a statement on "The Meaning of Democracy." It presumably is our duty to comply with such a request, and it is certainly our pleasure.

Surely the Board knows what democracy is. It is the line that forms on the right. It is the don't in don't shove. It is the hole in the stuffed shirt through which the sawdust slowly trickles; it is the dent in the high hat. Democracy is the recurrent suspicion that more than half of the people are right more than half of the time. It is the feeling of privacy in the voting booths, the feeling of communion in the libraries, the feeling of vitality everywhere. Democracy is a letter to the editor. Democracy is the score at the beginning of the ninth. It is an idea which hasn't been disproved yet, a song the words of which have not gone bad. It's the mustard on the hot dog and the cream in the rationed coffee. Democracy is a request from a War Board, in the middle of a morning in the middle of a war, wanting to know what democracy is.

From the *New Yorker*, July 3, 1943.

1. E. B. White uses figurative language in his stipulative definition of *democracy*. (For example, "It's the mustard on the hot dog" is a figure of speech.) What does White gain by using these images?
2. Is Humpty Dumpty's definition of *glory* similar to White's definition of *democracy*? Explain.
3. Write a stipulative definition for one of the following terms.

common sense	work ethic
Jeep	social responsibility
basketball	exercise

• Operational Definition

An **operational definition** focuses on what a term *does* rather than on what it *is*. Process writing and dynamic description frequently require operational definitions. In his journal (Jan. 7, 1844), Henry David Thoreau observes that we can define writing as a deed or as the record of a deed. He is pointing out one of the choices we face when we define. If we choose to define writing as a deed, then we are choosing an operational definition.

In the following essay on reading, "Reading, the Most Dangerous Game," Harold Brodkey examines literature operationally, from the reader's point of view. He is concerned with what literature does and how it works rather than with what it is.

READING, THE MOST DANGEROUS GAME

Reading is an intimate act, perhaps more intimate than any other human act. I say that because of the prolonged (or intense) exposure of one mind to another that is involved in it, and because it is the level of mind at which feelings and hopes are dealt in by consciousness and words.

Reading a good book is not much different from a love affair, from love, complete with shyness and odd assertions of power and of independence and with many sorts of incompleteness in the experience. One can marry the book: reread it, add it to one's life, live with it. Or it might be compared to pregnancy—serious reading even if you're reading trash: one is inside the experience and is about to be born; and one is carrying something, a sort of self inside oneself that one is about to give birth to, perhaps a monster. Of course, for men this is always verging on something else (part of which is a primitive rage with being masculine, a dismay felt toward women and the world, a reader's odd sense of women).

The act of reading as it really occurs is obscure: the decision to read a book in a real minute, how one selects the book, how one flirts with the choice, how one dawdles on the odd path of getting it read and then reread, the oddities of rereading, the extreme oddities of the procedures of continuing with or without interruptions to read, getting ready to read a middle chapter in its turn after going off for a while, then getting hold of the book physically, having it in one's hand, letting one's mind fill with thoughts in a sort of warm-up for the exercise of mind to come—one riffles through remembered scenes from this and other books, one diddles with half-memories of other pleasures and usefulnesses, one wonders if one can afford to read, one considers the limitations and possibilities of this book, one is humiliated in anticipation or superior or thrilled in anticipation, or nauseated in retrospect or as one reads. One has a sense of talk and of reviews and essays and of anticipation or dread and the will to be affected by the thing of reading, affected lightly or seriously. One settles one's body to some varying degree, and then one enters on the altered tempos of reading, the subjection to being played upon; one passes through phases, starting with reacting to or ignoring the cover of the book and the opening lines.

The piercing things, the stabbingly emotional stuff involved in reading, leads to envy, worse even than in sibling or neighborhood rivalry, and it leads to jealousy and possessiveness. If a book is not religious or trashy, the problem of salesmanship, always partly a con, arises in relation to it, to all the problems it presents. A good reader of Proust complains constantly as a man might complain of a wife or a woman of her husband. And Proust perhaps had such a marriage in mind with the reader. A good book, like pregnancy or a woman known to arouse love, or a man, is something you praise in the light of a general reluctance to risk the experience; and the quality of praise warns people against the book, warns them to take it seriously; you warn them about it, not wanting to be evangelical, a matchmaker or a malicious pimp for a troubled and troubling view of the world.

I can't imagine how a real text can be taught in a school. Even minor masterpieces, "Huckleberry Finn" or "The Catcher in the Rye," are too much for a classroom, too real an experience. No one *likes* a good book if they have actually read it. One is fanatically attached, restlessly attached, criminally attached, violently and criminally opposed, sickened, unable to bear it. In Europe, reading is known to be dangerous. Reading always leads to personal metamorphosis, sometimes irreversible, sometimes temporary, sometimes large-scale, sometimes less than that. A good book leads to alterations in one's sensibility and often becomes a premise in one's beliefs. One associates truth with texts, with impressive texts anyway; and when trashy books vanish from sight, it is because they lie too much and too badly and are not worth one's intimacy with them. Print has so much authority, however, that sometimes it is only at the beginning of an attempt at a second reading or at the end of it, and only then, if one is self-assured, that one can see whether a book was not really worth reading the first time; one tells by how alterable the truth in it seems in this more familiar light and how effective the book remains or, contrarily, how amazingly empty of meaning it now shows itself to be. It is a strange feeling to be a practiced enough reader and writer to see in some books that there is nothing there. It is eerie: why did the writer bother? What reward is there in being a fraud in one's language and in one's ideas? To believe they just didn't know is more unsettling than to doubt oneself or to claim to be superficial or prejudiced or to give up reading entirely, at least for a while.

Or, in our country, we deny what we see of this and even reverse it: fraud is presented as happiness; an empty book is said to be well constructed; a foolish argument is called innovative. This is a kind of bliss; but lying of that sort, when it is nearly universal, wrecks the possibility of our having a literary culture or even of our talking about books with each other with any real pleasure. It is like being phony yachtsmen who only know smooth water and who use their motors whenever they can. This guarantees an immense personal wretchedness, actually.

Of course, in Europe, cultural patterns exist which slow the rate of change in you as a reader (as well as supplying evidence to use in comprehending what happens and will happen to you if you change because of a book). Of course, such change is never entirely good or wise. In our country, we have nothing to hold us back from responding to any sort of idea. With us everything is for sale—everything is up for grabs; including ourselves—and we have very little tradition worth hanging onto except the antic.

The country is organized not by religion or political machinery but by what are seen as economic realities but which are fashions in making money and spending money. We are an army marching in the largest conceivable mass so entirely within cultural immediacy that it can be said this is new in the history in the world, emotionally new in that while this has been true of other cultures for brief periods in the past, it was never true as completely or for such a large part of the population or so continuously, with so few periods of stasis. We pretend to tradition but really, nothing prevents us changing.

And we do change. Divorce, born-again Christianity, the computer revolution, a return to the farm, a move to the city. In Boston, at college at Harvard, I first knew people who claimed to be cultivated to the degree they remained unchanged not only in spite of the reading they claimed to have done but with the help of it. They did not realize what an imbecile and provincial notion that was—it was simply untrue: you could see it, the untruth of it. A rule of thumb about culture is that personal or public yearning for a better time to come or one in the past and nostalgia of any sort are reliable signs of the counterfeit. The past is there to be studied in its reality, moment by moment and the future can be discussed in its reality to come, which will be a reality moment by moment; but doing that means being honest just as doing it makes you too busy to yearn; and doing it shows you that nostalgia is a swindler's trick. A sense of the real is what is meant by good sense. And because of the nature of time and because of how relentlessly change occurs, good sense has to contain a good deal of the visionary as well as of ironic apology to cover the inevitable mistakes. And this is doubly so with us, in the United States. Reality here is special. And part of reality here or elsewhere is that novels, plays, essays, fact pieces, poems, through conversion or in the process of argument with them, change you or else—to use an idiom—you haven't listened.

If the reader is not at risk, he is not reading. And if the writer is not at risk, he is not writing. As a rule, a writer and a book, or a poem are no good if the writer is essentially unchanged morally after having written it. If the work is really a holding operation, this will show in a closed or flat quality in the prose and in the scheme of the thing, a logiclessness, if you will pardon the neologism, in the writing. Writing always tends toward a kind of moral stance—this is because of the weight of logic and of truth in it—but judging the ways in which it is moral is hard for people who are not cultivated. Profoundly educated persons make the best judges.

The general risk in being a man or woman of cultivation is then very high, and this is so in any culture, and perhaps requires too much strength for even a small group to practice in ours. But should such a guerrilla group arise, it will have to say that cultivation and judgment issue from the mouths of books and can come from no other source. Over a period of centuries, ignorance has come, justifiably, to mean a state of booklessness. Movie-educated people are strained; they are decontextualized; they are cultivated in a lesser way. Television and contemporary music are haunted by the search for messiahs; the usual sign of mass inauthenticity is a false prophet (which usually means a war will shortly break out and be lost). The absence of good sense signals the decline of a people and of a civilization. Shrewdness without good sense is hell unleashed.

I would propose as a social cure that in fourth grade and in the first year at college, this society mandate that we undergo a year of reading with or without argument as the soul can bear, including argument with teachers and parents and local philosophers if there are any. Of course something like this happens anyway but we probably ought to institutionalize it in our faddish way.

After all, if you don't know what's in good books, how can your life not be utterly miserable all in all? Won't it fall apart with fearsome frequency? The best of what this species knows is in books. Without their help, how can you manage?

If I intend for my life to matter to me, I had better read seriously, starting with newspapers and working up to philosophy and novels. And a book in what it teaches, and in what it does in comforting and amusing us, in what it does in granting asylum to us for a while; had better be roughly equivalent to, or greater in worth than, an event involving other people in reality that teaches us or that grants us asylum for a while in some similar way, or there is no reason to bother with it. And I am careful toward books that offer refuge to my ego or my bad conscience. A writer who is opposed to notions of value and instruction is telling you he or she does not want to have to display loyalty or insight or sensitivity—to prose or to people: that would limit his or her maneuverability; and someone who does not believe that loyalty or insight or sensitivity or meaning has any meaning is hardly worth knowing in books or on the page although such people are unavoidable in an active life.

The procedures of real reading, if I may call it that, are not essentially shrewd, although certain writers, Twain and Proust for instance, often do play to the practice of shrewdness in their readers.

But the disappearance from the immediate world of one's attention, that infidelity to one's alertness toward outside attack, and then the gullibility required for a prolonged act of attention to something not directly inferior to one's own methods and experiences, something that emanates from someone else, that and the risk of conversion, the certainty that if the book is good, one will take on ideas and theories, a sense of style, a sense of things different from those one had before—if you think of those, you can see the elements of middle-class leisure and freedom, or upper-class insolence and power or lower-class rebelliousness and hiddenness and disloyalty to one's surroundings, that are required for real reading.

And you can also see what the real nature of literature is—it is a matter of one's attention being removed from the real world and regarding nature and the world verbally: it is a messy mathematics in its way; it is a kind of science dealing in images and language, and it has to be right in the things it says; it has to be right about things.

I learned very early that when you were infatuated with someone, you read the same books the other person read or you read the books that had shaped the other person or you committed an infidelity and read for yourself and it was the beginning of trouble. I think reading and writing are the most dangerous human things because they operate on and from that part of the mind in which judgments of reality are made; and because of the authority language has from when we learn to speak and use its power as a family matter, as an immediate matter, and from when we learn to read and see its modern, middle-class power as a public matter establishing our rank in the world.

When a book is technically uninteresting, when such a book is not a kind of comically enraged protest against the pretensions of false technique and ludicrously misconceived subject matter, it is bound to be a phony. The democratic subversion of objects, of techniques, can never without real dishonesty stray far from its ostensible purpose, which is the democratic necessity of making our lives interesting to us. Folk art is, inevitably, a kind of baby talk in relation to high art—and this is shaming, but so is much in life, including one's odor giving one's secrets away (showing one's nervousness or one's lechery), but it is better to do that than live messageless and without nerves or desire. The moral extravagance of reading—its spiritual element and its class element—is bound to reflect both an absence of humility and a new kind of humility and both in odd ways. Two of our most conceited writers, Gertrude Stein and Ernest Hemingway, overtly wrote baby talk. Nowadays the young like financial reporting as a window on the world, and television and the interview. They are pursuing fact in the plethora of baby talk, and they are trying to exercise judgment in the middle of the overenthusiastic marketing of trash.

American colleges have taught our intellectuals to read politically in order to enter and stay in a group or on a track. One reads skimmingly then, and one keeps placing the authority for what one reads outside oneself. But actually people cannot read in a two-souled way, shrewdly, and with a capacity to feel and learn. Learning involves fear and sometimes awe and just plain factually is not shrewd—it is supershrewd if you like, it is a very grand speculation indeed; and graduate school stuff won't open out into awe and discovery or recognition or personal knowledge of events but only onto academic hustling. I mean when you stop theorizing and think about what is really there. Do I need to go on? One of the primary rules of language is that there must be a good reason for the listener to attend to a second sentence after the first one; to supply a good reason is called "being interesting." Not to attend to the second sentence is called "not listening." The reasons to listen are always selfish, but that does not mean they are only selfish.

It is hard to listen. It is also hard to write well and to think. These ought not to be unfamiliar statements. This ought not to be news.

See you in the bookstores soon.

Harold Brodkey
From *New York Times Book Review*, November 24, 1985

1. What operational definition of literature does Brodkey offer? How does he develop it?
2. How would you modify Brodkey's operational definition of literature? You may choose to combine stipulative and operational definitions here.
3. Write an operational definition for "writing."

• Lexical Definition

A **lexical definition** is one which delves into the word itself, its history, etymology and evolution. *The Oxford English Dictionary* is a good data source for the lexical definition. As an example, take a look at the lexical definition of *recreation*. *The Oxford English Dictionary* tells us that this term comes to us from Italian via 14th century French. Its most common usage then, now obsolete, was to refresh by eating. Other citations in English, from 1390 onward, indicate that restoring energy so that one could get back to work was basic to the early meanings of this term.

Recreation[1] (rekrɪ͵ēɪ·ʃən). Also 4–6 -acioun, -acyon, etc. [a. F. *récréation* (13th c. in Littré), or ad. L. *recreātiōn-em* (Pliny), n. of action f. *recreāre* to RECREATE *v.*[1]]

†**1.** Refreshment by partaking of food; a refection; nourishment. *Obs.*

1390 GOWER *Conf.* III. 100 To sustienen hem and fede In time of recreacion. *c* **1489** CAXTON *Blanchardyn* 145 Blanchardyn, Sadoyne, and his wyff..were sittyng at the bord takynge their recreacyon. **1538** in Strype *Eccl. Mem.* (1721) I. II. App. xc. 251, I bequest to the Maister, Wardens and Felyshyp of the Drapers, v. pounde, for a recreation or a dyner. **1600** SURFLET *Countrie Farme* III. xlvi. 516 The tree must haue some recreation giuen it in winter, after his great trauell in bringing foorth of his fruite.

†**2.** Refreshment or comfort produced by something affecting the senses or body. *Obs.*

1390 GOWER *Conf.* III. 114 [Of the sun] alle erthly creatures..taken after the natures Here ese and recreacion. *c* **1430** LYDG. *Min. Poems* (Percy Soc.) 14 Wyne is a lycor of grete recreacioun. *c* **1440** *Gesta Rom.* ii. 6 (Harl. MS.) Ofte tyme he vsid to ligge ny the fire, for to haue comfort and recreacion of þe fire.

†**b.** Comfort or consolation of the mind; that which comforts or consoles. *Obs. rare.*

c **1410** HOCCLEVE *Mother of God* 138 The habitacion Of the holy goost our recreacion Be in myn herte. *c* **1440** *York Myst.* xlvi. 20 Vnkyndely þei kidde þem þer kyng for to kenne, With carefull comforth and cold recreacioun. *c* **1475** *Lament. Mary Magd.* cxcvii, My comforte, and al my recreacioun, Fare wel my parpetual saluacioun.

3. The action of recreating (oneself or another), or fact of being recreated, by some pleasant occupation, pastime or amusement.

c **1400** MAUNDEV. (Roxb.) xxxiv. 155 New thinges..to tell off for solace and recreacioun of þaim þat lykez to here þam. **1484** CAXTON *Fables of Alfonce* vi, To take his recreacion he entryd in to his gardyn. **1532** MORE *Confut. Tindale* Wks. 558/1 Tindall is as it semeth..set vpon reading of rydles for his recreacion. **1584** COGAN *Haven Health* ii. (1636) 20 Socrates..for recreation..blushed not to ride upon a Reed among his little children. **1651** HOBBES *Leviath.* II. xxiv. 129 Forrests, and Chases, either for his recreation, or for preservation of Woods. **1755** YOUNG *Centaur* ii. Wks. 1757 IV. 140 Too much recreation tires as much, as too much business. **1791** COWPER *Iliad* XXI. 56 Eleven days, at his return, he gave To recreation joyous with his friends. **1860** HOOK *Lives Abps.* I. i. 2 He sought his recreation in the study of Ecclesiastical History.

attrib. **1853** D. F. M'CARTHY *Dramas of Calderon* I. p. viii, Recreation-rambles into the enchanted regions of foreign song. **1859** *Act* 22 *Vict.* c. 27 § 8 This Act..may be cited..[as] 'The Recreation Grounds Act, 1859'.

b. An instance of this; a means of recreating oneself; a pleasurable exercise or employment.

c **1430** LYDG. *Min. Poems* (Percy Soc.) 82 Travaile requyrithe a recreacioune. **1477** EARL RIVERS (Caxton) *Dictes* 1 For a recreacion and a passyng of tyme I had delyte and axed to rede somme good historye. **1585** T. WASHINGTON tr. *Nicholay's Voy.* III. x. 86 The Turke hath observed the Palester of the Athletes..for one of his accustomed recreations. **1631** GOUGE *God's Arrows* III. § 11. 206 Such kind of recreations as make men fitter for warre. **1749** LAVINGTON *Enthus. Meth. & Papists* 23 Our love of Recreations and Diversions has indeed confessedly exceeded all bounds. **1849** MACAULAY *Hist. Eng.* vii. II. 169 The chase was his favourite recreation.

c. One who or that which supplies recreation.

1601 SHAKS. *Twel. N.* II. iii. 146 If I do not gull him into an ayword, and make him a common recreation [etc.]. **1863** *Sat. Rev.* 15 Aug. 224 These *Tragedies and other Plays* will live..not as the recreation of an idle hour [etc.].

†**4.** A place of refreshment or recreation. *Obs.*

c **1440** *Promp. Parv.* 426/1 Recreacyon', or howse of refreschynge, *recreatorium.* **1618** BOLTON *Florus* (1636) 29 Tiber which is now but a Suburbe, and Præneste but our Summer-recreation.

Recreation[2] (rīkrɪ͵ēɪ·ʃən). Also **re-creation.** [f. RE- 5 a + CREATION.] The action of creating again; a new creation.

1522 *World & Child* C iiij b, Christ,.. That craftly made euery creature by good recreacyon. **1584** R. SCOT *Discov. Witchcr.* v. ii. (1886) 74 But to what end should one dispute against these creations and recreations? **1611** BP. HALL *Serm.* v. 52 As in the Creation he could have made all at once, but he would take days for it: so in our recreation by grace. **1664** J. WEBB *Stone-Heng* (1725) 2 Not long after the Re-creation of Mankind we find recorded..the Tower of Babylon. **1850** R. I. WILBERFORCE *Holy Baptism* 42 Regeneration is a re-creation of man's nature. **1873** G. HENSLOW *Evolution* xiii. 204 The cataclysms and recreations of the early geological theorists.

This lexical definition was recently helpful to a writer investigating contemporary attitudes toward work and the importance of work in our lives.

• Extended Definitions

In many cases our writing will demand more than a precise, simple definition. Imagine facing this essay question in an international business course:

What is the balance of trade and how is it calculated?

Using our earlier model a simple definition would be:

TERM	= CLASS	+ DIFFERENTIATING CHARACTERISTIC
balance of trade	net difference over a period of time	between the value of a country's imports and exports of merchandise

Though this definition is technically correct, it is incomplete. Such a question as this calls for an extended definition. The writer could develop an essay using any of the expository patterns or a combination of them. These patterns include:

description (static, dynamic and process)
comparison and contrast
cause and effect

The extended definition draws on other expository patterns to allow the writer to explore the more subtle and interesting aspects of this topic, in this case, the balance of trade.

The writer could point out the finer aspects of the balance of trade by **describing a specific example**, such as the U.S. auto industry balance of trade in 1987. What this balance means to different groups of people, present and past, might also be included. For example, our psychological and emotional response to balance of trade figures may well rest on meanings the balance of trade figures had for our 16th century mercantilist ancestors and not on what the balance of trade means to today's more complex and smaller globe. Perhaps, too, the writer could indicate a grasp and control of the concept by exploring its different implications, the subtleties of its meanings, to citizens of the U.S. and of Japan. The topic could be further defined by exploring *what it is not*. The balance of trade is not, for example, any measure of American direct investment abroad or in that sense, of American wealth. An additional approach to an extended definition of balance of trade would be to explore why the balance is calculated and what the effect of this calculation is, economically, politically and socially.

In the following essay, Wayne W. Dyer offers his extended definition of freedom.

WHAT IS FREEDOM?

No one is handed freedom on a platter. You must make your own freedom. If someone hands it to you, it is not freedom at all, but the alms of a benefactor who will invariably ask a price of you in return.

Freedom means you are unobstructed in ruling your own life as you choose. Anything less is a form of slavery. If you cannot be unrestrained in making choices, in living as *you* dictate, in doing as you please with your body (provided your pleasure does not interfere with anyone else's freedom), then you are without the command I am talking about, and in essence you are being victimized.

To be free does not mean denying your responsibilities to your loved ones and your fellow man. Indeed, it includes the freedom to make choices to be responsible. But nowhere is it dictated that you must be what others want you to be when their wishes conflict with what you want for yourself. You can be responsible *and* free. Most of the people who will try to tell you that you cannot, who will label your push for freedom "selfish," will turn out to have measures of authority over your life, and will really be protesting your threat to the holds you have allowed them to have on you. If they can help you feel selfish, they've contributed to your feeling guilty, and immobilized you again.

The ancient philosopher Epictetus wrote of freedom in this line from his *Discourses*: "No man is free who is not master of himself."

Reread that quote carefully. If you are not the master of yourself, then by this definition you are not free. You do not have to be overtly powerful and exert influence over others to be free, nor is it necessary to intimidate others, nor to try to bully people into submission in order to prove your own mastery.

1. How does Dyer's definition of freedom differ from your own?
2. What techniques does Dyer use to develop his extended definition of freedom? Are they effective?
3. From this extended definition, draw what you think would be Dyer's simple definition of freedom.

The following essay, "What is a Wife?," is another example of extended definition. The essay is written by a student and is preceded by the sentence outline the student used when writing. As you read the essay, focus on the types of definition and the development techniques the writer uses.

What Is a Wife?

Thesis Statement and Introduction: Webster's New School Office Dictionary defines wife as "a married woman; a woman in relationship to her husband." I feel that a wife is a friend, partner, mother, and lover.

I. My wife is my friend.
- A. She is my confidant.
  - 1. She listens to my problems.
  - 2. She celebrates my successes with me.
- B. She is my companion.
  - 1. We enjoy being together.
  - 2. Life is not the same when we are not together.

II. My wife is my partner.
- A. She is my co-worker.
  - 1. She does her part at home.
  - 2. We undertake projects together.
- B. She is my associate.
  - 1. We discuss our finances.
  - 2. We discuss our long-term plans.

III. My wife is a mother.
- A. She provides for the physical needs of our child.
  - 1. She ensures our daughter receives the proper nutrition.
  - 2. She ensures our daughter remains healthy.
- B. She provides for the mental needs of our daughter.
  - 1. She has taught our daughter the meaning of love and affection.
  - 2. She has taught our daughter the basics of education.

IV. My wife is my lover.
- A. She provides for my sexual needs.
  - 1. She is exciting.
  - 2. She is willing.
- B. She provides for my psychological needs.
  - 1. She shows me affection.
  - 2. She really cares about me.

Conclusion: I feel that Webster's definition of a wife is too impersonal. In addition to being a married woman, a wife must also be a friend, partner, lover, and possibly a mother.

The Webster's New School and Office Dictionary defines wife as "a married woman; a wife in relationship to her husband." I feel that this definition is rather short and inexact, for it omits several personal qualities that I feel a woman should possess in order to be a real wife. For instance, my wife is not only a married woman; she is also a mother, a friend, a partner, and a lover. I have known several women who were married; however, they did not exhibit these qualities. I did not consider these women to be real wives.

To begin with, my wife is my dearest and most cherished friend. I have many friends; we joke around, we drink beer, and generally we have a good time. However, my wife is a different kind of friend. She is my confidant. She is the one who listens to my problems, and she is a very good listener. On several occasions she has assisted me in arriving at a proper solution to a problem I might have had. She is also the one who celebrates the successes of life with me. Recently I received word that I was to be promoted; we celebrated this event as a promotion for both of us, because she influenced me to prepare for the promotion test. As a result, my wife experienced the same positive emotions that I did. As my friend, she is also my constant companion. There is nothing in life I enjoy more than being with my wife. My job frequently dictates that I travel for extended periods of time; it is during these periods that we each feel lonely and isolated.

In addition to being my friend, my wife is also my most valuable partner. In a sense, she is my co-worker. By this I do not mean that we work side by side at the office. Rather, while I work at the office, she works at home. We each realize the importance of our roles, and we each accept those roles. We also cooperate as partners at home. We have a beautiful home, and we accomplished that by being partners. Many of our projects have been possible only through her ability to conceive an idea, and my ability to work with my hands. For example, we recently decorated our patio with a beautiful flower bed. My wife designed the floral layout, and I did the actual planting. We could not have accomplished this without our mutual efforts. As my partner, my wife is also my associate. We carefully discuss our financial matters and long-term plans which may affect our future.

Another important role that my wife plays is that of being a mother. We have one daughter, and we are very proud of her. Most people compare their children with others and when I do this, the result is clear: my wife has proven herself as the type of mother most husbands desire. For example, not only does my wife provide for the physical needs of our child, she also provides for the mental needs as well. Our child receives proper nourishment and medical attention, such as immunizations when necessary. In addition, my wife has taught our daughter the meaning of love and affection. My daughter always greets me with hugs and kisses, and sometimes she will stop right in the middle of her playtime to come sit on my lap to ask for a kiss or a hug. My wife has also taught our child the basics of education such as pre-school counting and singing.

Finally, my wife is the best lover I have ever known. She is the one who best knows how to satisfy my sexual needs. She is a very exciting and passionate sexual partner. She is also ready and willing whenever I am. Sometimes, I must be the one who is ready and willing whenever she is. Not only does she provide for my physical needs; she also knows how to satisfy my psychological needs. For instance, she shows me caring and affection. She seems to sense that there are times when I need extra emotional support. These are the times when I value her companionship the most. However, she is careful not to go overboard and crowd me with her affections. I have known women who actually repulse a man by constantly invading his personal space. This tends to give a man a sense of not being able to breathe. I appreciate my wife for giving me the right amount of space and the right amount of affection.

In conclusion, I do not know whether Webster was a married man or not, but I am sure of one thing. He has definitely done most wives an injustice by portraying them in such a narrow role. I, for one, feel that his definition should have read, "wife—a married woman, who in addition to possibly being a mother, is the friend, partner, and lover to her husband."

1. Notice that this definition of wife uses several forms of definitions we have discussed in this chapter. Can you spot them?
2. Does the paper follow the outline? What functions does the outline fill for the writer?
3. Do you agree or disagree with the definition developed in this paper? Explain.
4. What suggestions for improvement would you make to the author of this essay?

Now let's focus on the use of a specific technique to develop an extended definition. In this following paper, the student-writer builds on what he already knew how to write, using the comparison-contrast technique to define.

The "Good Life"

When I was ten years old, my parents decided they were fed up with the hustle and bustle of city life. One decision led to another, and, before I knew it, we were headed for the serene, relaxing beauty found in country life.

My siblings and I made a fuss, but to no avail. Not two weeks into the transition, I discovered that what my parents called the "good life" was turning into a nightmare for me.

When they had talked about a relaxing life in the country, I assumed that meant I did not have to mow the lawn, shovel the sidewalks, or deliver newspapers. Much to my dismay, these simple chores were replaced by more demanding, physical (not to mention smelly) work.

My insides turned when they made me clean the chicken coop. I grumbled a lot when they made me slop the hogs and feed the rest of the animals every morning. But, they went too far when they told me to milk the cow. "You want me to squeeze what?" I exclaimed. I was not about to mess with any private parts on a 650-pound beast.

A firm command and a threat on my allowance helped me to decide it may be in my better interest to at least try. I must admit, I was a natural. I had the milk flowing rather well. But, then, a feeble bawl from a hungry calf caused the motherly bovine to realize I was an impostor. The next thing I knew, my ear was stinging from a swat I received from her tail, and all my effort was spilled onto the barn floor and immediately soaked up by some dry straw.

About this time, I was thinking back to the "good old days" when all I had to worry about was dodging rocks when mowing the lawn or slipping on a patch of ice while shoveling the walk.

They told me the country is the good life . . . Ha! I had never hustled and bustled so much in my life.

I did my best to adjust, but it seemed the harder I tried, the worse things got. My troubles peaked when I found out I did not even get to sleep in on weekends anymore. The animals still needed to be fed. Sundays were not even a day of rest.

It was not until I met my best friend that I finally started to see some advantages to country living. He had a motorcycle, horses, and, best of all, a cute sister with golden hair and a bright smile.

He showed me the best fishing spots and took me duck hunting at a nearby pond. My attitude started to change rapidly. I even discovered little ways to control that ornery milk cow. Getting up early was not a problem after awhile, because my internal clock adjusted to it.

I soon found a lot of interesting things that the city was missing. Snakes, lizards and bullfrogs were in abundance, and they proved to be handy devices for bribing a terrified sister.

But, even with my newly found entertainment, I missed the city. So, when my sister and her husband invited me to visit their place in the city—my old neighborhood—I jumped at the chance.

When I arrived at my old hangout, I was looking forward to riding "wheelies" on a bicycle, "hanging ten" on a skateboard, and watching the neighbor's poodle do the tricks it was so famous for.

However, the bike and skateboard did not quite live up to the excitement of climbing hills on a motorcycle and racing horses over the meadows. And, the neighbor's poodle was okay, but that old milk cow sure made my life a lot more interesting and exciting.

The polluted atmosphere the city offered surely did not beat the country's fresh air. As a matter of fact, it barely outshined the rank odor of the pig pen. The smog dimmed, and sometimes nearly blocked out, the bright, clear picture of stars that I was able to view in the country.

Things picked up a little when I visited the video arcade, and the shopping mall was still a fun place to spend the day. But by the time I finished my city visit, I was ready to rejoin my parents in the "good life," or as my dad came to call it . . . "God's country."

1. How do you define "the good life"?
2. Try your hand at defining and developing this topic *without* using comparison-contrast.

In the following essay, which is less successful than those we've already considered, the student writer is trying to define the difference between offensive and defensive in football.

Offense or Defense?

In the game of football there are basically two teams. One team is offensive and the other is defensive. The most crowd-pleasing is the offense, because they have the excitement of showing numbers on the scoreboard. The defense usually isn't too crowd-pleasing because they don't score points. The crowd sees that points win games. The defense is not thought of too much, but, without any defense, there would be no opposition. The offensive goals are to gain real estate and, if possible, score. The goals of the defense are quite different. The defensive players are to oppose opposite forces and stop the offense, if possible. The less ground they give up and the more times they give their offense the ball, the better chance they have of winning. I think the crowd should give the defense and offense support as one. Looking at both sides of football usually changes people's attitudes toward the defense.

1. Where do you feel the student had problems?
2. Would the student have been better off defining only one type of team?
3. If you knew nothing about football, would you understand what the student is defining here?
4. Try defining a term used in a sport you're familiar with.

Let's conclude with a more successful student essay which defines the basic trainee. Notice the use of cliche as an organizational element.

A Basic Trainee

When you arrive at basic training, you discover that a trainee seems to be one of the lowest forms of life on the planet Earth. The species "basic trainee" is told what to wear, when to wear it, and how it is worn. He learns to speak only when spoken to, and learns he will live longer by listening to what is being said. He is told how and where to position his head, arms, hands and eyes at "attention," "parade rest," and "at ease." He is informed that his eyes are for looking at only what he is told to look at. He learns to perform each movement in a precise military manner, and to execute that movement only when told to do so. He is told when he may eat, drink, sleep and see others. He learns never to leave anything lying around, and that his most important roles in life are to work with others as a team, become the best, and be second to none. Yes, a trainee believes that he is the lowest form of life when he enters basic training, but he knows that when he graduates, he will be one of the finest, toughest, and most dedicated fighting men that America may call "her own."

1. Would this essay be better if the writer had not used a cliche to open the definition?
2. Do you think the cliches add humor? Immediacy?
3. Has the writer left out any ideas which you would consider essential to what a basic trainee is? If so, what are they?
4. Try writing an essay in which you define a novice in any field, remembering to incorporate what all novices have in common.

Cross-curricular Essay Questions

1. What is meant by the term distribution channel?
2. Is currency fluctuation a risk in barter trade? Explain.
3. Is the Supply/Demand curve a critical concept in a centralized economy such as we find in the Eastern Bloc countries?

4. Describe country risk assessment and its role in market analysis.
5. What is the thematic role of the voyage in Mark Twain's *Huckleberry Finn*?
6. What is the purpose of a progress report?
7. What is the function of the World Bank in Third World debt control?
8. Define the relationship between form and content in a technical document.

CHAPTER

• FOUR •

Cause and Effect

"A Horse! A Horse! My kingdom for a horse!"

William Shakespeare,
From *Richard the Third*

"A little neglect may breed great mischief . . . for want of a nail the shoe was lost; for want of a shoe the horse was lost; and for want of a horse the rider was lost."

Benjamin Franklin,
From *Preface: Courteous Reader*

Right after learning how to say "no," most children seem to learn the word "why?" Not only do children ask "why?" and "what happens if?" or "what happened because of?" but so also do professors. History instructors all too often want to know why certain events happened: what were the causes of wars, of changes in society, of changes in governments, or of the growth of ideas and movements. Sociologists and psychologists, too, use expressions like, "What were the underlying causes of," "What event or series of events resulted in," or "What was the effect of?" Conversely, marketing instructors, businessmen, and statisticians inquire "What caused this effect to come about?" "Why are sales down?" Philosophers have asked the same two questions from earliest times: "Why does man suffer?" and "Why does man die?" These queries are echoed by all human beings as we try to come to terms with cause and effect in real life.

• Discovering Causes

To discover a cause, or causes, of a given effect is a common writing problem. For example, why was there a high rate of absenteeism last week at the factory? Investigation shows that 97% of the absenteeism is due to a highly contagious virus. Why does the average freshman dread taking English composition? Instructors discover from talking with students that many students are genuinely afraid that they really don't know enough about grammar, spelling, and punctuation to do well enough in an English writing course to pass it.

In the first of these two situations, it is possible to establish a definite or final cause—one that evidence proves beyond question is the true cause. The second of the two situations is not so clear-cut. Often a definite cause cannot be established.

A possible or probable cause, or causes, must suffice. Why was the Edsel such a flop? Why is a particular patient so antagonistic toward the nurses? Why is my sister Jean so popular? Why is red hair associated with a quick temper? Like the question "Why does the average freshman dread taking English composition?" questions such as these cannot be answered with complete certainty, yet causes that answer them need to be established and examined.

The basic types of causal relationships can best be understood by examining the following diagrams. Try your hand at outlining the structures of the student and professional essays in this chapter to see how closely they follow the standard patterns. Applying these diagrams to your own writing will help in organizing your own cause and effect compositions.

TYPES OF CAUSAL RELATIONSHIPS

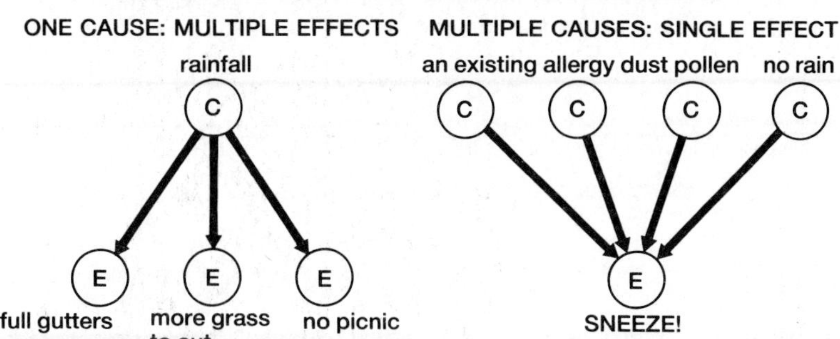

CHAIN REACTION

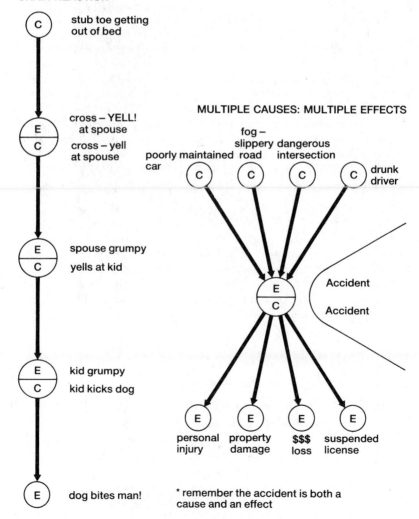

C — stub toe getting out of bed

E — cross – YELL! at spouse
C — cross – yell at spouse

E — spouse grumpy
C — yells at kid

E — kid grumpy
C — kid kicks dog

E — dog bites man!

MULTIPLE CAUSES: MULTIPLE EFFECTS

C — poorly maintained car
C — fog – slippery road
C — dangerous intersection
C — drunk driver

E — Accident
C — Accident

E — personal injury
E — property damage
E — $$$ loss
E — suspended license

* remember the accident is both a cause and an effect

The following essay shows how one student used cause and effect in writing about a difficult problem child.

Erik—Problem Child

Erik is known as a "problem child" at the Little Bo-Peep Child Care Center. As part of my practicum, I have attempted to discover why Erik is a disruptive element in the center and how he can be helped.

Erik is a physically attractive four year old boy: curly red hair, bright blue eyes, and a sturdy, healthy body. In the classroom he often shouts, interrupts others, pushes and shoves the smaller children, and even bites. Although he is already four, he still uses "me" exclusively in place of "I"—as is common with children three years and under—and he shouts "no" almost exclusively to requests and direction much as the stereotypic two year old does. Erik is reluctant to follow the nursery room rules, refuses to rest in the afternoon, and frequently will not eat the lunch served at the center.

The causes for his behavior can be attributed to several problems. Erik's hearing was, at my insistence, tested. He does have a hearing loss from an adenoid problem that can be corrected by minor surgery and follow-up speech therapy. His inability to hear certainly would contribute to his boisterous, angry behavior, perhaps even to his biting. Very often a child bites when he or she is frustrated by his or her inability to communicate.

Another reason for Erik's disruptive behavior may be the present stressful family environment. His parents are getting a divorce, and Erik, too, feels tension and anxiety in his daily life. This situation may account for some of his most recent obnoxious behavior towards his playmates and the child care givers.

In addition to these significant reasons for Erik's actions, I feel I should also point out that much of his behavior falls well within the normal range of the noisy, active four year old child. The everyday working experience that I have gained from my practicum has given me a better awareness of the practical realities of dealing with children than merely studying child development theory ever did. Not all disruptive behavior is "caused" by anything; much is just ordinary "kid stuff." Erik is not particularly less troublesome than before I undertook this study; he is simply more tolerable now that I am more experienced and understanding than I was initially.

Warm-up Exercises

EXERCISE 1

a. What is the controlling idea?

b. Using a blocking-out pattern establish the causes and effects that form the framework of this essay.

c. Where would you say the student had trouble getting smoothly from the evidence of Erik's behavior to the causes?

• Multiple Causes

In the process of establishing a probable cause, or causes, a writer must consider **all** the possible causes. After examining each possible cause, he or she then has only three choices: to eliminate the unlikely cause or causes; to keep the cause or causes as possibilities or to decide that—all things considered—one or all are probable causes. The writer needs to remember that in life, in history, or in business there is seldom only one probable cause; instead usually a number of contributing factors complicate the issue, some obviously more significant than others.

In the investigation of possible causes, a writer's reasoning must be logical, reasonable, and relevant. Each possible cause must be examined on the basis of reason, and not on the basis of emotions or preconceived ideas; each possible cause must really be seen as a possibility, not a figment of wishful thinking, a sentiment, or a stereotype. The student-writer of the following short essay had these points in mind.

Mirror, Mirror

"Mirror, mirror on the wall. Who's the fattest kid of all?"

"Good old Jeannie Jolly."

Jeannie looked at her globby, fat self in the mirror. She hated her fat cheeks that made her look thirty instead of seventeen; she hated her overblown body that nobody ever looked at except herself.

"Mirror, mirror on the wall. Why's Jeannie the fattest slob of all?"

"Poor little duckie—here—have a piece of cake. Granny loves you." Granny cut a big piece of layer cake and sighed, "Poor little duckie, Mommie's just gone away. Maybe she'll be back someday when she knows how much she misses her sweetie and her poor, good mother."

The mirror's voice changed from Granny's wheedle to Aunt Sarah's whine, "All the Jolly girls are plump. It's just in our genes. That little, itsy, bitsy, teeny chocolate wouldn't cause anyone else to gain an ounce, but I'll just balloon."

The mirror sounded so like her Granny again, "I declare, that child's just a sweet tooth. I know she got it from my side; all my sisters had sweet tooths too. I'll have just one of those spice drops myself. I need to keep my strength up."

Jeannie looked at the mirror again; this time at her "bosom." "I won't win any Playmate awards." Her breasts weren't appealingly rounded; they were like fat, drooping melons. She tried to explain to the mirror much as she had to Miss Kaiser, the school's guidance counselor, "I just can't help it. When ever I get nervous or tired, I have to eat. When I'm unhappy, I eat twice as much. It cheers me up."

"Does it cheer you up the next day when you're even bigger and even more unhappy that nobody—that is—no boys like you?"

"But my mother left me with Granny when I was four. It's all her fault!"

"But you're seventeen now. Aren't you just a little bit responsible for your own self?"

"Mirror, mirror on the wall. Who is responsible for it all?"

EXERCISE 2

a. Working with the effects—overweight, lousy self-image—as developed in "Mirror, Mirror," list the causes in order of their importance.

b. This student who describes Jeannie Jolly makes use of narration. Contrast this essay's structure with "Erik—Problem Child." When would you choose to use one approach over another? Why?

Reliable Conclusions

Whether the conclusion that the writer reaches is the definite (final) cause or the most probable cause of a situation, the conclusions must be arrived at through logical investigation. A conclusion, to be logical, must be based on **reliable**, relevant evidence, a significant amount of evidence, and intelligent analysis of the evidence.

Reliable Evidence: reliable evidence is the proof that can be gathered from trustworthy sources.

Relevant Evidence: relevant evidence is information that directly influences the situation.

Sufficient Evidence: sufficient evidence means enough information with no significant facts omitted that would alter the situation.

Evidence that is reliable, relevant, and sufficient must be analyzed intelligently. For the most plausible conclusion or conclusions to be reached, the significance of the individual pieces of information must be considered together.

Consider this student's answer to a typical essay examination question in a small business class.

QUESTION 7: Using your knowledge of the facts and statistics given in the textbook example of the small business known as Snow White Laundromat, to what do you attribute its dramatic drop in profits?

STUDENT ANSWER: The Snow White Laundromat showed a dramatic drop in profits from last fiscal year to this one for several important reasons. One of the primary reasons is that the original owner, Mr. Frances Kowalski, died early this year. His son, Mr. John Kowalski, inherited. Unfortunately, for the laundromat, Mr. John Kowalski is a pharmacist with three very successful drugstores to manage. Unlike old Mr. Kowalski, he has neither the time nor the interest to devote to the management of the laundromat.

Probably just as significant a factor as the change in management is that there has been a rise in crimes of violence in the neighborhood where the Snow

White Laundromat is located. The Polar Bear Beer and Wine Store, which shares the same building with the laundromat, has been held up by armed robbers twice in the past six months. Many former customers are afraid to use the laundromat after dark. In the past, the cleaners have been supplied by the nearby old folks home; however, the women who used to work there are unwilling to come from St. Aloysius any later than four in the afternoon. Many of the cleaners have stopped coming entirely. The newly hired firm has not had the personal pride in the job nor shown an interest in the clientele that the old folks did in the past.

In addition to the laundromat's being dirty and unattractive, many of the machines are regularly out of order. Old Mr. Kowalski repaired them himself, but his son does not have the time to do this. The laundromat has also become a hang out for the local "toughs" now that game machines have been installed. The police have reported drug deals and a lot of unsavory activity at the Snow White Laundromat. It is only a matter of time until the laundromat will be closed down completely or sold at a loss.

EXERCISE 3

a. Has the student considered all the possible causes and the resulting effects?

b. Has the writer answered the question in a way that moves smoothly from one idea to the next? Are there any places where the transition from one point to another is too abrupt?

c. Can you easily sketch a working outline of the main points of this essay? Why or why not?

• Insufficient Causes

In any investigation of **why** a certain phenomenon exists, pitfalls in reasoning need to be guarded against lest an illogical or insufficient cause be reached. One should never assume that a preceding event causes the following event. If a student helps a little old lady across the street and then comes to class and gets an "A" on a math test, one should never presume that this kindness was cause for the student's scoring well on the test. Now, if this same student helps a pitiful, little old lady across the street and he discovers later during class that his wallet is missing, there is a possibility that when the grateful, old gal leaned against him, she may have relieved him of the burden of his wallet. The second scenario, although not too likely, is still a valid possibility.

Neither should a writer oversimplify a situation by thinking that the situation has been created by only one cause, when there is a distinct possibility of several causes. If Lisa says she did not get the job for which she interviewed for because she was too nervous during the interview to reveal her best self, she may be oversimplifying the situation. She may not be taking into consideration such possibilities as her inadequate training, lack of experience, poor recommendations from a previous job, or the better qualifications of another applicant. Often a writer is confronted with a cause and wants to know what the effects are or will be.

EXAMPLE 1: *if a piece of stock is not perfectly entered into a lathe* (cause), what will happen (effect)?

EXAMPLE 2: *If a television antenna is not properly installed* (cause), what will be the consequences (effect)?

EXAMPLE 3: *If the swelling of an injured foot is not attended to* (cause), what will happen to the patient (effect)?

Whether the occasion warrants approaching a problem by moving from effect to cause or from cause to effect, the writing principles are the same. The following essays illustrate the many variations possible using the process of cause and effect.

Not Time Enough

Making time for everybody and everything, plus still having enough time for studying is hard. It is especially hard if you're married and have a family. Since my wife and I both work, it seems that there's not enough time in a day for everyone/everything. I had to make some sacrifices, and so did my family, if I wanted to do well in college.

Before I started taking college courses, there was plenty of time available that I would spend with my wife. She didn't care if we didn't go anywhere, just as long as I was there with her, which was fine with me. So when I started taking courses, the spare time my wife was receiving was gone. With all of the other things I'm into such as working, playing ball and hanging out with the guys, I just didn't have *any* time for her. So my wife and I got together, sacrificed certain activities, compromised on subjects we disagreed on, and made time for us. It appeared to me everything was starting to fall in place. I was wrong.

Now I was neglecting the children. The only time I saw them was in the morning, when I would look in on them as I was leaving for work, and in the evening after work. At that time I would rest before dinner. So it was back to the drawing board. I had to make more time for my kids. I explained to them what I was doing and what I expected from them to help in our search for attention. I made it clear to them and myself that if all I can give them is a few minutes every now and then, it would be the best minutes they would have all day. Also, I designated Saturday as family day for us. No playing ball, studying and working (if I don't have to) on that day.

I've talked about how I had to make time for everyone/everything but I hardly mentioned (if at all) the time I have for studying. At work, during the day I have numerous breaks that I'll use to catch up on homework and exercises. At home, I'll stay up after hours studying when everyone is asleep. Studying in this manner is tiring but I'm able to handle it. However, through all the problems I think I'm doing pretty well in the course I'm taking.

In the beginning my wife supported me, but now I think she gives me more and the kids are cooperating, so it looks like we're making it together. Realizing how important education is made it easier for me to give up a few things or just alter them a bit. You learn by your mistakes and trials so maybe the next time I take a course we'll have a smoother plan and perhaps, more time.

Students will have to make sure, before attending college, that they can make time for studying skills, make sure their going to be dedicated to college, and make sure that finances will be constant to pay for college.

The reason you should make sure you have a sufficient amount of time to study is because if you don't have a sufficient amount of time to study, it could lead to overworking yourself, failure in a subject and dropping out of school. When I was in high school, I had a job and was also trying to pass my classes. A few months later I started failing easy classes and almost came to the conclusion I was going to drop out. I decided to ask the store manager to shift my work hours, whereas, I would have time to study and work. Comprehension in my class subjects began to rise in a matter of weeks. College students need to do the same. They will have to find a job, which does not go into conflict with their studying time. In order to be successful in college.

Also, students will have to be dedicated to college. Dedication in a college course means you will have lots of interest which will enable you to "breeze" through the course and maybe become an expert in the field.

I found that the reason I didn't do so well in some of my college courses is because I either didn't care too much for the subject or the teacher was usually boring. If you are dedicated to a college course it will enable you to have a greater understanding in the course. In no time you'll find yourself passing every test that's given to you. After finding out how easy the course is because of your interest in it, you may go on to become an expert in the subject.

EXERCISE 4

a. Make a blocking-out pattern or outline for this essay to see where the student needs to restructure it.

b. This essay, although it has many good ideas, needs a *lot* of revision. What things would you change before you handed it in to the instructor?

c. Does the student really have a conclusion? Try your hand at designing a conclusion that does just that: conclude the essay.

Trade In Time

For several reasons, I've decided that it's time to trade in my present car because of its' dependability, appearance and the economical advantage of its' usage.

First of all, I like a car that will take me from point A to point B in the least amount of time. Also, I like a car that is very dependable because I do not enjoy being late for social or business functions. I long for the times when I can go grocery or clothes shopping without having to limit myself to a few items at a time. This would be highly impossible to achieve without the use of a car.

Secondly, I cannot stand the sight of a car that has been damaged in a car accident. I guess this is a very good reason to get rid of my old car. It used to look suave. Recently, it was in the shop for a body repair job. The service that was performed really dented my pocketbook.

Finally, I would enjoy a car which wouldn't put a dent in my pocket along money lines. I usually stay away from cars I don't know anything about. It takes a lot of money nowadays, to keep a car in good running condition. Therefore I would buy a car that has such qualities. Everyone has different reasons for buying a car, but I believe that these are the most important reasons for even thinking of buying a car to begin with.

EXERCISE 5

a. Like the previous student essay, this one is badly flawed. What changes in the mechanics, i.e. spelling, punctuation, grammar, would you make?

b. Bearing in mind that introductions and conclusions are truly vital parts of an essay and not just superfluous trimming, how would you introduce this essay? Conclude it?

c. How could the student have given a bit more life and interest to the essay? How would you "jazz" it up a bit?

The following essay is a professional example of cause and effect writing combined with humor.

WHY I QUIT WATCHING TELEVISION

I remember the exact moment I quit watching television. It was 10 years ago. I had a girlfriend who was a compulsive viewer. We were at her apartment on a Sunday afternoon, sitting on the couch, and I was . . . Well, I was nuzzling her ear, making little kissy noises, and generally acting like a boyfriend. Then, all of a sudden, I experienced one of those devastating realizations: She was watching a *Star Trek* rerun over my shoulder.

We had a big fight. I'm still wondering where our relationship went wrong. She's still wondering if Captain Kirk got beamed up in time to escape from the Klingons.

I was tired of watching television anyway. TV was too dumb. And TV was too much trouble. Not too much trouble to watch, of course, but there was too much trouble on the screen. Every show seemed to be about murder, theft, car chases or adultery. I was living in Manhattan at the time, and if I wanted to see those things, I could look out my window. Even comedy shows like *M*A*S*H* were about people getting blown apart. I figured there was enough real tragedy every day. Why get four more hours of it on TV every night? I gave my television set away.

TV is such a waste of time, I thought. I never considered how else

I'd fill my evenings and weekends. It turns out there are worse things to do with time than waste it; more expensive things, anyway.

In my newfound leisure hours, I fixed up my apartment. This cost $12,000—$600 for the do-it-yourself remodeling and $11,400 for the carpenters, painters and plasterers to repair the damage I'd done. I also took up downhill skiing and paid $1500 for equipment when I probably could have gotten somebody to break my leg for free. And I began to read. This sounds worthwhile, but anyone who worries about the lewdness and mayhem on TV ought to peek into *The Satyricon* by Petronius or *Gargantua and Pantagruel* by Rabelais or some Shakespeare plays or even the Old Testament. Most of my reading, though, wasn't quite so brainy. I read paperbacks like *Murder for Brunch*. It's hard to call these more intellectual than *The Gong Show*.

Without a TV set (and with a new girlfriend), I had time for conversation. But a lot of conversations, if they go on long enough, turn into arguments. What's dumber—watching *Family Feud* or arguing about whether to get a TV so we *could* watch *Family Feud*?

Not having a TV is supposed to bring families closer together. I didn't have a family, so this didn't help me.

Not having a TV turns out to be more strange than virtuous. I don't see any trend-setting shows like *Miami Vice*, so I don't know what to wear. I still dress like John Cameron Swayze. Without TV advertising, I don't understand new consumer products. Styling mousse, for instance—is it edible? And since, as a spectator, I'm limited to home teams, I've lost interest in most professional sports. I'm honestly not sure what the Seattle Seagulls are. They may be a girls' field hockey team, for all I know. (Editor's note: They're the Sea*hawks*—a football team.)

People magazine, newspaper gossip columns and friends' conversations are filled with names that mean nothing to me—"Prince," "Sting," "Peewee," "Apollonia." Sounds like a litter of puppies. And the celebrities I do recognize are mystifying. Imagine Mr. T completely out of *The A-Team* context: What kind of character could he possibly play?

Lack of a television set has more severe effects too. No TV means no VCR. That is, I actually paid to see *Flashdance* and couldn't even fast-forward through the parts where Jennifer Beals has all her clothes on. Furthermore, I'm getting fat. When you don't have to wait for a commercial to get up and get a sandwich and a beer, you can get up and get a lot more beer and sandwiches.

So maybe television isn't so bad for us as it's supposed to be. To research this story, I borrowed my next-door neighbor's TV—or, rather, I borrowed his whole TV room, since televisions are connected to cables now, so you can get 100 silly channels instead of five or six. I watched some shows at the start of the new season: *Hell Town*, *Hometown*, *Crazy Like a Fox*, *Stir Crazy*, etc. There were a few surprises. On MTV, I saw the video of a song I thought was a tender love ballad. I turns out to be sung by guys in leather underwear chasing a girl through a sewer.

But, mostly, television was just the same. It was kind of comforting to see Johnny Carson again, a little grayer but with the same slack gags. Most of the shows are still violent, but I live in New Hampshire these days, and we don't have as much murder, theft or car-chasing (and not even as much adultery) as some might like. The shows are still dumb, but I'm 10 years older, and I've forgotten how perfect everything is in the television world. The people are all pretty. The pay phones all work. And all the endings are hopeful. That's not so bad. Most of us real people are a bit homely, and lots of our endings are hopeless. TV's perfect world was a relief. So I was sitting, comfortable as a pig, in my neighbor's armchair, punching remote-control buttons with my snout.

But I didn't enjoy it. No, sir. Not me. I've spent a whole decade acting superior to everybody because I don't watch television. I'm not about to back down and start liking it now. (Though I might drop in next door about 8 tonight. That's when *Amazing Stories* comes on.)

P. J. O'Rourke
From *Parade*, December 8, 1985

EXERCISE 6

a. Notice the beginning and the conclusion. How does the author capture your interest and keep it?

b. Do you think that either of the previous two student writers could have done something in a humorous vein with their essays rather than using the rather plodding approaches taken?

Barbara Tuchman, a major twentieth-century historian, poses the oft-asked question of the value of history as a guide to the future. Best known for her works on World War I, Dr. Tuchman emphasizes the relationships between the past and the present and frequently draws uncomfortable, but needed parallels that force her readers to think, to reconsider, and, frequently, to act to bring about change.

IS HISTORY A GUIDE TO THE FUTURE?

The commonest question asked of historians by laymen is whether history serves a purpose. Is it useful? Can we learn from the lessons of history?

When people want history to be utilitarian and teach us lessons, that means they also want to be sure that it meets scientific standards. This, in my opinion, it cannot do, for reasons which I will come to in a moment. To practice history as a science is sociology, an altogether different discipline which I personally find antipathetic—although I suppose the sociologists would consider that my deficiency rather than theirs. The sociologists plod along with their noses to the ground assembling masses of statistics in order to arrive at some obvious conclusion which a reasonably perceptive historian, not to mention a large part of the general public, knows anyway, simply from observation—that social mobility is increasing, for instance, or that women have different problems from men. One wishes they would just cut loose someday, lift up their heads, and look at the world around them.

If history were a science, we should be able to get a grip on her, learn her ways, establish her patterns, know what will happen tomorrow. Why is it that we cannot? The answer lies in what I call the Unknowable Variable—namely, man. Human beings are always and finally the subject of history. History is the record of human behavior, the most fascinating subject of all, but illogical and so crammed with an unlimited number of variables that it is not susceptible of the scientific method nor of systematizing.

I say this bravely, even in the midst of the electronic age when computers are already chewing at the skirts of history in the process called Quantification. Applied to history, quantification, I believe, has its limits. It depends on a method called "data manipulation," which means that the facts, or data, of the historical past—that is, of human behavior—are manipulated into named categories so that they can be programmed into computers. Out comes—hopefully—a pattern. I can only tell you that for history "data manipulation" is a built-in invalidator, because to the degree that you manipulate your data to suit some extraneous requirement, in this case the requirements of the machine, to that degree your results will be suspect—and run the risk of being invalid. Everything depends on the naming of the categories and the assigning of facts to them, and this depends on the quantifier's individual judgment at the very base of the process. The categories are not revealed doctrine nor are the results scientific truth.

The hope for quantification, presumably, is that by processing a vast quantity of material far beyond the capacity of the individual to encompass, it can bring to light and establish reliable patterns. That remains to be seen, but I am not optimistic. History has a way of escaping attempts to imprison it in patterns. Moreover, one of its basic data is the human soul. The conventional historian, at least the one concerned with truth, not propaganda, will try honestly to let his "data" speak for themselves, but data which are shut up in prearranged boxes are helpless. Their nuances have no voice. They must carry one fixed meaning or another and weight the result accordingly. For instance, in a quantification study of the origins of World War I which I have seen, the operators have divided all the diplomatic documents, messages, and utterances of the July crisis into categories labeled "hostility," "friendship," "frustration," "satisfaction," and so on, with each statement rated for intensity on a scale from one to nine, including fractions. But no pre-established categories could match all the private character traits and public pressures variously operating on the nervous monarchs and ministers who were involved. The massive effort that went into this study brought forth a mouse—the less than startling conclusion that the likelihood of war increased in proportion to the rise in hostility of the messages.

Quantification is really only a new approach to the old persistent effort to make history fit a pattern, but *reliable* patterns, or what are otherwise called the lessons of history, remain elusive.

For instance, suppose Woodrow Wilson had not been President of the United States in 1914 but instead Theodore Roosevelt, who had been his opponent in the election of 1912. Had that been the case, America might have entered the war much earlier, perhaps at the time of the *Lusitania* in 1915, with possible shortening of the war and incalculable effects on history. Well, it happens that among the Anarchists in my book *The Proud Tower* is an obscure Italian named Miguel Angiolillo, whom nobody remembers but who shot dead Premier Canovas of Spain in 1897. Canovas was a strong man who was just about to succeed in quelling the rebels in Cuba when he was assassinated. Had he lived, there might have been no extended Cuban insurrection for Americans to get excited about, no Spanish-American War, no San Juan Hill, no Rough Riders, no Vice-Presidency for Theodore Roosevelt to enable him to succeed when another accident, another Anarchist, another unpredictable human being, killed McKinley. If Theodore had never been President, there would have been no third party in 1912 to split the Republicans, and Woodrow Wilson would not have been elected. The speculations from that point on are limitless. To me it is comforting rather than otherwise to feel that history is determined by the illogical human record and not by large immutable scientific laws beyond our power to deflect.

I know very little (a euphemism for "nothing") about laboratory science, but I have the impression that conclusions are supposed to be logical; that is, from a given set of circumstances a predictable result should follow. The trouble is that in human behavior and history it is impossible to isolate or repeat a given set of circumstances. Complex human acts cannot be either reproduced or deliberately initiated—or counted upon like the phenomena of nature. The sun comes up every day. Tides are so obedient to schedule that a timetable for them can be printed like that for trains, though more reliable. In fact, tides and trains sharply illustrate my point: One depends on the moon and is certain; the other depends on man and is uncertain.

In the absence of dependable recurring circumstance, too much confidence cannot be placed on the lessons of history.

There *are* lessons, of course, and when people speak of learning from them, they have in mind, I think, two ways of applying past experience: One is to enable us to avoid past mistakes and to manage better in similar circumstances next time; the other is to enable us to anticipate a future course of events. (History could tell us something about Vietnam, I think, if we would only listen.) To manage better next time is within our means; to anticipate does not seem to be.

World War II, for example, with the experience of the previous war as an awful lesson, was certainly conducted, once we got into it, more intelligently than World War I. Getting into it was another matter. When it was important to anticipate the course of events, Americans somehow failed to apply the right lesson. Pearl Harbor is the classic example of failure to learn from history. From hindsight we now know that what we should have anticipated was a surprise attack by Japan in the midst of negotiations. Merely because this was dishonourable, did that make it unthinkable? Hardly. It was exactly the procedure Japan had adopted in 1904 when she opened the Russo-Japanese War by surprise attack on the Russian fleet at Port Arthur.

In addition we had every possible physical indication. We had broken the Japanese code, we had warnings on radar, we had a constant flow of accurate intelligence. What failed? Not information but *judgment*. We had all the evidence and refused to interpret it correctly, just as the Germans in 1944 refused to believe the evidence of a landing in Normandy. Men will not believe what does not fit in with their plans or suit their prearrangements. The flaw in all military intelligence, whether twenty or fifty or one hundred percent accurate, is that it is no better than the judgment of its interpreters, and this judgment is the product of a mass of individual, social, and political biases, prejudgments, and wishful thinkings; in short, it is human and therefore fallible. If man can break the Japanese code and yet not believe what it tells him, how can he be expected to learn from the lessons of history?

Would a computer do better? In the case of Pearl Harbor, probably yes. If one could have fed all the pieces of intelligence available in November 1941 into a computer, it could have hardly failed to reply promptly, "Air attack, Hawaii, Philippines" and probably even "December 7." But will this work every time? Can we trust the lessons of history to computers? I think not, because history will fool them. They may make the right deductions and draw the right conclusions, but a twist occurs, someone sneezes, history swerves and takes another path. Had Cleopatra's nose been shorter, said Pascal, the whole aspect of the world would have been changed. Can a computer account for Cleopatra?

Once long ago when the eternal verities seemed clear—that is, during the Spanish Civil War—I thought the lessons of history were unmistakable. It appeared obvious beyond dispute that if fascism under Franco won, Spain in the foreshadowed European war would become a base for Hitler and Mussolini, the Mediterranean would become an Italian lake, Britain would lose Gibraltar and be cut off from her empire east of Suez. The peril was plain, the logic of the thing implacable, every sensible person saw it, and I, just out of college, wrote a small book published in England to point it up, all drawn from the analogy of history. The book showed how, throughout the eighteenth and nineteenth centuries, Britain had consistently interposed herself against the gaining of undue influence over Spain by whatever power dominated the continent. The affair of the Spanish marriages, the campaigns of Wellington, the policies of Castlereagh, Canning, and Palmerston all were directed toward the same objective: The strongest continental power must be prevented from controlling Spain. My treatise was, I thought, very artful and very telling. It did not refer to the then current struggle, but let the past speak for itself and make the argument. It was an irrefutable one—until history refuted it. Franco, assisted by

Hitler and Mussolini, *did* win, European war *did* follow, yet unaccountably Spain remained neutral—at least nominally. Gibraltar did not fall, the portals of the Mediterranean did *not* close. I, not to mention all the other "premature" anti-fascists, as we were called, while morally right about the general danger of fascism, had been wrong about a particular outcome. The lessons of history I had so carefully set forth simply did not operate. History misbehaved.

Pearl Harbor and Spain demonstrate two things: One, that man fails to profit from the lessons of history because his prejudgments prevent him from drawing the indicated conclusions; and, two, that history will often capriciously take a different direction from that in which her lessons point. Herein lies the flaw in systems of history.

When it comes to systems, history played her greatest betrayal on Karl Marx. Never was a prophet so sure of his premises, never were believers so absolutely convinced of a predicted outcome, never was there an interpretation of history that seemed so foolproof. Analyzing the effects of the Industrial Revolution, Marx exposed the terrible riddle of the nineteenth century: that the greater the material progress, the wider and deeper the resulting poverty, a process which could only end, he decided, in the violent collapse of the existing order brought on by revolution. From this he formulated the doctrine of *Verelendung* (progressive impoverishment) and *Zusammenbruch* (collapse) and decreed that since working-class self-consciousness increased in proportion to industrialization, revolution would come first in the most industrialized country.

Marx's analysis was so compelling that it seemed impossible history could follow any other course. His postulates were accepted by followers of his own and later generations as if they had been graven on the tablets of Sinai. Marxism as the revealed truth of history was probably the most convincing dogma ever enunciated. Its influence was tremendous, incalculable, continuing. The founder's facts were correct, his thinking logical and profound; he was right in everything but his conclusions. Developing events did not bear him out. The working class grew progressively better, not worse, off. Capitalism did not collapse. Revolution came in the least, not the most, industrialized country. Under collectivism the state did not wither but extended itself in power and function and in its grip on society. History, ignoring Marx, followed her own mysterious logic, and went her own way.

When it developed that Marx was wrong, men in search of determinism rushed off to submit history to a new authority—Freud. His hand is now upon us. The Unconscious is king. At least it was. There are new voices, I believe, claiming that the Unconscious is a fraud—iconoclasm has reached even Freud. Nevertheless, in his effect on the modern outlook, Freud, I believe, unquestionably was the greatest influence for change between the nineteenth and twentieth centuries. It may well be that our time may one day be named for him and the Freudian Era be said to have succeeded the Victorian Era. Our understanding of human motivation has taken on a whole new dimension since his ideas took hold. Yet it does not seem to me that unconscious sexual and psychological drives are as relevant in all circumstances as they are said to be by the Freudians, who have become as fixed in their system as were the orthodox Marxists. They can supply historians with insights but not with guidance to the future because man *en masse* cannot be relied upon to behave according to pattern. All salmon swim back to spawn in the headwaters of their birth; that is universal for salmon. But man lives in a more complicated world than a fish. Too many influences are at work on him to make it applicable that every man is driven by an unconscious desire to swim back to the womb.

It has always seemed to me unfortunate, for instance, that Freud chose the experiences of two royal families to exemplify his concept of the Oedipus and Elektra complexes. Royalty lives under special circumstances, particularly as regards the issue of power between the sovereign and his heir, which are not valid as universal experience. The legend of Oedipus killing his father may have derived from the observed phenomenon that every royal heir has always hated his father, not because he wants to sleep with his mother but because he wants to ascend the throne. If the parental sovereign happens to be his mother, he hates her just as much. She will dislike him equally from birth because she knows he is destined to take her place, as in the case of Queen Victoria and her eldest son, who became Edward VII. That is not Freudian, it is simply dynastic.

As for Elektra, it is hard to know what to make of that tale. The House of Atreus was a very odd family indeed. More was going on there than just Elektra being in love with her father. How about Orestes, who helped her to kill their mother, or killed her himself, according to another version? Was not that the wrong parent? How come he did not kill his father? How about Iphigenia, the sister, whom Agememnon killed as a sacrifice? What is the Freudian explanation for that? They do not say, which is not being historical. A historian cannot pick and choose his facts; he must deal with all the evidence.

Or take Martin Luther. As you know, Professor Erik Erikson of Harvard has discovered that Luther was constipated from childhood and upon this interesting physiological item he has erected a system which explains everything about his man. This is definitely the most camp thing that has happened to history in years. It even made Broadway. Nevertheless I do not think Luther pinned the 95 Theses on the church door at Wittenberg solely or even mainly because of the activity, or inactivity rather, of his anal muscle. His personal motive for protest may have had an anal basis for all I know, but what is important historically is the form the protest took, and this had to do with old and deep social grievances concerned with the worldliness of the church, the sale of indulgences, corruption of the clergy, and so on. If it had not been Luther who protested, it would have been someone else; Protestantism would have come with or without him, and its causes had nothing whatever to do with his private physiological impediment. Professor Erikson, I am sure, was attempting to explain Luther, not Protestantism, but his book has started a fad for psycho-history among those without the adequate knowledge or training to use it.

Following Freud there flourished briefly a minor prophet, Oswald

Spengler, who proclaimed the Decline of the West, based on an elaborate study of the lessons of history. Off and on since then people have been returning to his theme, especially since World War II and the end of colonialism. The rise of China and the rash of independence movements in Asia and Africa have inspired many nervous second looks at Spengler. Europe is finished, say the knowing ones; the future belongs to the colored races and all that.

People have been burying Europe for quite some time. I remember a political thinker for whom I had great respect telling me in the thirties that Europe's reign was over; the future belonged to America, Russia, and China. It was a new and awful thought to me then and I was immensely impressed. As I see it now, his grouping has not been justified. I do not think Russia and America can be dissociated from Europe; rather, we are extensions of Europe. I hesitate to be dogmatic about Russia, but I am certain about the United States. American culture stems from Europe, our fortunes are linked with hers, in the long run we are aligned. My impression is that Europe, and by extension the white race, is far from finished. Europe's vitality keeps reviving; as a source of ideas she is inexhaustible. Nuclear fission, the most recent, if unwanted, advance, came from the work of a whole series of Europeans: Max Planck, the Curies, Einstein, Rutherford, Fermi, Nils Bohr, Szilard. Previously the three great makers of the modern mind, Darwin, Marx, and Freud, were Europeans. I do not know of an original idea to have importantly affected the *modern* world which has come from Asia or Africa (except perhaps for Gandhi's concept of non-violent resistance or civil disobedience, and, after all, Thoreau had the same idea earlier).

It does not seem to me a passing phenomenon or an accident that the West, in ideas and temporal power, has been dominant for so long. Far from falling behind, it seems to be extending its lead, except in the fearful matter of mere numbers and I like to think the inventiveness of the West will somehow eventually cope with that. What is called the emergence of the peoples of Asia and Africa is taking place in Western terms and is measured by the degree to which they take on Western forms, political, industrial, and otherwise. That they are losing their own cultures is sad, I think, but I suppose it cannot be helped. The new realm is space, and that too is being explored by the West. So much for Spengler.

Theories of history go in vogues which, as is the nature of vogues, soon fade and give place to new ones. Yet this fails to discourage the systematizers. They believe as firmly in this year's as last year's, for, as Isaiah Berlin says, the "obstinate craving for unity and symmetry at the expense of experience" is always with us. When I grew up, the economic interpretation of history, as formulated with stunning impact by Charles Beard, was the new gospel—as incontrovertible as if it had been revealed to Beard in a burning bush. Even to question that financial interests motivated our Founding Fathers in the separation from Britain, or that equally mercenary considerations decided our entrance into the First World War, was to convict oneself of the utmost naïveté. Yet lately the fashionable—indeed, what appears to be the required—exercise among historians has been jumping on Beard with both feet. He and the considerable body of his followers who added to his system and built it up into a dogma capable of covering any historical situation have been knocked about, analyzed, dissected, and thoroughly disposed of. Presently the historical establishment has moved on to dispose of Frederick Jackson Turner and his theory of the Frontier. I do not know what the new explanation is, but I am sure there must be some thesis, for, as one academic historian recently ruled, the writing of history requires a "large organizing idea."

I visualize the "large organizing idea" as one of those iron chain mats pulled behind by a tractor to smooth over a plowed field. I see the professor climbing up on the tractor seat and away he goes, pulling behind his large organizing idea over the bumps and furrows of history until he has smoothed it out to a nice, neat, organized surface—in other words, into a system.

The human being—you, I, or Napoleon—is unreliable as a scientific factor. In combination of personality, circumstance, and historical moment, each man is a package of variables impossible to duplicate. His birth, his parents, his siblings, his food, his home, his school, his economic and social status, his first job, his first girl, and the variables inherent in all of these, make up that mysterious compendium, personality—which then combines with another set of variables: country, climate, time, and historical circumstance. Is it likely, then, that all these elements will meet again in their exact proportions to reproduce a Moses, or Hitler, or De Gaulle, or for that matter Lee Harvey Oswald, the man who killed Kennedy?

So long as man remains the Unknowable Variable—and I see no immediate prospect of his ever being pinned down in every facet of his infinite variety—I do not see how his actions can be usefully programmed and quantified. The eager electronic optimists will go on chopping up man's past behavior into the thousands of little definable segments which they call Input, and the machine will whirr and buzz and flash its lights and in no time at all give back Output. But will Output be dependable? I would lay ten to one that history will pay no more attention to Output than it did to Karl Marx. It will still need historians. Electronics will have its uses, but it will not, I am confident, transform historians into button-pushers or history into a system.

Barbara Tuchman
From Address, Chicago Historical Society, October 1966

One of the most shocking things that has happened in the past few decades in New York City was the killing of Kitty Genovese. Here is Martin Gansberg's account in *The New York Times* at the time of this crime in 1964. Immediately following is A. M. Rosenthal's more recent *New York Times* article commenting on parallels to the Genovese case as he perceives them.

38 WHO SAW MURDER DIDN'T CALL THE POLICE

For more than half an hour 38 respectable, law-abiding citizens in Queens watched a killer stalk and stab a woman in three separate attacks in Kew Gardens.

Twice their chatter and the sudden glow of their bedroom lights interrupted him and frightened him off. Each time he returned, sought her out, and stabbed her again. Not one person telephoned the police during the assault; one witness called after the woman was dead.

That was two weeks ago today.

Still shocked is Assistant Chief Inspector Frederick M. Lussen, in charge of the borough's detectives and a veteran of 25 years of homicide investigations. He can give a matter-of-fact recitation on many murders. But the Kew Gardens slaying baffles him—not because it is a murder, but because the "good people" failed to call the police.

"As we have reconstructed the crime," he said, "the assailant had three chances to kill this woman during a 35-minute period. He returned twice to complete the job. If we had been called when he first attacked, the woman might not be dead now."

This is what the police say happened beginning at 3:20 a.m. in the staid, middle-class, tree-lined Austin Street area:

Twenty-eight-year-old Catherine Genovese, who was called Kitty by almost everyone in the neighborhood, was returning home from her job as manager of a bar in Hollis. She parked her red Fiat in a lot adjacent to the Kew Gardens Long Island Railroad Station, facing Mowbray Place. Like many residents of the neighborhood, she had parked there day after day since her arrival from Connecticut a year ago, although the railroad frowns on the practice.

She turned off the lights of her car, locked the door, and started to walk the 100 feet to the entrance of her apartment at 87-70 Austin Street, which is in a Tudor building, with stores on the first floor and apartments on the second.

The entrance to the apartment is in the rear of the building because the front is rented to retail stores. At night the quiet neighborhood is shrouded in the slumbering darkness that marks most residential areas.

Miss Genovese noticed a man at the far end of the lot, near a seven-story apartment house at 82-40 Austin Street. She halted. Then, nervously, she headed up Austin Street toward Lefferts Boulevard, where there is a call box to the 102nd Police Precinct, in nearby Richmond Hill.

She got as far as a street light in front of a bookstore before the man grabbed her. She screamed. Lights went on in the ten-story apartment house at 82-67 Austin Street, which faces the bookstore. Windows slid open and voices punctuated the early-morning stillness.

Miss Genovese screamed: "Oh, my God, he stabbed me! Please help me! Please help me!"

From one of the upper windows in the apartment house, a man called down: "Let that girl alone!"

The assailant looked up at him, shrugged, and walked down Austin Street toward a white sedan parked a short distance away. Miss Genovese struggled to her feet.

Lights went out. The killer returned to Miss Genovese, now trying to make her way around the side of the building by the parking lot to get to her apartment. The assailant stabbed her again.

"I'm dying!" she shrieked. "I'm dying!"

Windows were opened again, and lights went on in many apartments. The assailant got into his car and drove away. Miss Genovese staggered to her feet. A city bus, 0-10, the Lefferts Boulevard line to Kennedy International Airport, passed. It was 3:35 a.m.

The assailant returned. By then, Miss Genovese had crawled to the back of the building, where the freshly painted brown doors to the apartment house held out hope for safety. The killer tried the first door; she wasn't there. At the second door, 82-62 Austin Street, he saw her slumped on the floor at the foot of the stairs. He stabbed her a third time—fatally.

It was 3:50 by the time the police received their first call, from a man who was a neighbor of Miss Genovese. In two minutes they were on the scene. The neighbor, a 70-year-old woman, and another woman were the only persons on the street. Nobody else came forward.

The man explained that he had called the police after much deliberation. He had phoned a friend in Nassau County for advice and then he had crossed the roof of the building to the apartment of the elderly woman to get her to make the call.

"I didn't want to get involved," he sheepishly told the police.

Six days later, the police arrested Winston Moseley, a 20-year-old business machine operator, and charged him with the homicide. Moseley had no previous record. He is married, has two children, and owns a home at 133-19 Sutter Ave., South Ozone Park, Queens. On Wednesday, a court admitted him to Kings County Hospital for psychiatric observation.

When questioned by the police, Moseley also said that he had slain Mrs. Annie May Johnson, 24, of 146-12 133rd Ave., Jamaica, on Feb. 29 and Barbara Kralik, 15, of 174-17 140th Ave., Springfield Gardens, last July. In the Kralik case, the police are holding Alvin L. Mitchell, who is said to have confessed that slaying.

The police stressed how simple it would have been to have gotten in touch with them. "A phone call," said one of the detectives, "would have done it." The police may be reached by dialing 0 for operator or SPring 7-3100.

Today witnesses from the neighborhood, which is made up of one-family homes in the $35,000 to $60,000 range with the exception of the two apartment houses near the railroad station, find it difficult to explain why they didn't call the police.

A housewife, knowingly if quite casual, said, "We thought it was a lover's quarrel." A husband and wife both said, "Frankly, we were afraid." They seemed aware of the fact that events might have been different. A distraught woman wiping her hands on her apron, said, "I didn't want my husband to get involved."

One couple, now willing to talk about that night, said they heard the first screams. The husband looked thoughtfully at the bookstore where the killer first grabbed Miss Genovese.

"We went to the window to see what was happening," he said, "but the light from our bedroom made it difficult to see the street." The wife, still apprehensive, added: "I put out the light and we were able to see better."

Asked why they hadn't called the police, she shrugged and replied: "I don't know."

A man peeked out from a slight opening in the doorway to his apartment and rattled off an account of the killer's second attack. Why hadn't he called the police at the time? "I was tired," he said without emotion. "I went back to bed."

It was 4:25 a.m. when the ambulance arrived to take the body of Miss Genovese. It drove off. "Then," a solemn police detective said, "the people came out."

Martin Gansberg
From *The New York Times*, March 27, 1964

I HEAR PEOPLE SCREAMING; OF COURSE, I PASS THEM BY

New York—In the early morning of March 13, 1964, a woman named Catherine Genovese walked to her home on Austin Street in the borough of Queens and was stabbed to death. Her killer attacked her once, ran when she screamed, returned again, attacked again and then once more. And while she screamed her young life out on Austin Street, 38 people, by police count, heard her. Some raised their windows. Not one did anything to come to her help or even called the police.

In life, few knew her outside her family but in the manner of her dying, and because of the silent witnesses, she lives. Studies have been made of the Genovese case, psychologists have dissected it and seminars are still held about it in universities. She lives on in many individual memories, including my own.

I was involved, as an editor, in the coverage of her death. For a long time I could not drive the story from my mind. I hoped that I would never be a silent witness. But I know that now I am.

Almost every day I see a body sprawled on the sidewalk. Some days I see quite a number. Some show signs of life; others are still. I assume they are all alive but I never stop to find out, or bend over to see if I could be of help.

They do not scream, as did Catherine Genovese. If they did I would probably walk away even faster. They are dirty, sometimes foul, unattractive victims.

I do hear people screaming, almost every day and sometimes several times a day. They do not lie on the ground but run about the streets.

I feel better about passing them by than the quiet ones. After all, the screamers could be dangerous. And if the government and police and doctors let them run around the street screaming in pain, who am I to try to do anything. I become a slightly less concerned 39th witness, even a mildly self-righteous one. Why don't Mayor Edward Koch and Governor Mario Cuomo do something about it, aren't they elected to do things like that, for God's sake?

When it is very cold, I see people wrapped in cardboard, bag ladies shuffling in the night streets to keep warm. I tell myself: It's really better when it is cold. Don't the cops have to take them off the street when it freezes, whether they like it or not?

Sometimes I get very angry—angry at the bodies for making me so uncomfortable, angry at the cops and the hospital people for not taking them somewhere they can be taken care of, angry at the judges and the civil libertarians who have changed the vagrancy laws so the police can't make people get off the streets and into someplace or other.

The new laws hold that homelessness is not a crime; all right, as long as they don't park themselves outside my door. I do not like that at all.

And what about really sick people, sick in the head? The law says that in New York state a mentally ill person must be a danger to himself or others and unable to "survive safely outside a hospital" before being taken off the street. Is that surviving safely, running up and down the street screaming? What about my rights? Do I have to hear them and see them? What do I pay taxes for?

It helps a little, getting mad at the lawyers and the judges and the mayor and the governor, mad at the bodies lying still on the ground or the bodies running screaming through the street.

Then, sometimes, and more often recently, I think of Catherine Genovese and the way she died and the 38 witnesses. I check out a little book I wrote about the case then and find that I didn't really attack the 38 and wrote that anyone might have done the same.

I am glad that I was not too high and mighty about those witnesses because now I am the 39th. And if you live in a city where living bodies lie in the streets or roam them in pain, and walk by, so are you.

Of course you and I could search out some of the people and organizations who do help the street sleepers and the street screamers and maybe do something ourselves. But, I don't know about you, but I am pretty busy these days, so maybe some other time.

A. M. Rosenthal
From *The New York Times*, February 12, 1987

The following essays, one light-hearted by the humorist S. J. Perelman, "Insert Flap A and Throw Away" and one serious like Roger Lewin's "On the Benefits of Being Eaten", show the close relationship between causes and effects.

EXERCISE 7

a. As you read these two professionally written articles, try to identify and list the linking chain of causes to results.

b. As conclusions are inextricably tied to causes, pay especial attention to the conclusions that these professional writers use. Look at your own cause and effect essay and list the causes that led to your conclusions.

c. Go through the openings to both essays and note how the writers get your attention. What lessons can you learn from the professional writers to use in your own writing?

INSERT FLAP "A" AND THROW AWAY

One stifling summer afternoon last August, in the attic of a tiny stone house in Pennsylvania, I made a most interesting discovery: the shortest, cheapest method of inducing a nervous breakdown ever perfected. In this technique (eventually adopted by the psychology department of Duke University, which will adopt anything), the subject is placed in a sharply sloping attic heated to 340°F. and given a mothproof closet known as the Jiffy-Cloz to assemble. The Jiffy-Cloz, procurable at any department store or neighborhood insane asylum, consists of half a dozen gigantic sheets of red cardboard, two plywood doors, a clothes rack, and a packet of staples. With these is included a set of instructions mimeographed in pale-violet ink, fruity with phrases like "Pass Section F through Slot AA, taking care not to fold tabs behind washers (see Fig. 9)." The cardboard is so processed that as the subject struggles convulsively to force the staple through, it suddenly buckles, plunging the staple deep into his thumb. He thereupon springs up with a dolorous cry and smites his knob (Section K) on the rafters (RR). As a final demonic touch, the Jiffy-Cloz people cunningly omit four of the staples necessary to finish the job, so that after indescribable purgatory, the best the subject can possibly achieve is a sleazy, capricious structure which would reduce any self-respecting moth to helpless laughter. The cumulative frustration, the tropical heat, and the soft, ghostly chuckling of the moths are calculated to unseat the strongest mentality.

In a period of rapid technological change, however, it was inevitable that a method as cumbersome as the Jiffy-Cloz would be superseded. It was superseded at exactly nine-thirty Christmas morning by a device called the Self-Running 10-Inch Scale-Model Delivery-Truck Kit Powered by Magic Motor, costing twenty-nine cents. About nine on that particular morning, I was spread-eagled on my bed, indulging in my favorite sport of mouth-breathing, when a cork fired from a child's air gun mysteriously lodged in my throat. The pellet proved awkward for a while, but I finally ejected it by flailing the little marksman (and his sister for good measure) until their welkins rang and sauntered in to breakfast. Before I could choke down a healing fruit juice, my consort, a tall, regal creature indistinguishable from Cornelia, the Mother of the

Gracelu, except that her foot was entangled in a roller skate, swept in. She extended a large, unmistakable box covered with diagrams.

"Now don't start making excuses," she whined. "It's just a simple cardboard toy. The directions are on the back—"

"Look, dear," I interrupted, rising hurriedly and pulling on my overcoat, "it clean slipped my mind. I'm supposed to take a lesson in crosshatching at Zim's School of Cartooning today."

"On Christmas?" she asked suspiciously.

"Yes, it's the only time they could fit me in," I countered glibly. "This is the big week for crosshatching, you know, between Christmas and New Year's."

"Do you think you ought to go in your pajamas?" she asked.

"Oh, that's O.K.," I smiled. "We often work in our pajamas up at Zim's. Well, goodbye now. If I'm not home by Thursday, you'll find a cold snack in the safe-deposit box." My subterfuge, unluckily, went for naught, and in a trice I was sprawled on the nursery floor, surrounded by two lambkins and ninety-eight segments of the Self-Running 10-Inch Scale-Model Delivery-Truck Construction Kit.

The theory of the kit was simplicity itself, easily intelligible to Kettering of General Motors, Professor Millikan, or any first-rate physicist. Taking as my starting point the only sentence I could comprehend, "Fold down on all lines marked 'fold down'; fold up on all lines marked 'fold up.'" I set the children to work and myself folded up with an album of views of Chili Williams. In a few moments, my skin was suffused with a delightful tingling sensation and I was ready for the second phase, lightly referred to in the directions as "Preparing the Spring Motor Unit." As nearly as I could determine after twenty minutes of mumbling, the Magic Motor ("No Electricity—No Batteries—Nothing to Wind—Motor Never Wears Out") was an accordion-pleated affair operating by torsion, attached to the axles. "It is necessary," said the text, "to cut a slight notch in each of the axles with a knife (see Fig. C). To find the exact place to cut this notch, lay one of the axles over diagram at bottom of page."

"Well, *now* we're getting someplace!" I boomed, with a false gusto that deceived nobody. "Here, Buster, run in and get Daddy a knife."

"I dowanna," quavered the boy, backing away. "You always cut yourself at this stage." I gave the wee fellow an indulgent pat on the head that flattened it slightly, to teach him civility, and commandeered a long, serrated bread knife from the kitchen. "Now watch me closely, children," I ordered. "We place the axle on the diagram as in Fig. C, applying a strong downward pressure on the knife handle at all times." The axle must have been a factory second, because an instant later I was in the bathroom grinding my teeth in agony and attempting to stanch the flow of blood. Ultimately, I succeeded in contriving a rough bandage and slipped back into the nursery without awakening the children's suspicions. An agreeable surprise awaited me. Displaying a mechanical aptitude clearly inherited from their sire, the rascals had put together the chassis of the delivery truck.

"Very good indeed," I complimented (naturally, one has to

exaggerate praise to develop a child's self-confidence). "Let's see—what's the next step? Ah, yes. 'Lock into box shape by inserting tabs, C, D, E, F, G, H, J, K, and L into slots C, D, E, F, G, H, J, K, and L. Ends of front axle should be pushed through holes A and B.'" While marshaling the indicated parts in their proper order, I emphasized to my rapt listeners the necessity of patience and perseverance. "Haste makes waste, you know," I reminded them. "Rome wasn't built in a day. Remember, your daddy isn't always going to be here to show you."

"Where *are* you going to be?" they demanded.

"In the movies, if I can arrange it," I snarled. Poising tabs C, D, E, F, G, H, J, K, and L in one hand and the corresponding slots in the other, I essayed a union of the two, but in vain. The moment I made one set fast and tackled another, tab and slot would part company, thumbing their noses at me. Although the children were too immature to understand, I saw in a flash where the trouble lay. Some idiotic employee at the factory had punched out the wrong design, probably out of sheer spite. So that was his game, eh? I set my lips in a grim line and, throwing one hundred and fifty-seven pounds of fighting fat into the effort, pounded the component parts into a homogeneous mass.

"There," I said with a gasp, "that's close enough. Now then, who wants candy? One, two, three—everybody off to the candy store!"

"We wanna finish the delivery truck!" they wailed. "Mummy, he won't let us finish the delivery truck!" Threats, cajolery, bribes were of no avail. In their jungle code, a twenty-nine-cent gewgaw bulked larger than a parent's love. Realizing that I was dealing with a pair of monomaniacs, I determined to show them who was master and wildly began locking the cardboard units helter-skelter, without any regard for the directions. When sections refused to fit, I gouged them with my nails and forced them together, cackling shrilly. The side panels collapsed; with a bestial oath, I drove a safety pin through them and lashed them to the roof. I used paper clips, bobby pins, anything I could lay my hands on. My fingers fairly flew and my breath whistled in my throat. "You want a delivery truck, do you?" I panted. "All right, I'll show you!" As merciful blackness closed in, I was on my hands and knees, bunting the infernal thing along with my nose and whinnying, "Roll, confound you, roll!"

"Absolute quiet," a carefully modulated voice was saying, "and fifteen of the white tablets every four hours." I opened my eyes carefully in the darkened room. Dimly I picked out a knifelike character actor in pince-nez lenses and a morning coat folding a stethoscope into his bag. "Yes," he added thoughtfully, "if we play our cards right, this ought to be a long, expensive recovery." From far away, I could hear my wife's voice bravely trying to control her anxiety.

"What if he becomes restless, Doctor?"

"Get him a detective story," returned the leech. "Or better still, a nice, soothing picture puzzle—something he can do with his hands."

S. J. Perelman
From *The Most of S. J. Perelman*

ON THE BENEFITS OF BEING EATEN

Experiments on a western mountain herb, scarlet gilia, show that its fitness is enhanced after being partially browsed

What advantage—if any—do plants gain from being eaten by grazing or browing animals? This question has been debated vigorously by ecologists for more than a decade, with no clear consensus emerging. "The most common view," says Ken Paige of the University of Utah and Thomas Whitham of Northern Arizona University, "is that herbivory is detrimental to plants and represents a selective pressure for the evolution of plant defenses." The opposing view, which Paige and Whitham favor, is that "plants can benefit by overcompensating, ultimately achieving greater fitness."

When Joy Belsky of Cornell University last year reviewed some 40 papers that are often cited in support of the grazing-advantage hypothesis she concluded the following: "Although herbivores may benefit certain plants by reducing competition or removing senescent tissue, no convincing evidence supports the theory that herbivory benefits grazed plants." In other words, there is no sound evidence that plants' fitness can be enhanced through being eaten. Now, however, Paige and Whitham present what they consider to be the first clear-cut data—from natural and experimental observations—that plants can be fitter as a consequence of being eaten.

"Our studies are unique," they say, "because they represent a closer approximation of true plant fitness in that seed quality and subsequent survival were examined." David Inouye of the University of Maryland is impressed, though not surprised, by the results. "It makes a lot of sense that plants would respond like this," he says. "In fact, I've collected similar, though less detailed, data at the Rocky Mountain Biological Laboratory in Colorado."

Paige and Whitham studied scarlet gilia, a red-flowered herb that grows in the western mountains, and showed that compared with uncropped plants, cropped plants not only sprout more in what is termed overcompensation, but ultimately also produce more seeds of high viability. This measure of potential future reproduction is crucial in comparisons of fitness.

There are many examples in nature of what is known as coevolution, in which a pair of organisms become evolutionarily modified in concert as a result of their interaction. The adaptations of certain insects and the flowers they pollinate provide multiple examples of coevolution, for example. And so it is sometimes for plants and the animals that eat them.

The open grassland plains of the Old World are relatively recent in its natural history, having arisen somewhat haltingly over the past 15 million years or so. During the same time there evolved a range of grazing animals, the modern forms of which appeared within the past couple of million years. Part of the coevolution between grasses and grazers was the introduction of abrasive pieces of silica into the leaves and the development of bigger teeth equipped with thick enamel in the animals that ate the leaves.

This aspect of coevolution was a kind of arms race between grass and grazer, between defense and offense. A second consequence of the interaction, according to a proposal made a couple of years ago by Samuel McNaughton of Syracuse University, was a behavioral one for the grazers. He showed that the animals benefited if they ate in herds, because plants cropped in this systematic way, rather than by a scatter of lone animals, tended to be more productive, yielding about twice the normal biomass. The question addressed by Paige and Whitham was, do the plants benefit too, not just in increased biomass but in Darwinian fitness? Do grazed plants have the potential for leaving more offspring than ungrazed plants?

In preliminary observations on scarlet gilia in two locations in Arizona, Paige and Whitham noted that almost three-quarters of all plants were fed upon by their natural grazers—mule deer and elk—at some point during the flowering season, the immediate result of which was the loss of 95% of the plant above ground. Once cropped, the stub of the original single stalk rapidly regrows four replacements . . . which bear 2.76 times as many flowers and 3.05 as many fruits as unbrowsed plants. This field observation led Paige and Whitham to suspect that "mammalian herbivory plays a beneficial role in the survival and reproductive success of scarlet gilia."

The notion had to be tested experimentally, which was done by taking 40 plants into the laboratory and artificially cropping half of them. The result was that although experimentally cropped plants produced on average fewer flowers than naturally browsed plants, there were still 1.86 as many as on uncropped plants. The number of fruits produced, however, were rather similar for the naturally and experimentally cropped plants. Cropping therefore does seem to benefit scarlet gilia.

There are, however, many examples of plant growth increase following cropping, which is nevertheless accompanied by the production of poorer quality seeds. For instance, when Fraser fir is cropped naturally the weight of its seeds declines 39% and germination rate drops 43%. In the case of scarlet gilia, by contrast, neither seed weight nor germination success suffered from cropping. And once germinated, the seedlings derived from cropped plants thrived as well as those from noncropped plants. Paige and Whitham were therefore able to conclude that "Cumulative estimates of plant performance demonstrate that browsed plants achieve a 2.4-fold increase in relative fitness over uneaten control plants."

The mechanisms by which growth of cropped scarlet gilia is stimulated are still unclear, but Paige and Whitham say they can eliminate two popular proposals. The first is that overcompensation in above-ground growth is at the expense of root structure. In this case, however, cropping also enhances root growth, producing roots twice as big as in uncropped plants. The second idea is that saliva from the browsing animal acts as a form of growth-stimulating hormone. The fact that natural and experimental cropping produced similar growth promotion rules this out as being important in scarlet gilia.

Paige and Whitham's results do seem to imply an evolutionary response by scarlet gilia to herbivory. Although the plant does not absolutely depend on being cropped in order to reproduce—as has occasionally happened in some coevolutionary pairs—its fitness is apparently enhanced through being eaten.

The Northern Arizona and Utah researchers do not yet know how common a phenomenon this might be among cropped plants. According to Inouye, "it is likely to be common enough to make it worthwhile looking for in other species." Paige and Whitham urge that investigations with other plants must include analysis of seed quality so that fitness, not just the immediate growth response to being eaten, can be truly measured.

Roger Lewin
From *SCIENCE*, May 1, 1987

Cross-curricular Essay Questions

1. Why did the novel develop in eighteenth century England and what, then, in turn were the effects of this new art form, the novel, on society in the nineteenth century? (English Literature)
2. (a) What were the causes of the depression of 1929?
   (b) What were the immediate effects on the world economy and what are the continuing effects today? (Economics)
3. Examine briefly the causes of World War I and describe the unexpected social ramifications as well as the more predictable changes that occurred in twentieth-century Europe as a result of the Great War? (European History)
4. What factors in American society in the 1870s led to the great migration from the farms and the small towns to the cities? How did the rise of urbanism affect the American family structure? (Sociology)
5. What has caused the changes in the atmosphere that have led to acid rain? What are both the short-range and long-range effects of this phenomenon on world ecology? (Science)
6. Name three causes of major psychological problems that frequently occur in the development of an emotionally disturbed, pre-school child and discuss the possible, even probable, adolescent behavior that may be linked later to these early childhood difficulties. (Psychology)

CHAPTER

• FIVE •

Classification

NAMING OF PARTS

Today we have naming of parts. Yesterday,
we had daily cleaning. And tomorrow morning,
we shall have to do after firing. But today,

Today we have naming of parts. Japonica
glistens like coral in all of the neighbouring
gardens, and today we have naming of parts.

This is the lower sling swivel. And this
Is the upper sling swivel, whose use you will
see, when you are given your slings. And this
is the piling swivel, which in your case you
have not got. The branches hold in the
gardens their silent, eloquent gestures,
which in our case we have not got.

This is the safety-catch, which is always
released with an easy flick of the thumb. And
please do not let me see anyone using his
finger. You can do it quite easy if you have

any strength in your thumb. The blossoms are
fragile and motionless, never letting anyone
see any of them using their finger.

And this you can see is the bolt. The purpose
of this is to open the breech, as you see. We
can slide it rapidly backwards and forwards:
we call this easing the spring. And rapidly
backwards and forwards the early bees are
assaulting and fumbling the flowers: they
call it easing the Spring.

They call it easing the Spring: it is perfectly
easy if you have any strength in your
thumb: like the bolt, and the breech, and the
cocking-piece and the point of balance, which
in our case we have not got; and the
almond-blossom silent in all of the gardens
and the bees going backwards and forwards,
for today we have naming of the parts.

Henry Reed.
From *A Map of Verona*

In order to grasp the underlying principles of **classification**, and by natural extension **division**, we'll examine these approaches by using a device called the ladder of abstraction. The top rung of the ladder will be the highest in abstraction, that is, furthest away from the concrete and specific entry on our ladder. Many of us played a game based on this ladder device when, as children, we addressed a letter:

Miss Raven McCrory
1234 Pleasant Street
Groton, MA 01045
U.S.A.
North America
Planet Earth
Galaxy Milky Way
Nebula Orion.

Another example

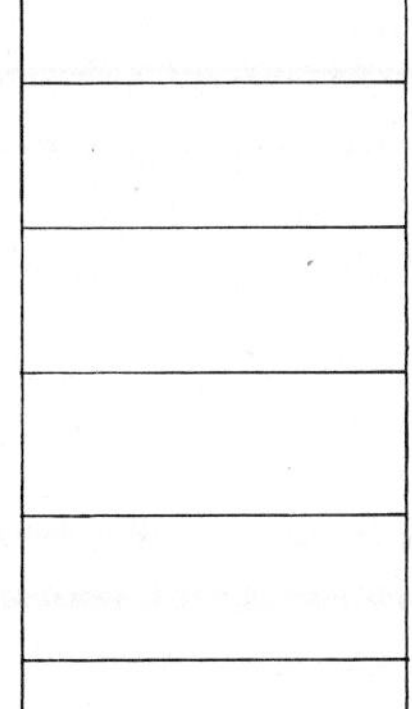

Material objects: this is quite an abstract idea. Any tangible thing will fit into this category.
Furniture: We've moved down a rung on the ladder. Now our category will be more specific.
Chair: The class of chairs is narrower but still includes all types of chairs—deck chairs, kitchen chairs, office chairs, living room chairs.
Living room chair: We further limit our group of chairs, but it still includes all the types of living room chairs.
Nick's living room chair: Now we have a specific chair in mind. We can describe it precisely.

In the process of classification we move up the ladder, grouping diverse data into more abstract categories. In division, in contrast, we move down the ladder, dividing a more abstract category into its component and more specific parts (classify up; divide down). This distinction between classification and division is sometimes glossed over when the term **classification** is used to describe both processes. As you can see, they are distinct.

• Classification as a Process

Classification as a process is useful for writers because it helps them sort and give meaning to the vast array of data which most research yields. That is, classification helps the writer analyze collected facts. It is a valuable thinking skill. Suppose we are writing an activity report to summarize a business trip to sales regions I and II of our hypothetical national-level company. In chronological order, we did the following on our trip:

4/15 met with area director responsible for region I
4/16 met with region I advertising agent
4/16 met with Bruce Wallace, a region I retailer
4/18 talked on the phone with Emma Smith, a region II retailer
4/19 visited four retail outlets in region II
4/20 met with region II distribution manager.

Simply to list our business trip activities in chronological order will not help our reader give meaning to our trip. If we were to look for categories into which we could **classify** our activity (up the ladder of abstraction), we might well find an organizing method which would give continuity, coherence and order to our activities. The first possibility for classification might be whether we had direct contact or indirect contact, a meeting or a phone call. A moment's reflection will indicate though, that although this would classify, the principle of classification—type of contact—wouldn't be of much use in helping our boss understand how we spent a week of our work time and our company's money. Another possibility for classification might occur as we review our activities. This possibility is at what level in the organization the contract occurred. There are three levels represented here, area, regional and retail. Classifying by these levels provides coherence to our data, emphasizes that our activity has continuity in and of itself and with our company's organization, and orders our data into a structure which will, we hope, make sense to our boss. Using the level of contact as the principle for our classification would, in this particular case, be sensible.

Now let's look at another logical way to arrange the same data. If our boss has been under pressure to show that he covers all of his regions equally well, he may find our trip report data most useful when it is organized by region. In such a case, classifying by region, and then following the chronology would be a wise approach. Note that, as in this example, the classification structure may often be suggested by the needs of the audience.

• The Divisional Process

The process of **division** is useful also. In fact, you may well have noticed that once we classify, we've already set up the ladder of abstraction. Division consists of going down the rungs rather than up them. Using our business trip activity report example, if our classification principle is the organizational level, then we could look at all the possible levels into which we might divide our activities. In addition to the area level, the regional level and the retail level, we might also have been concerned with the head office level, where our boss is located.

Use Equal Categories. There are several hints which help ensure effective classification and division. One of these is to **use categories of equal abstraction**. In our business example, imagine that in addition to the area, regional and retail levels, we included the personnel relation level.

area activity
regional activity
retail activity
personnel activity

This last level, personnel, is not equal to our others because it does not follow the same classification principle. It segments on the basis of a function (personnel) rather than on the basis of level in the organization. Be careful. Use one classification or division principle at a time. In effective classification and division, the segments don't overlap or do so as little as possible. Since we live in a complex world of interlocking relationships, some overlap is a given, but do try to keep it to a minimum.

Classification and division are specific ways to develop extended definition, as are narrative description, dynamic description, example, comparison and contrast and cause and effect. Use any or a combination of these techniques to develop the following essays.

1. Explain the effects protectionist trade legislation in the U.S. could have on the American consumer.
2. Provide an extended definition for one of the following terms:

chair	dictionary
racquet-ball racket	Jeep
sweater	charity

3. Develop an essay which clearly illustrates your grasp of one of the following topics. Do this for a specific audience.

culture	patience
knowledge	heavy metal music
wisdom	calculus
bravery	social responsibility

4. When we encounter a question of the form, "What is the difference between . . . (any two ideas or objects)," we are actually being asked to compare and contrast two definitions in an extended essay. Combining what you know about comparison and contrast and definition, write an essay of this form answering a question of your own choice.

The following student essay is a good example of the process of classification.

First Date Foods

A first date can be embarrassing enough without the help of food, and the results of ordering the wrong kind of food can be hilariously disastrous. Three types of food that should not be eaten on a first date are: food that is eaten with the hands, food that requires great dexterity to eat, and food that falls apart when eaten.

Of the edibles in the first category, food that is eaten with the hands, pizza is the best at making a couple on their first date feel unpleasantly awkward. Anyone who has gone out to eat with a person for the first time, and ordered pizza, knows the problems that eating pizza can cause.

How can anyone casually remove the long string of cheese that dangles between a person's mouth and a piece of pizza without being noticed? The nervous pizza-eater will wonder if it's acceptable to chew down the cheesy string until the cheese on the piece of pizza, or if it is better to break the cheese free from the pizza with one's fingers, hoping that no one will notice the following surreptitious finger-licking. The real problem with the long string of cheese that dangles between the person's mouth and the pizza itself, however, is that when the stringy line of cheese snaps in two, half of it ends up twirled around the nose. And, just when the pizza eater thinks that no further embarrassment could be humanly possible, the soda that he or she has been drinking with the pizza comes back up the wrong way, and the thought of slithering beneath the table doesn't seem like such a bad one. Some other hand-eaten foods that could cause a great deal of embarrassment on a first date are chicken and barbecued ribs.

Spaghetti is a type of food that requires great dexterity to eat, and a person should think twice before ordering it on a first date. Probably the most embarrassing thing about eating spaghetti is the slurping sound one makes while trying inconspicuously to suck in the errant strand of spaghetti hanging from one's mouth. Would it be acceptable, the spaghetti-dangler wonders, to cut the hanging strand of spaghetti with the teeth, letting the hanging strand fall to the plate, or would it be a better idea to suck the hanging strand of spaghetti into the mouth, running the risk of making an awful slurping sound, and possibly slobbering spaghetti sauce all over a clean shirt? The spaghetti-eater would probably be better off cutting up the spaghetti and eating it with a spoon. Another problem with spaghetti is the meatballs that come with it. As the spaghetti-eater tries to cut a meatball with the side of a fork, the meatball slides out from under the fork, leaps off the plate, and lands onto the table. The flustered diner is then presented with the following problems: does one use his or her fingers to replace the meatball quickly on the plate, or should silverware be used instead as a sort of lever to slide the meatball back into its former position, saving what little dignity the diner has left by now? No matter what one does in this situation, the chances of placing the meatball back onto the plate without anyone noticing are almost zero. Other types of food that require great dexterity to eat include unboned fish, crab and lobster.

Tacos are a kind of food that falls apart when eaten and are a gigantic mistake on a first date. No matter how a taco-eater approaches a taco, the taco creates a mess. The loud CRUNCH caused by the collapsing taco shell makes the muncher think that the entire restaurant is watching this disaster, but the truth is that only his or her date is staring. As a bite of taco is taken, the meat, tomatoes, lettuce, and anything else on the taco begin to slide, drip and ooze out the taco's sides. How should one go about getting the food back into the taco? Would it be acceptable to use one's fingers to push the food back into the taco, or is it a better idea to place the spilled food back into the taco with a spoon? Overall, a taco may not be as hard to eat as pizza or spaghetti, but it's definitely a type of food that should be avoided on a first date. Probably the best solution is not to order a taco on a first date, or for that matter, any food that is eaten with the hands, that requires great dexterity to eat, or that falls apart when eaten.

1. This essay examines three categories into which specific foods may be classified. Are the classifications based on the same principle? What is it? Can you think of other principles that would have been more effective?
2. If you use teaching methods as a classification principle, how would you classify the professors of courses in which you're now enrolled?
3. In chemistry we learned early on that all material objects are divided into two categories, those containing carbon (organic) and those not containing carbon (inorganic). Within each classification, how are further divisions made?

4. Write an essay which divides the members of this category (teachers, brothers, First Sergeants, friends, homes) into smaller groups. Be sure to consider all its members.

The next student essay we'll consider divides dogs by disposition into three distinct categories: friendly, ferocious, or fickle, often briefly mentioning and rejecting two other principles of division, size and genealogy.

Dogs I've Known

Many kinds of dogs provide companionship for people around the world, and some folks even say they are "man's best friend." But as a former paperboy, I can tell you that "man's best friend" can be a "boy's worst fiend." This is especially true during the "wee" hours of the morning on a deserted neighborhood street.

Small, medium, or large is not much of a factor to the wary paperboy. Fullbreed, halfbreed and mutt usually do not come into the picture either. A paperboy worries about three kinds of dogs: friendly, ferocious, or fickle.

The friendly dog usually causes limited problems for the delivery boy. He provides the boy with company and a break from the loneliness of walking the barren streets. He will just tag along for awhile, beg for an occasional scratch behind the ear, and then be on his merry way.

He also can be a security blanket for the nervous paperboy, especially on spooky mornings when the air is thick with fog.

So, if the friendly dog gives so much, why does the paperboy have to worry about him? If you have to ask that question, I would like to throw a delivery bag over your head, load you down with Sunday newspapers, and introduce you to Max.

Max was a good dog, with a big, friendly heart. Of course, his heart had to be big to keep the blood flowing through his massive body. I suppose he was not really that huge, but, at the time, his shaggy frame seemed nothing short of a 1,000-pound bear to his wide-eyed deliverer.

I believe he was some sort of sheepdog, but being too friendly was his folly. It never failed. Everytime I was struggling to reach the summit of Fremont Drive (a steep hill along my route), Max would appear—loveable, huggable, jump-on-the-paperboy-and-knock-him-down Max. I could have forgiven him for scattering my newspapers halfway across the street. I could have even dismissed my skinned elbow or knee. But I could never forget the mushy, slobbery kisses that made me want to sterilize my face in boiling water.

About the only good thing that came out of these little meetings was the fact that his paws, which seemed to be wet and muddy even on the driest summer morning, would always smudge at least one newspaper. This paper I would gladly leave at the Biernacki's, who did not even give me a tip on Christmas.

I suppose the worst thing about a friendly dog is he attracts the next category of canines—the ferocious dog. These beasts are the meanest, loudest, scariest, and a lot of times the most violent creatures the paperboy faces.

The least harmful of this category is the yapper. This is the dog that follows you from the beginning to the end of his territory, making such a ruckus you would think the neighborhood was being invaded. For the most part, this dog keeps his distance, and you soon learn that his bark is worse than his bite.

Of course, we cannot forget the growler. The growler is the one that chases you into a corner, sometimes nipping at your heels. As long as you remain motionless, you are relatively safe. Most of the time, this dog finally gets bored and lets you pass, or he is shooed away by an early-rising neighbor.

The last dog in the ferocious category is the least common (thank goodness), but the most dangerous. This canine will not hesitate to bite you if you look at him, talk to him, offend or irritate him in any other manner. I ran into one of this sort, who showed no mercy, gave no breaks, and made you pay a price for wandering in his domain. This fiend, whom I came to call Jaws, seemed to take a chunk out of you for simply breathing air. I armed myself with a quick bicycle and a long stick before entering his neighborhood. Even with all of my precautions, he managed to put his signature on my ankles more than once. This unfriendly foe seemed to enjoy sinking his teeth into trembling flesh.

The last kind of dog on the paperboy's worry list falls under the fickle category. The fickle canine is unpredictable. One day he may walk up to you wagging his tail, bite your fingers when you try to pet him, and then lick your wounds—all in a matter of seconds. The next day he may bark at you fiercely, then suddenly roll on his back, begging for you to scratch his belly. This mixed up canine keeps you on your toes and is another dog to avoid.

Friendly, ferocious, or fake canines may have their own menacing characteristics, but they have at least one thing in common. For the survival conscious paperboy, they will always be a "boy's worst fiend."

1. In the final paragraph, summing up the major point of his essay, the student writer changes his categories a bit. Probably this is done to avoid redundancy. Evaluate this decision.
2. Work out classification and division schemes for one of the following subjects and then develop the essay choosing from description, comparison and contrast, definition and cause and effect techniques.

jobs	children
goodness	education
sacrifice	spouses

"13 Ways of Looking at a Blackbird," a poem by Wallace Stevens, lets us know immediately that the poet is categorizing ways of looking at a blackbird. As you read the poem, decide whether it is classifying or dividing.

THIRTEEN WAYS OF LOOKING AT A BLACKBIRD

I

Among twenty snowy mountains,
The only thing
Was the eye of the blackbird.

II

I was of three minds,
Like a tree
In which there are three blackbirds.

III
The blackbird whirled in the autumn winds.
It was a small part of the pantomime.

IV
A man and a woman
Are one.
A man and a woman and a blackbird
Are one.

V
I do not know which to prefer,
The beauty of inflections
Or the beauty of innuendoes,
The blackbird whistling
Or just after.

VI
Icicles filled the long window
With barbaric glass.
The shadow of the blackbird
Crossed it, to and fro.
The mood
Traced in the shadow
An indecipherable cause.

VII
O thin men of Haddam,
Why do you imagine golden birds?
Do you not see how the blackbird
Walks around the feet
Of the women about you?

VIII
I know noble accents
And lucid, inescapable rhythms;
But I know, too
That the blackbird is involved
In what I know.

IX
When the blackbird flew out of sight
It marked the edge
Of one of many circles.

X
As the sight of blackbirds
Flying in a green light,
Even the bawds of euphony
Would cry out sharply.

XI
He rode over Connecticut
In a glass coach.
Once, a fear pierced him,
In that he mistook
The shadow of his equipage
For blackbirds.

XII
The river is moving.
The blackbird must be flying.

XIII
It was evening all afternoon.
It was snowing
And it was going to snow.
The blackbird sat
In the cedar-limbs.

Wallace Stevens
From *The Collected Poems of Wallace Stevens*

Actually, since Stevens is sharing his random thoughts with us, strictly categorizing his work as classification or division is difficult. In contrast, John Updike's essay on the Masters Golf Tournament at the Augusta (Georgia) National Golf Club is a study in classification. Notice how he playfully uses Wallace Stevens' categories.

THIRTEEN WAYS OF LOOKING AT THE MASTERS

1. As an Event in Augusta, Georgia

In the middle of downtown Broad Street a tall white monument—like an immensely heightened wedding cake save that in place of the bride and groom stands a dignified Confederate officer—proffers the thought that

No nation rose so white and fair;
None fell so pure of crime.

Within a few steps of the monument, a movie theater, during Masters Week in 1979, was showing *Hair*, full of cheerful miscegenation and anti-military song and dance.

This is the Deep/Old/New South, with its sure-enough levees, railroad tracks, unpainted dwellings out of illustrations to Joel Chandler Harris, and stately homes ornamented by grillework and verandas. As far up the Savannah River as boats could go, Augusta has been a trading post since 1717 and was named in 1735 by James Oglethorpe for the mother of George III. It changed hands several times during the Revolutionary War, thrived on tobacco and cotton, imported textile machinery from Philadelphia in 1828, and during the Civil War housed the South's largest powder works. Sherman passed through here, and didn't leave much in the way of historical sites.

The Augusta National Golf Club is away from the business end of town, in a region of big brick houses embowered in magnolia and dogwood. A lot of people retire to Augusta, and one of the reasons that Bobby Jones wanted to build a golf course here, instead of near his native Atlanta, was the distinctly milder climate. The course, built in 1931–32 on the site of the Fruitlands Nursery property, after designs by Dr. Alister Mackenzie (architect of Cypress Point) and Jones himself, has the venerable Augusta Country Club at its back, and at its front, across Route 28, an extensive shopping-center outlay. At this point the New South becomes indistinguishable from New Jersey.

2. As an Event Not in Augusta, Georgia

How many Augusta citizens are members of the Augusta National Golf Club? The question, clearly in bad taste, brought raised eyebrows and a muttered "Very few" or, more spaciously, "Thirty-eight or forty." The initial membership fee is rumored to be $50,000, there is a waiting list five years long, and most of the members seem to be national Beautiful People, Golfing Subspecies, who jet in for an occasional round during the six months the course is open. When Ike, whose cottage was near the clubhouse, used to show up and play a twosome with Arnold Palmer, the course would be cleared by the Secret Service. Cliff Roberts, chairman of the tournament from its inception in 1934 until his death in 1977, was a Wall Street investment banker; his chosen successor, William H. Lane, is a business executive from faraway Houston.

A lot of Augusta's citizens get out of town during Masters Week, renting their houses. The lady in the drugstore near the house my wife and I were staying in told me she had once gone walking on the course. *Once*: the experience seemed unrepeatable. The course had looked deserted to her, but then a voice shouted "Fore" and a ball struck near her. The ghost of Lloyd Mangrum, perhaps. The only Augustans conspicuous during the tournament are the black caddies, who know the greens so well they can call a putt's break to the inch while standing on the fringe.

3. As a Study in Green

Green grass, green grandstands, green concession stalls, green paper cups, green folding chairs and visors for sale, green-and-white ropes, green-topped Georgia pines, a prevalence of green in the slacks and jerseys of the gallery, like the prevalence of red in the crowd in Moscow on May Day. The caddies' bright green caps and Sam Snead's bright green trousers. If justice were poetic, Hubert Green would win it every year.

4. As a Rite of Spring

"It's become a rite of spring," a man told me with a growl, "like the Derby." Like Fort Lauderdale. Like Opening Day at a dozen ballparks. Spring it was, especially for us Northerners who had left our gray skies, brown lawns, salt-strewn highways, and plucky little croci for this efflorescence of azaleas and barefoot *jeunes filles en fleurs*. Most of the gallery, like most of the golfers, had Southern accents. This Yankee felt a little as if he were coming in late on a round of equinoctial parties that had stretched from Virginia to Florida. A lot of young men were lying on the grass betranced by the memories of last night's libations, and a lot of matronly voices continued discussing Aunt Earlene's unfortunate second marriage, while the golf balls floated overhead. For many in attendance, the Masters is a ritual observance; some of the old-timers wore sun hats festooned with over twenty years' worth of admission badges.

Will success as a festival spoil the Masters as a sporting event? It hasn't yet, but the strain on the tournament's famous and exemplary organization can be felt. Ticket sales are limited, but the throng at the main scoreboard is hard to squeeze by. The acreage devoted to parking would make a golf course in itself. An army of over two thousand policemen, marshals, walkway guards, salespersons, trash-gleaners, and other attendants is needed to maintain order and facilitate the pursuit of happiness. To secure a place by any green it is necessary to arrive at least an hour before there is anything to watch.

When, on the last two days, the television equipment arrives, the crowd itself is watched. Dutifully, it takes its part as a mammoth unpaid extra in a national television spectacular. As part of it, patting out courteous applause at a good shot or groaning in chorus at a missed putt, one felt, slightly, *canned*.

5. As a Fashion Show

Female fashions, my wife pointed out, came in three strata. First, young women decked out as if going to a garden party—makeup, flowing dresses, sandals. Next, the trim, leathery generation of the mothers, dressed as if they themselves were playing golf—short skirts, sun visors, cleated two-tone shoes. Last, the generation of the grandmothers, in immaculately blued hair and amply filled pants suits in shades we might call electric pastel or Day-Glo azalea.

6. As a Display Case for Sam Snead and Arnold Palmer

Though they no longer are likely to win, you wouldn't know it from their charismas. Snead, with his rakishly tilted panama and slightly pushed-in face—a face that has known both battle and merriment—swaggers around the practice tee like the Sheriff of Golf Country, testing a locked door here, hanging a parking ticket there. On the course, he remains a golfer one has to call beautiful, from the cushioned roll of his shoulders as he strokes the ball to the padding, panther-like tread with which he follows it down the center of the fairway, his chin tucked down while he thinks apparently rueful thoughts. He is one of the great inward golfers, those who wrap the dazzling difficulty of the game in an impassive, effortless flow of movement. When, on the green, he stands beside his ball, faces the hole, and performs the curious obeisance of his "side-winder" putting stroke, no one laughs.

And Palmer, he of the unsound swing, a hurried slash that ends as though he is snatching back something hot from a fire, remains the monumental outward golfer, who invites us into the game to share with him its heady turmoil, its call for constant courage. Every inch an agonist, Palmer still hitches his pants as he mounts the green, still strides between the wings of his army like Hector on his way to yet more problematical heroism. Age has thickened him, made him look almost muscle-bound, and has grizzled his thin, untidy hair; but his deportment more than ever expresses vitality, a love of life and of the game that rebounds to him, from the multitudes, as fervent gratitude. Like us golfing commoners, he risks looking bad for the sake of some fun.

Of the younger players, only Lanny Wadkins communicates Palmer's reckless determination, and only Fuzzy Zoeller has the captivating blitheness of a Jimmy Demaret or a Lee Trevino. The Masters, with its clubby lifetime qualification for previous winners, serves as an annual exhibit of Old Masters, wherein one can see the difference between the reigning, college-bred pros, with their even teeth, on-camera poise, and abstemious air, and the older crowd, who came up from caddie sheds, drove themselves in cars along the dusty miles of the Tour, and hustled bets with the rich to make ends meet. Golf expresses the man, as every weekend foursome knows; amid the mannerly lads who dominate the money list, Palmer and Snead loom as men.

7. As an Exercise in Spectatorship

In no other sport must the spectator move. The builders and improvers of Augusta National built mounds and bleachers for the crowds to gain vantage from, and a gracefully written pamphlet by the founder, Robert Jones, is handed out as instruction in the art of "letting the Tournament come to us instead of chasing after it." Nevertheless, as the field narrows and the interest of the hordes focuses, the best way to see anything is to hang back in the woods and use binoculars. Seen from within the galleries, the players become tiny walking dolls, glimpsable, like stars on a night of scudding clouds, in the gaps between heads.

Examples of Southern courtesy in the galleries: (1) When my wife stood to watch an approach to the green, the man behind her mildly observed, "Ma'am, it was awful nice when you were sittin' down." (2) A gentleman standing next to me, not liking the smell of a cigar I was smoking, offered to buy it from me for a dollar.

Extraordinary event in the galleries: on the fourth hole a ball set in flight by Dow Finsterwald solidly struck the head of a young man sitting beside the green. The sound of a golf ball on a skull is remarkably like that of two blocks of wood knocked together. *Glock*. Flesh hurts; bone makes music.

Single instance of successful spectatorship by this reporter: I happened to be in the pines left of the seventh fairway on the first day of play, wondering whether to go for another of the refreshment committee's standardized but economical ham sandwiches, when Art Wall, Jr., hooked a ball near where I was standing. Only a dozen or so gathered to watch his recovery; for a moment, then, we could breathe with a player and experience with him—as he waggled, peered at obtruding branches, switched clubs, and peered at the branches again—that quintessential golfing sensation, the loneliness of the bad-ball hitter.

Sad truth, never before revealed: by sticking to a spot in the stands or next to the green, one can view the field coming through, hitting variants of the same shots and putts, and by listening to the massed cheers and grunts from the other greens, one can guess at dramas unseen; but the unified field, as Einstein discovered in a more general connection, is unapprehendable, and the best way to witness a golf tournament is at the receiving end of a television signal. Many a fine golf reporter, it was whispered to me, never leaves the set in the press tent.

The other sad truth about golf spectatorship is that for today's pros it all comes down to the putting, and that the difference between a putt that drops and one that rims the cup, though teleologically enormous, is intellectually negligible.

8. As a Study in Turf-Building

A suburban lawn-owner can hardly look up from admiring the weedless immensity of the Augusta National turf. One's impression, when first admitted to this natural Oz, is that a giant putting surface has been dropped over acres of rolling terrain, with a few apertures for ponds and trees to poke through. A philosophy of golf is expressed in Jones's pamphlet: "The Augusta National has much more fairway and green area than the average course. There is little punishing rough and very few bunkers. The course is not intended so much to punish severely the wayward shot as to reward adequately the stroke played with skill—and judgment."

It is an intentional paradox, then, that this championship course is rather kind to duffers. The ball sits up on Augusta's emerald carpet looking big as a baseball. It was not always such; in 1972, an invasion of *Poa annua*, a white-spiked vagabond grass, rendered conditions notoriously bumpy; in remedy a fescue called Pennlawn and a rye called Pennfine were implanted on the fairways and greens respectively and have flourished. Experimentation continues; to make the greens even harder and slicker, they are thinking of rebuilding them on a sand base—and have already done so on the adjacent par-three course.

From May to October, when the course is closed to play, everything goes to seed and becomes a hayfield, and entire fairways are plowed up: a harrowing thought. The caddies, I was solemnly assured, never replace a divot; they just sprinkle grass seed from a pouch they carry. Well, this is a myth, for I repeatedly saw caddies replace divots in the course of the tournament, with the care of tile-setters.

9. As Demography

One doesn't have to want to give the country back to the Indians to feel a nostalgic pang while looking at old photos of the pre-World War II tournaments, with their hatted, necktied galleries strolling up the fairways in the wake of the baggy-trousered players, and lining the tees and greens only one man deep.

The scores have grown crowded, too. The best then would be among the best now—Lloyd Mangrum's single-round 64 in 1940 has not been bettered, though for the last two years it has been equalled. But the population of the second-best has increased, producing virtually a new winner each week of the Tour, and stifling the emergence of stable constellations of superstars like Nelson-Hogan-Snead and Palmer-Player-Nicklaus. In the 1936 and 1938 Masters, only seven players made the thirty-six-hole score of 145 that cut the 1979 field to forty-five players. Not until 1939 did the winner break 280 and not again until 1948. The last total over 280 to win it came in 1973. In 1936, Craig Wood had a first-day round of 88 and finished in the top two dozen. In 1952, Sam Snead won the Masters in spite of a third-round 77. That margin for intermittent error has been squeezed from tournament golf. Johnny Miller chops down a few trees, develops the wrong muscles, and drops like a stone on the lists. Arnold Palmer, relatively young and still strong and keen, can no longer ram the putts in from twenty feet, and becomes a father figure. A cruel world, top-flight golf, that eats its young.

10. As Race Relations

A Martian skimming overhead in his saucer would have to conclude that white Earthlings hit the ball and black Earthlings fetch it, that white men swing the sticks and black men carry them. The black caddies of Augusta, in their white coveralls, are a tradition that needs a symbolic breaking, the converse of Lee Elder's playing in the tournament.

To be fair, these caddies are specialists of a high order, who take a cheerful pride in their expertise and who are, especially during Masters Week, well paid for it. Gary Player's caddie for his spectacular come-from-nowhere victory of 1978 was tipped $10,000—a sum that, this caddie assured an impudent interrogator, was still safe in the bank. In the New South, blacks work side by side with whites in the concession stands and at the fairway ropes, though I didn't see any in a green marshal's coat. I was unofficially informed that, at the very time when civil rightists were agitating for a black player to be invited to play even if one did not earn qualification—as Elder did in 1975—blacks were not being admitted to the tournament *as spectators*. I wonder about this. On pages 26–27 of the green souvenir album with a text by Cliff Roberts, one can see a photograph of Henry Picard hitting out of a bunker; behind him in the scattering of spectators are a number of ebony gentlemen not dressed as caddies. At any rate, though golf remains a white man's game, it presents in the Masters player and caddie an active white-black partnership in which the white man is taking the advice and doing the manual work. Caddies think of the partnership as "we," as in "We hit a drive down the center and a four-iron stiff to the pin, but then *he* missed the putt."

11. As Class Relations

Though the Augusta National aspires to be the American St. Andrews, there is a significant economic difference between a Scottish golf links thriftily pinked out on a wasteland—the sandy seaside hills that are "links"—and the American courses elaborately, expensively carved from farmland and woods. Though golf has plebeian Scottish roots, in this country its province is patrician. A course requires capital and flaunts that ancient aristocratic prerogative, land. In much of the world, this humbling game is an automatic symbol of capitalist-imperialist oppression; a progressive African novelist, to establish a character as a villain, has only to show him coming off a golf course. And in our own nation, for all the roadside driving ranges and four o'clock factory leagues, golf remains for millions something that happens at the end of a long driveway, beyond the MEMBERS ONLY sign.

Yet competitive golf in the United States came of age when, at The Country Club, in Brookline, Massachusetts, a twenty-year-old ex-caddie and workingman's son, Francis Ouimet, beat the British legends Vardon and Ray in a playoff for the U.S. Open. And ever since, the great competitors have tended to come from the blue-collar level of golf, the caddies and the offspring of club pros. Rare is the Bobby Jones who emerges from the gentry with the perfectionistic drive and killer instinct that make a champion in this game which permits no let-up or loss of concentration, yet which penalizes tightness also. Hagen acted like a swell and was called Sir Walter, but he came up from a caddie's roost in Rochester. The lords of golf have been by and large gentlemen made and not born, while the clubs and the management of the Tour remain in the hands of the country-club crowd. When genteel Ed Sneed and Tom Watson fell into a three-way playoff for the 1979 Masters title, you knew in your bones it was going to be the third player, a barbarian called Fuzzy with a loopy all-out swing, who would stroll through the gates and carry off the loot.

12. As a Parade of Lovely Golfers, No Two Alike

Charles Coody, big-beaked bird. Billy Casper, once the king of touch, now sporting the bushy white sideburns of a turn-of-the-century railroad conductor, still able to pop them up from a sandtrap and sink the putt. Trevino, so broad across he looks like a reflection in a funhouse mirror, a model of delicacy around the greens and a model of affable temperament everywhere. Player, varying his normal black outfit with white slacks, his bearing so full of fight and muscle he seems to be restraining himself from breaking into a run. Nicklaus, Athlete of the Decade, still golden but almost gaunt and faintly grim, as he feels a crown evaporating from his head. Gay Brewer, heavy in the face and above the belt, nevertheless uncorking a string-straight mid-iron to within nine inches of the long seventh hole in the par-three tournament. Miller Barber, Truman Capote's double, punching and putting his way to last year's best round, a storm-split 64 in two installments. Bobby Clampett, looking too young and thin to be out there. Andy Bean, looking too big to be out there, and with his perennially puzzled expression seeming to be searching for a game more his size. Hubert Green, with a hunched flicky swing that would make a high-school golf coach scream. Tom Weiskopf, the handsome embodiment of pained near-perfection. Hale Irwin, the picture-book golfer with the face of a Ph.D. candidate. Johnny Miller, looking heavier than we remember him, patiently knocking them out on the practice tee, wondering where the lightning went. Ben Crenshaw, the smiling Huck Finn, and Tom Watson, the more pensive Tom Sawyer, who, while the other boys were whitewashing fences, has become, politely but firmly, the best golfer in the world.

And many other redoubtable young men. Seeing them up close, in the dining room or on the clubhouse veranda, one is struck by how young and in many cases how slight they seem, with their pert and telegenic little wives—boys, really, anxious to be polite and to please even the bores and boors that collect in the interstices of all well-publicized events. Only when one sees them at a distance, as they walk alone or chatting in twos down the great green emptiness of the fairway, does one sense that each youth is the pinnacle of a buried pyramid of effort and investment, of prior competition from pre-teen level up, of immense and it must be at times burdensome accumulated hopes of parents, teachers, backers. And with none of the group hypnosis and exhilaration of team play to relieve them. And with the difference between success and failure so feather-fine.

13. As a Religious Experience

The four days of 1979's Masters fell on Maundy Thursday, Good Friday, Holy Saturday, and Easter Sunday. On Good Friday, fittingly, the skies darkened, tornadoes were predicted, and thousands of sinners ran for cover. My good wife, who had gone to divine services, was prevented from returning to the course by the flood of departing cars, and the clear moral is one propounded from many a pulpit: golf and churchgoing do not mix. Easter Sunday also happened to be the anniversary of the assassination of Abraham Lincoln and the sinking of the *Titanic*, and it wasn't such a good day for Ed Sneed either.

About ninety-nine percent of the gallery, my poll of local vibes indicated, was rooting for Sneed to hold off disaster and finish what he had begun. He had played splendidly for three days, and it didn't seem likely he'd come this close soon again. When he birdied the fifteenth and enlarged his once huge cushion back to three strokes, it seemed he would do it. But then, through no flagrant fault of his own, he began "leaking." We all knew how it felt, the slippery struggle to nurse a good round back to the clubhouse. On the seventeenth green, where I was standing, his approach looked no worse than his playing partner's; it just hit a foot too long, skipped onto the sloping back part of the green, and slithered into the fringe. His putt back caught the cup but twirled away. And his putt to save par, which looked to me like a gimme, lipped out, the same way my two-footers do when I lift my head to watch them drop, my sigh of relief all prepared. Zoeller, ten minutes before, had gently rolled in a birdie from much farther away. Sneed's fate seemed sealed then: the eighteenth hole, a famous bogey-maker, waited for him as ineluctably as Romeo's missed appointment with Juliet.

He hadn't hit bad shots, and he hadn't panicked; he just was screwed a half-turn too tight to get a par. The gallery of forty thousand felt for him, right to the pits of our golf-weary stomachs, when his last hope of winning it clean hung on the lip of the seventy-second hole. It so easily might have been otherwise. But then that's life, and that's golf.

John Updike
From *Hugging the Shore*

In one final professionally-written essay, "Proxemics in the Arab World," by Edward T. Hall, consider how this anthropologist divides the study of proxemics (spatial relationships) in the Arab world.

PROXEMICS IN THE ARAB WORLD

In spite of over two thousand years of contact, Westerners and Arabs still do not understand each other. Proxemic research reveals some insights into this difficulty. Americans in the Middle East are immediately struck by two conflicting sensations. In public they are compressed and overwhelmed by smells, crowding, and high noise levels; in Arab homes Americans are apt to rattle around, feeling exposed and often somewhat inadequate because of too much space! (The Arab houses and apartments of the middle and upper classes which Americans stationed abroad commonly occupy are much larger than the dwellings such Americans usually inhabit.) Both the high sensory stimulation which is experienced in public places and the basic insecurity which comes from being in a dwelling that is too large provide Americans with an introduction to the sensory world of the Arab.

Behavior in Public

Pushing and shoving in public places is characteristic of Middle Eastern culture. Yet it is not entirely what Americans think it is (being pushy and rude) but stems from a different set of assumptions concerning not only the relations between people but how one experiences the body as well. Paradoxically, Arabs consider northern Europeans and Americans pushy, too. This was very puzzling to me when I started investigating these two views. How could Americans who stand aside and avoid touching be considered pushy? I used to ask Arabs to explain this paradox. None of my subjects was able to tell me specifically what particulars of American behavior were responsible, yet they all agreed that the impression was widespread among Arabs. After repeated unsuccessful attempts to gain insight into the cognitive world of the Arab on this particular point, I filed it away as a question that only time would answer. When the answer came, it was because of a seemingly inconsequential annoyance.

While waiting for a friend in a Washington, D.C., hotel lobby and wanting to be both visible and alone, I had seated myself in a solitary chair outside the normal stream of traffic. In such a setting most Americans follow a rule, which is all the more binding because we seldom think about it, that can be stated as follows: as soon as a person stops or is seated in a public place, there balloons around him a small sphere of privacy which is considered inviolate. The size of the sphere varies with the degree of crowding, the age, sex, and the importance of the person, as well as the general surroundings. Anyone who enters this zone and stays there is intruding. In fact, a stranger who intrudes, even for a specific purpose, acknowledges the fact that he has intruded by beginning his request with "Pardon me, but can you tell me . . . ?"

To continue, as I waited in the deserted lobby, a stranger walked up to where I was sitting and stood close enough so that not only could I easily touch him but I could even hear him breathing. In addition, the dark mass of his body filled the peripheral field of vision on my left side. If the lobby had been crowded with people, I would have understood his behavior, but in an empty lobby his presence made me exceedingly uncomfortable. Feeling annoyed by this intrusion, I moved my body in such a way as to communicate annoyance. Strangely enough, instead of moving away, my actions seemed only to encourage him, because he moved even closer. In spite of the temptation to escape the annoyance, I put aside thoughts of abandoning my post, thinking, "To hell with it. Why should I move? I was here first and I'm not going to let this fellow drive me out even if he is a boor." Fortunately, a group of people soon arrived whom my tormentor immediately joined. Their mannerisms explained his behavior, for I knew from both speech and gestures that they were Arabs. I had not been able to make this crucial identification by looking at my subject when he was alone because he wasn't talking and he was wearing American clothes.

In describing the scene later to an Arab colleague, two contrasting patterns emerged. My concept and my feelings about my own circle of privacy in a "public" place immediately struck my Arab friend as strange and puzzling. He said, "After all, it's a public place, isn't it?" Pursuing this line of inquiry, I found that an Arab thought I had no rights whatsoever by virtue of occupying a given spot; neither my place nor my body was inviolate! For the Arab, there is no such thing as an intrusion in public. Public means public. With this insight, a great range of Arab behavior that had been puzzling, annoying, and sometimes even frightening began to make sense. I learned, for example, that if *A* is standing on a street corner and *B* wants his spot, *B* is within his rights if he does what he can to make *A* uncomfortable enough to move. In Beirut only the hardy sit in the last row in a movie theater, because there are usually standees who want seats and who push and shove and make such a nuisance that most people give up and leave. Seen in this light, the Arab who "intruded" on my space in the hotel lobby had apparently selected it for the very reason I had: it was a good place to watch two doors and the elevator. My show of annoyance, instead of driving him away, had only encouraged him. He thought he was about to get me to move.

Another silent source of friction between Americans and Arabs is in an area that Americans treat very informally—the manners and rights of the road. In general, in the United States we tend to defer to the vehicle that is bigger, more powerful, faster, and heavily laden. While a pedestrian walking along a road may feel annoyed he will not think it unusual to step aside for a fast-moving automobile. He knows that because he is moving he does not have the right to the space around him that he has when he is standing still (as I was in the hotel lobby). It appears that the reverse is true with the Arabs who apparently *take on rights to space as they move*. For someone else to move into a space an Arab is also moving into is a violation of his rights. It is infuriating to an Arab to have someone else cut in front of him on the highway. It is the American's cavalier treatment of moving space that makes the Arab call him aggressive and pushy.

Concepts of Privacy

The experience described above and many others suggested to me that Arabs might actually have a wholly contrasting set of assumptions concerning the body and the rights associated with it. Certainly the Arab tendency to shove and push each other in public and to feel and pinch women in public conveyances would not be tolerated by Westerners. It appeared to me that they must not have any concept of a private zone outside the body. This proved to be precisely the case.

In the Western world, the person is synonymous with an individual inside a skin. And in northern Europe generally, the skin and even the clothes may be inviolate. You need permission to touch either if you are a stranger. This rule applies in some parts of France, where the mere touching of another person during an argument used to be legally defined as assault. For the Arab the location of the person in relation to the body is quite different. The person exists somewhere down inside the body. The ego is not completely hidden, however, because it can be reached very easily with an insult. It is protected from touch but not from words. The dissociation of the body and the ego may explain why the public amputation of a thief's hand is tolerated as standard punishment in Saudi Arabia. It also sheds light on why an Arab employer living in a modern apartment can provide his servant with a room that is a boxlike cubicle approximately 5 by 10 by 4 feet in size that is not only hung from the ceiling to conserve floor space but has an opening so that the servant can be spied on.

As one might suspect, deep orientations towards the self such as the one just described are also reflected in the language. This was brought to my attention one afternoon when an Arab colleague who is the author of an Arab-English dictionary arrived in my office and threw himself into a chair in a state of obvious exhaustion. When I asked him what had been going on, he said: "I have spent the entire afternoon trying to find the Arab equivalent of the English word 'rape.' There is no such word in Arabic. All my sources, both written and spoken, can come up with no more than an approximation, such as 'He took her against her will.' There is nothing in Arabic approaching your meaning as it is expressed in that one word."

Differing concepts of the placement of the ego in relation to the body are not easily grasped. Once an idea like this is accepted, however, it is possible to understand many other facets of Arab life that would otherwise be difficult to explain. One of these is the high population density of Arab cities like Cairo, Beirut, and Damascus. According to the animal studies described in the earlier chapters, the Arabs should be living in a perpetual behavioral sink. While it is probable that Arabs are suffering from population pressures, it is also just as possible that continued pressure from the desert has resulted in a cultural adaptation to high density which takes the form described above. Tucking the ego down inside the body shell not only would permit higher population densities but would explain why it is that Arab communications are stepped up as much as they are when compared to northern European communication patterns. Not only is the sheer noise level much higher, but the piercing look of the eyes, the touch of the hands, and the mutual bathing in the warm moist breath during conversation represent stepped-up sensory inputs to a level which many Europeans find unbearably intense.

The Arab dream is for lots of space in the home, which unfortunately many Arabs cannot afford. Yet when he has space, it is very different from what one finds in most American homes. Arab spaces inside their upper middle-class homes are tremendous by our standards. They avoid partitions because Arabs *do not like to be alone*. The form of the home is such as to hold the family together inside a single protective shell, because Arabs are deeply involved with each other. Their personalities are intermingled and take nourishment from each other like the roots and soil. If one is not with people and actively involved in some way, one is deprived of life. An old Arab saying reflects this value: "Paradise without people should not be entered because it is Hell." Therefore, Arabs in the United States often feel socially and sensorially deprived and long to be back where there is human warmth and contact.

Since there is no physical privacy as we know it in the Arab family, not even a word for privacy, one could expect that the Arabs might use some other means to be alone. Their way to be alone is to stop talking. Like the English, an Arab who shuts himself off in this way is not indicating that anything is wrong or that he is withdrawing, only that he wants to be alone with his own thoughts or does not want to be intruded upon. One subject said that her father would come and go for days at a time without saying a word, and no one in the family thought anything of it. Yet for this very reason, an Arab exchange student visiting a Kansas farm failed to pick up the cue that his American hosts were mad at him when they gave him the "silent treatment." He only discovered something was wrong when they took him to town and tried forcibly to put him on a bus to Washington, D.C., the headquarters of the exchange program responsible for his presence in the U.S.

Arab Personal Distances

Like everyone else in the world, Arabs are unable to formulate specific rules for their informal behavior patterns. In fact, they often deny that there are any rules, and they are made anxious by suggestions that such is the case. Therefore, in order to determine how the Arab sets distances, I investigated the use of each sense separately. Gradually, definite and distinctive behavioral patterns began to emerge.

Olfaction occupies a prominent place in the Arab life. Not only is it one of the distance-setting mechanisms, but it is a vital part of a complex system of behavior. Arabs consistently breathe on people when they talk. However, this habit is more than a matter of different manners. To the Arab good smells are pleasing and a way of being involved with each other. To smell one's friend is not only nice but desirable, for to deny him your breath is to act ashamed. Americans, on the other hand, trained as they are not to breathe in people's faces, automatically communicate shame in trying to be polite. Who would expect that when our highest diplomats are putting on their best manners they are also communicating shame? Yet this is what occurs constantly, because diplomacy is not only "eyeball to eyeball" but breath to breath.

By stressing olfaction, Arabs do not try to eliminate all the body's odors, only to enhance them and use them in building human relationships. Nor are they self-conscious about telling others when they don't like the way they smell. A man leaving his house in the morning may be told by his uncle, "Habib, your stomach is sour and your breath doesn't smell too good. Better not talk too close to people today." Smell is even considered in the choice of a mate. When couples are being matched for marriage, the man's go-between will sometimes ask to smell the girl, who may be turned down if she doesn't "smell nice." Arabs recognize that smell and disposition may be linked.

In a word, the olfactory boundary performs two roles in Arab life. It enfolds those who want to relate and separates those who don't. The Arab finds it essential to stay inside the olfactory zone as a means of keeping tab on changes in emotion. What is more, he may feel crowded as soon as he smells something unpleasant. While not much is known about "olfactory crowding," this may prove to be as significant as any other variable in the crowding complex because it is tied directly to the body chemistry and hence to the state of health and emotions. It is not surprising, therefore, that the olfactory boundary constitutes for the Arabs an informal distance-setting mechanism in contrast to the visual mechanisms of the Westerner.

Facing and Not Facing

One of my earliest discoveries in the field of intercultural communication was that the position of the bodies of people in conversation varies with the culture. Even so, it is used to puzzle me that a special Arab friend seemed unable to walk and talk at the same time. After years in the United States, he could not bring himself to stroll along, facing forward while talking. Our progress would be arrested while he edged ahead, cutting slightly in front of me and turning sideways so we could see each other. Once in this position, he would stop. His behavior was explained when I learned that for the Arabs to view the other person peripherally is regarded as impolite, and to sit or stand back-to-back is considered very rude. You must be involved when interacting with Arabs who are friends.

One mistaken American notion is that Arabs conduct all conversations at close distances. This is not the case at all. On social occasions, they may sit on opposite sides of the room and talk across the room to each other. They are, however, apt to take offense when Americans use what are to them ambiguous distances, such as the four- to seven-foot social-consultative distance. They frequently complain that Americans are cold or aloof or "don't care." This was what an elderly Arab diplomat in an American hospital thought when the American nurses used "professional" distance. He had the feeling that he was being ignored, that they might not take good care of him. Another Arab subject remarked, referring to American behavior, "What's the matter? Do I smell bad? Or are they afraid of me?"

Arabs who interact with Americans report experiencing a certain flatness traceable in part to a very different use of the eyes in private and in public as well as between friends and strangers. Even though it is rude for a guest to walk around the Arab home eying things, Arabs look at each other in ways which seem hostile or challenging to the American. One Arab informant said that he was in constant hot water with Americans because of the way he looked at them without the slightest intention of offending. In fact, he had on several occasions barely avoided fights with American men who apparently thought their masculinity was being challenged because of the way he was looking at them. As noted earlier, Arabs look each other in the eye when talking with an intensity that makes most Americans highly uncomfortable.

Involvement

As the reader must gather by now, Arabs are involved with each other on many different levels simultaneously. Privacy in a public place is foreign to them. Business transactions in the bazaar, for example, are not just between buyer and seller, but are participated in by everyone. Anyone who is standing around may join in. If a grownup sees a boy breaking a window, he must stop him even if he doesn't know him. Involvement and participation are expressed in other ways as well. If two men are fighting, the crowd must intervene. On the political level, *to fail to intervene* when trouble is brewing is to take sides, which is what our State Department always seems to be doing. Given the fact that few people in the world today are even remotely aware of the cultural mold that forms their thoughts, it is normal for Arabs to view *our* behavior as though it stemmed from *their* own hidden set of assumptions.

Feelings About Enclosed Spaces

In the course of my interviews with Arabs the term "tomb" kept cropping up in conjunction with enclosed space. In a word, Arabs don't mind being crowded by people but hate to be hemmed in by walls. They show a much greater overt sensitivity to architectural crowding than we do. Enclosed space must meet at least three requirements that I know of if it is to satisfy the Arabs: there must be plenty of unobstructed space in which to move around (possibly as much as a thousand square feet); very high ceilings—so high in fact that they do not normally impinge on the visual field; and, in addition, there must be an unobstructed view. It was spaces such as these in which the Americans referred to earlier felt so uncomfortable. One sees the Arab's need for a view expressed in many ways, even negatively, for to cut off a neighbor's view is one of the most effective ways of spiting him. In Beirut one can see what is known locally as the "spite house." It is nothing more than a thick, four-story wall, built at the end of a long fight between neighbors, on a narrow strip of land, for the express purpose of denying a view of the Mediterranean to any house built on the land behind. According to one of my informants, there is also a house on a small plot of land between Beirut and Damascus which is completely surrounded by a neighbor's wall built high enough to cut off the view from all windows!

Boundaries

Proxemic patterns tell us other things about Arab culture. For example, the whole concept of the boundary as an abstraction is almost impossible to pin down. In one sense, there are no boundaries. "Edges" of towns, yes, but permanent boundaries out in the country (hidden lines), no. In the course of my work with Arab subjects I had a difficult time translating our concept of a boundary into terms which could be equated with theirs. In order to clarify the distinctions between the two very different definitions, I thought it might be helpful to pinpoint acts which constituted trespass. To date, I have been unable to discover anything even remotely resembling our own legal concept of trespass.

Arab behavior in regard to their own real estate is apparently an extension of, and therefore consistent with, their approach to the body. My subjects simply failed to respond whenever trespass was mentioned. They didn't seem to understand what I meant by this term. This may be explained by the fact that they organize relationships with each other according to closed social systems rather than spatially. For thousands of years Moslems, Marinites, Druses, and Jews have lived in their own villages, each with strong kin affiliations. Their hierarchy of loyalties is: first to one's self, then to kinsman, townsman, or tribesman, co-religionist and/or countryman. Anyone not in these categories is a stranger. Strangers and enemies are very closely linked, if not synonymous, in Arab thought. Trespass in this context is a matter of who you are, rather than a piece of land or a space with a boundary that can be denied to anyone and everyone, friend and foe alike.

In summary, proxemic patterns differ. By examining them it is possible to reveal hidden cultural frames that determine the structure of a given people's perceptual world. Perceiving the world differently leads to differential definitions of what constitutes crowded living, different interpersonal relations, and a different approach to both local and international politics.

Edward T. Hall
From *The Hidden Dimension*

1. Within each category what techniques does Hall use to develop his points?
2. Are Hall's principles of division parallel? Can you suggest other principles he might have used?
3. Drawing on your own cross-cultural experience, write an essay using classification or division. Remember that "kinds of"/"types of" indicate the division process.

Cross-curricular Essay Material

1. Discuss motivational problems in adult education.
2. Trade barriers present the importer and exporter with complex hurdles, especially since some of these barriers are not capable of forecast. Describe the major types of barriers and how you can best prepare for them.
3. Review major foreign policy imitators of the Carter-era and classify them by level of effectiveness. Compare these results to a similar list for the Reagan-era.
4. Review the basic approaches to promotional activity and describe their strengths and weaknesses.
5. Discuss the image of women in early American fiction.
6. Kohlberg's levels of moral maturity serve as a good basis for classifying recent business scandals. Review several of the recent scandals covered by the press and discuss the level of moral maturity they indicate.

CHAPTER

• SIX •

Making a Case

"Persuade me! Go ahead, persuade me that I should extend at Comisco. . . . It can't be done!!! Nobody can persuade me to extend."

"You're right, I can't. It is too tough a job. I'll never be able to convince you of *that*."

"You're darn tootin!"

"But what if I told you that the Air Force will pay you $1,000 to say here another year. . . ."

"Hell no. Not for $5,000. No way. . . . I'm not intere . . . you said $1,000?"

"Also, you'll receive an invitation to the White House, to dine with the President and the Secretary of Defense."

"You must be kidding. I don't believe any of it."

"Well, suit yourself. I'm not trying to persuade you. . . ."

"Are these the facts or not?"

"Of course not. If you don't want to extend to help your country and preserve the peace, well, that's your problem. Let the Russians take over the world."

"Now, that is a real crock-of . . ."

"You're right. My only point is to prove how hard it is to persuade people of something they're really against. It is almost most impossible. So, pick something that is reasonable, ok?"

In exposition, we are most concerned with sharing our ideas with our readers. In argumentation, we use the expository patterns, but our goal is to persuade, to convince our readers that our position on an issue is one they ought to adopt as theirs. This need to convince others to share our way of thinking, our convictions, arises daily. For example, we try to convince our family that the best family vacation would be in Maine, while our spouse thinks France would be better.

Let's take a closer look at how we might approach our task, to convince our spouse that Maine is where we should head in August. One tack might be to review the positive aspects of a vacation in Maine and compare them with the positive aspects of a vacation in France. Our goal here would be to show that Maine offers us more of what we want in a vacation than does France. Our first approach might outline as follows:

Maine vacation

1. Transportation costs would be lower, as would room and board.
2. We would encounter no language difficulties, as Maniacs speak English.
3. Dollars are weak now, so a home vacation makes good economic sense.
4. We should know the U.S. first before we venture abroad.
5. The hassle factor of a rural vacation will be minimal.

French vacation

1. We could practice and improve our high school French.
2. We can enjoy French wine, cheese, cooking.
3. The museums and castles will be interesting and help us appreciate our European heritage.

Examples of reasoning and argumentation in our daily lives abound. Take the conversation we've just had with our son, Bob, who prefers soccer to chemistry homework. We attempt to help him understand the role of education and of deferred gratification in his future by presenting arguments from which he can learn. Or take a broader example that concerns us all at least once every four years. In a democracy, public debate, a form of argument, is critical. Ideally, we decide which are the important issues and what our position on them is as a result of argumentation. Making the intelligent political decisions necessary for a democracy to function well presumes an ability to reason logically. The following editorial, first printed in the *Asian Wall Street Journal*, March 17, 1987, is a good example of such reasoning. Herbert Stein was chairman of the Council of Economic Advisers under Presidents Nixon and Ford.

LEAVE THE TRADE DEFICIT ALONE

WASHINGTON—To say that the U.S. has a trade deficit is to use a figure of speech. I believe the word for it is "metonymy"—the use of one word to signify another with which it is associated. It is like saying that New York won baseball's World Series when we really mean that the New York Mets, a team of young men who mostly live elsewhere, won it.

The fact is that a certain (unknown) number of Americans bought more abroad than they sold abroad and a certain other (unknown) number of Americans sold more than they bought abroad. The trade deficit is the excess of the net foreign purchases of the first group over the net foreign sales of the second group. Unlike the budget deficit, which is the responsibility of a certain legal entity, the government of the U.S., the trade deficit does not belong to any individual or institution. It is a pure statistical aggregate, like the number of eggs laid in the U.S. or the number of bald-headed men living here.

My interest here is not simply in verbal precision. I am raising the questions why any of us should worry about this particular statistic, and why the U.S. government should take any responsibility for it. The people who have the trade deficit—who are buying more abroad than they are selling—are doing so voluntarily. If they were worried much they would stop. I had a trade deficit in 1986 because I took a vacation in France. I didn't worry about it; I enjoyed it.

No Guidance

There are statistics about which we do worry and for which the government takes responsibility. One such statistic is the consumer price index. The government's responsibility for doing something about the CPI is commonly accepted because there is a substantial consensus on what the optimum behavior of the CPI would be and also that the optimum would not be achieved by market behavior alone. The optimum is a stable and not very large rate of change in the CPI, and the essential contribution is in the domain of government monetary policy.

Does anyone know an optimum rate of the trade deficit other than what emerges in the market? I think not. Certainly the optimum rate is not zero. A cliche of these days is that a trade deficit of the present size cannot go on forever. This is not axiomatically true, but it is probably true. That does not, however, give any guidance. As I have said in this space before, if something cannot go on forever it will stop. Government action to stop it is not required.

The trade deficit is one of a number of things, harmless or even beneficient while they continue, that cannot go on forever and that may even cause some disturbance when they stop. I suppose (but don't know)—that the Dow Jones Industrial Average cannot go on rising by 35% a year forever. But no one thinks the government has a responsibility for deciding when the rise has gone too far and stopping it. The market will determine that. The trade deficit will end when Americans are no longer willing to borrow enough or foreigners are no longer willing to lend enough to finance it. These borrowers and lenders have a lot of their own money at stake and are at least as well informed and as well motivated as the government to decide when the deficit has gone too far.

Concern about the trade deficit as a "national problem" (distinguished from the problems of particular industries that should be considered and dismissed on their own merits) has shifted from the damage alleged to occur while the deficit goes on to the damage predicted to occur when the deficit stops. We have seen that it is possible at least to have normal growth of output and employment alongside a high and rising trade deficit. Even the slowdown of the economy in 1986 cannot reasonably be blamed on the trade deficit, which rose less during 1986 than during any other year of the recovery.

In the scenario envisaged for the ending of the U.S. trade deficit, the rest of the world no longer wants to go on accumulating dollar assets; the dollar declines in exchange markets, raising prices here and interest rates rise here, depressing investment. So we get the specter of rising inflation, due to the higher prices, alongside recession, due to the lower investment. But the decline of the dollar will only give back the temporary gain on inflation that we had when the dollar rose. And the depressing effect of lower investment will be offset by the stimulating effect of higher net exports.

These two may not balance out exactly, but no one can tell whether the net effect will be depressing or stimulating. In the longer run, just as we can have high employment and output with a trade deficit so can we have them without one.

The point is sometimes made that the ending of the trade deficit and associated capital inflow would not be so bad if the capital inflow had been invested in productive assets that would yield a return to service the debt. But in fact the net capital inflow was invested in productive assets; private investment in the U.S. would have been much lower without it.

In 1986, for example, U.S. individuals and corporations saved $680 billion gross, and government (federal, state and local) borrowed $143 billion to finance its deficits. If there had been no capital inflow, private investment in the U.S. could not have exceeded $537 billion. Since there was a capital inflow of $144 billion, however, private investment of $686 billion was possible and occurred. (Forgive me a statistical discrepancy of $5 billion.) This $144 billion of investment will yield a return to service the debt incurred through the capital inflow.

A great source of confusion today is the common association of the term "trade deficit" with the term "competitiveness." The term "competitiveness" raises all kinds of images that give the trade deficit a popular emotional force that the mere economist's term does not have. Competitiveness evokes the spirit of a game, and suggests that the U.S. is losing. National pride is involved. Politicians are inspired to promise that they will make America "No. 1" again.

But the fact of trade deficit does not mean that the U.S. is losing anything, and it is not a sign of economic weakness. Total output in the U.S. and per-capita output are both higher now than when America last had a trade surplus (1982). America has a trade deficit because although it produces much, it uses more, including what it invests for the future and uses for the defense of the entire Free World. The U.S. can have a trade deficit only because the rest of the world has confidence in the U.S. economy and U.S. policy and is willing to invest here. No one has to hold dollars. Willingness of foreigners to do so is a sign of the strength of the U.S., not of its weakness. Taiwan and South Korea have large trade surpluses. That does not make them stronger economies or countries than the U.S.

No Advantage

Anyway, the belief that the U.S. is in economic competition with the other industrial countries that are its principal allies and trading partners is a mistake. To have high real output per capita in the U.S. is a good thing, but there is no advantage for America in its being higher than that of America's friends. This is important to realize, because America cannot expect to have more output per capita than its friends forever.

Knowledge and capital move around the world with increasing ease. There is a strong tendency for levels of output per capita to converge—for the difference between the lowest and the highest to diminish. We will have to get used to living in a world in which we are no longer No. 1 in that sense, or at least not No. 1 by much.

There must be something serious to worry about.

Herbert Stein
From the *Asian Wall Street Journal*, March 17, 1987

1. What is Stein's major point in his argument?
2. With what facts does he support his major point?
3. Are you convinced? Explain why or why not.
4. Draft a counter argument.

• Reasoning Patterns: Induction and Deduction

There are two basic reasoning patterns, and since they are fundamental to our thinking, a familiarity with them will help us to form better arguments and to analyze better the arguments of others. *Induction* occurs when we make a series of observations and from them induce or infer a generalization. *Deduction* is the pattern which uses generalizations to arrive at particular applications or assertions. Let's look more closely at each of these patterns.

INDUCTION

This pattern consists of moving from a series of particular observations to a generalization. The Latin root of induction may help to illustrate how induction works: *inducere* means to *lead into*. Induction is a quite common pattern of thinking and is especially obvious when we are trying to understand something a new—a new environment, a new friend, a new language. We collect evidence through observation and from this evidence, infer or induce a generalization about our environment.

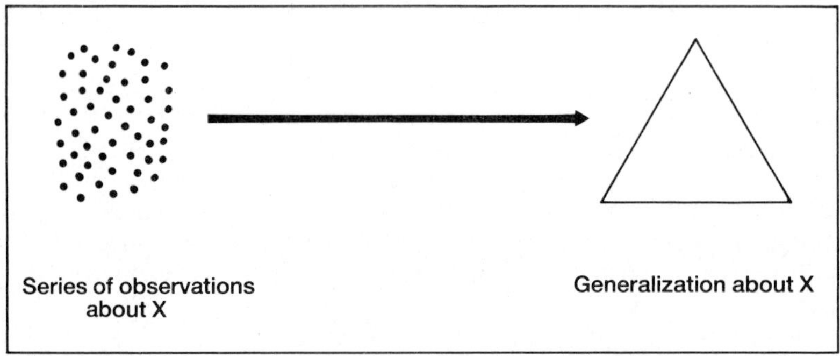

Induction is the method used in science. The scientist collects evidence which leads to a new generalization about our world. We can also see induction at work in our legal system. In jury trials, for example, lawyers present evidence, and the jury is asked to make the judgement, an inference, to decide which generalization, guilty or innocent, best describes the total set of evidence it has been presented with.

In your writing, induction will probably be dominant in two situations:

1. when you generalize from observation; and
2. when you attribute a cause to a set of observed circumstances.

1. Generalizing from observation. You've recently moved to Tokyo. One of the many surprises you've had in adjusting to this different culture is how older women and men push and shove, elbowing their ways on public transportation. Every day now for two weeks, you've collected evidence on this particular topic, both from your own experience and from watching local nationals. They, by the way, seem to regard this pushing as normal, as far as you can tell. At the end of two weeks, you make what is known as an inductive leap and generalize that in Tokyo, pushing by the elderly on public transportation is not rude.

2. Attributing a cause to a set of observed circumstances. Using the data above and evidence that you have seen no one offer his seat to an elderly person during these two weeks of data collection, you make a further inductive leap, using your observations as evidence to suggest that the cause of the pushing is the elderly people's need to get the few available seats.

Note that a paper reasoned inductively using this example could be written either using the evidence and leading to the generalization or beginning with the generalization and supporting it with your collected evidence.

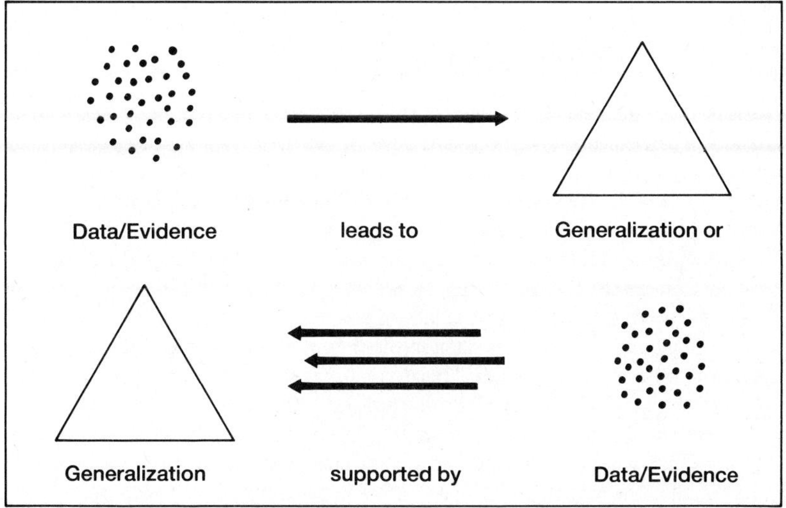

In induction, we make a leap from our evidence to our generalization, from a finite number of observations to a rule or generalization or conclusion based on those observations. This inductive leap is the "thin ice" part of inductive reasoning.

When we make this leap, we assume that what is applicable in one set of circumstances, in our data, for example, will be so in another, different set of circumstances.

DEDUCTION

In deduction, we use a generalization combined with a fact or another piece of evidence to conclude that a certain situation or event is likely to happen. The classic example of deduction (from the Latin *deducere*, to lead out of or from) is the syllogism

All men are mortal.	**Major premise**
Aristotle is a man.	**Minor premise**
Aristotle is mortal.	**Conclusion**

In the study of logic, the first two parts of the syllogism, the broad generalization and the more specific fact, are called premises, and the third part is the conclusion.

With the parts of an argument clearly labeled, its analysis is fairly easy. Our real lives offers us another situation, though, in which an argument's parts are rarely labeled. The ability to recognize their parts is helpful in analyzing their strengths and weaknesses. The application of such analysis to our writing ensures stronger reasoning.

Let's apply argument analysis to see why it can be useful. Please read the following student essay and consider its argument.

The Misconceptions About Mental Patients

Beliefs about the behavior of mental patients display many false ideas. People tend to look at mental patients in an odd way, but never stop to realize that mental patients are people who have a problem and are in desperate need of help. There is the false belief that abnormal behavior of mental patients is always bizarre. People in mental hospitals are often pictured as weird, spending their time ranting and raging or posing as Napoleon. In fact, most hospitalized patients are aware of what is going on around them and only a small percentage exhibit behavior that is labeled bizarre. There is the false belief that normal and abnormal are different in kind, whereas a dividing line between these two does not exist. There is no person in this world to say who is normal and who is abnormal. The behavior of different individuals ranges from normal to abnormal and from time to time most people shift their position. Both normal and abnormal behavior are attempts to cope with life problems as the individual sees them. People have different methods of coping adaptive resources and have different degrees of success. Most former mental patients are viewed as unstable and dangerous. Due to this factor, formal mental patients are discriminated against in job employment. Most mental patients respond well to treatment and achieve a higher level of personality adjustment. The Diagnostic and Statistical Manual of Mental Disorders states that less than one percent of patients released is considered dangerous or criminally violent. There is a misconception that a mental disorder is something to be ashamed of. A mental disorder should be considered no more disgraceful than a physical disorder. People do not hesitate to consult a dentist or a lawyer, but yet there is still a tendency to judge a person differently who goes to a psychiatrist for help. Society tends to reject the emotionally disturbed. People are sympathetic toward a crippled child or an adult with cancer, but tend to turn away from a person with a mental problem. These people are no different than anyone else except that they have a different kind of problem. People never stop to realize what it is really like to have a mental disorder. A mental disorder is an illness within the mind and is curable. These people need all of the love and attention that a physically ill person needs. Society needs to be much more educated on the misconceptions of the mentally ill. People need to realize that having a mental disorder is just as serious as having a physical illness.

ARGUMENT ANALYSIS

1. How would you state the major point of this argument? That is, what positions does the author want the reader to share?

2. List the strengths of this paper's argument.
3. What are the weaknesses of this paper's argument?
4. Working with several of your classmates, can you outline this paper's major premise, minor premise, and conclusion?
5. Label the following syllogisms and discuss their strengths and weaknesses.

   A. All men play football.
   Albert is a man.
   Albert plays football.

   B. All women are good at learning foreign languages.
   Rebecca is a woman.
   Rebecca will be a successful student of French.

   C. English 101 papers with sentence fragments earn a grade of F.
   Mary's paper contains three fragments.
   Mary's paper will earn an F.

Example B is a good use of the form of the syllogism, but there is something wrong with the major premise. It is false. Certainly we can all think of at least one counterexample to this generalization, and that's all it takes. Therefore, although the minor premise is true, the conclusion is false. The same holds for example A. All men do not play football. Remember, a valid syllogism is one whose major and minor premises both are true.

• Argumentative Essays

In argumentative essays, the deductive method is quite effective. We begin with a generalized observation and a more specific fact. Then from them we deduce a certain course of action, position, set of beliefs, the conclusion of our argument. In argumentative essays, there are two sources of difficulty writers encounter in using deductive reasoning:

1. sometimes an argument is based on unstated premises, which makes for a weak argument; and
2. sometimes the premises are overstated, which also makes for a weak argument.

UNSTATED PREMISE

Consider this syllogism.

Family harmony exists when children respect their elders.
Making relatives comfortable is one way to show respect.
John should get a haircut and take out his earring when Uncle Harold visits next weekend.

The unstated premise here is that John's long hair and earring will make Uncle Harold feel uncomfortable and is therefore a sign of disrespect.

As you read the following student essay, focus in on what the premise might be.

Its Time Had Come

President Reagan's visit to the cemetery in Bitburg is an event whose time had come. The media have covered the emotional protests of World War II veterans. One of their objections is that interred there are Waffen SS soldiers who had fought against the allies in the Battle of the Bulge (this is an untruth; Waffen SS did fight in that battle, but not these; they died before the battle). President Reagan's reply and justification that these soldiers were also victims should be judged on its merit. One must recall the severe depression that gripped Germany and aided Hitler's rise to power—one loaf of bread cost millions of marks. His early reign benefited the country and its people. He revalued the currency and created work programs; the autobahn is one example. Who could have foreseen the impending dementia? Are men not obliged to serve their country militarily? This is not an easily avoided obligation. And what if their leader is a madman? Then a reasonable assertation is that they are also his victims.

Jewish groups, who feel Reagan's allegiance should lie with them, claim this visit honors these Nazi criminals and will lead people to forget the painfully sobering reality of the Holocaust. But if heads of state postponed any controversial ceremony until every possible victim or perpetrator (or anyone who would be offended) were dead, there would be a greater possibility, indeed probability, the atrocities could be forgotten since there would be no one to remind us. Open, publicized ceremonies, such as President Reagan's visit to the cemetery in Bitburg along with his countervailing trip to the site that was Bergen-Belsen concentration camp, will ensure the searing truth can not be buried.

At what point does some forgiveness begin? At what point should it begin? Do we blame and damn Germans forever? Should we continue to fault those who had no say in their ancestor's sins? Isn't this akin to faulting Americans for their previous involvement with slavery? Need we wait 160 years to absolve them? And what of the forty years of progress Germany has made? It is not the same nation that perpetrated the world wars—and is not likely to be again. This very nationalism that we condemn Germans of is the same nationalism we partake of when we refuse to view this visit for what it really is. Two nations, once adversaries and now allies responsible for world peace, are ceremoniously honoring and acknowledging the ones who paid the highest price, whether considered war criminals or honorable soldiers. President Reagan's visit is not to deny the past nor to try to justify it, but rather, to strengthen the bond between these allies.

OVERSTATED PREMISE

Women are too emotional to serve in combat units.
Sue is a woman.

Sue is too emotional to serve combat duty.

The major premise here over-generalizes and oversimplifies a complex situation.

Note that the major premise of a deductive syllogism is often the result of inductive reasoning. These two patterns work together to help us move from specific evidence to generalizations and then to additional applications of those generalizations.

This student essay offers a good illustration of these patterns.

My Worst Enemy

Ever since, at the age of four, I tried to ride my tricycle up too steep an incline and cracked my skull open, I've proven to be my own worst enemy.

Shortly after recovering from the tricycle accident, I tried to imitate Superman by jumping out of a tree house; I smashed a bone in each ankle. Several months later I got in the way of my brother's baseball bat and received another wound on my skull. People may say that this was all part of growing up, but in growing up I've managed to acquire an uncanny bent for self-destruction.

In high school I became a football player and by the end of the first season, I had broken my nose and thumb and was sporting a steel brace on each ankle. Unfortunately, I didn't get my fill of football until I had smashed three toes and contracted a bone infection I was to fight for the better part of a year. I had also acquired a charlie horse on my left leg and a broken clavicle on my right side.

While playing football, I developed an interest in two other methods of suicide. First I started skiing. I was fortunate here at first for I failed to suffer any injuries that usually plague beginners. But when I became quite an expert at skiing, I made up for lost time. First I broke my collar bone. Then I dislocated my jaw and tore the ligaments in my left ankle.

Perhaps something in my subconscious suicidal bent told me that skiing wasn't enough, so I became interested in sports cars and racing. My interest wilted a bit when I took a ride with a friend in his MG and we hit a station wagon at sixty-five miles per hour. I received a broken back, lacerated face, mutilated ear, and (of all things) a broken toe.

It is not that I go out of my way to meet self-destruction, but I do have a knack for it. Although I've given up football, skiing, and racing, I manage to maim myself in ways no one else would. For instance, if a dog is going to go mad and bite someone, he'll bite me. My uncle's dog went mad and roamed the neighborhood all day without biting anyone. Then I came home and he got me. If a car door is going to slam on anyone's fingers, mine will be the fingers. My fingers have been mangled by house doors, garage doors, and even shower stall doors. Recently I got a job operating a printing press and what did I do the very first day but jam my fingers in the press.

I have to think what the future holds for me. Recently I've felt drawn to take up flying. Who knows, I might break my neck and get it over with. But suspense is killing me.

EVIDENCE

Once we outline an argument, we must give evidence to support our points. Evidence should be reliable, relative to our point, and ample. Back in our summer vacation dilemma (see p. 138), were we to support our first point about the vacation in Maine, that costs in Maine would be less than in France, by relying on an opinion from a neighbor who went to France six summers ago, our evidence would be weak and our family would be justified in rejecting it. We could find better evidence in the exchange rate section of the newspaper and in contemporary travel guides to both France and Maine. Factual evidence is more reliable and convincing than is opinion.

LOGICAL FALLACIES

Mistakes in reasoning are called fallacies (Latin root: *fallacia*, a trick or deceit). We'll review eight of the more common ones so that you can check your reasoning to make certain it is not fallacious.

The following student essay commits several fallacies. As you read, pay special attention to the meaning. Can you spot the weak areas?

A Popular Misconception

A conception held by many people is that all fat people are jolly. But since the jolly fatties spend so much money annually on items to make them less chubby, and perhaps, less jolly, I feel that the conception is not always valid.

Doctors who specialize in treating overweight patients have made a great deal of money helping fat people lose their extra pounds which people believe make fat people happy. Food manufacturers and dietitians have made fortunes from sales of special, low-calorie foods. Publishers and writers have made large sums of money from sales of low-calorie diets and menus and describing weight-reducing exercises. Health clubs have acquired much money by selling memberships in reducing salons to the jovial overweight people.

Other evidence leads me to believe that the conception about fat people being jolly is false. In the first place rotund ones have many more problems than their slimmer friends have. It is a proven fact that fat people die younger than slimmer people. Insurance companies charge fat policy-holders higher premiums and require frequent physical examinations. Furthermore, fat people have more respiratory ailments and tire more easily than slimmer people; consequently, overweight people have to be more limited in their activities and lose part of the fun of life.

Because fat people have so much trouble with operations, they are, many times, forced to go on strict diets before a necessary operation can be performed on them. Since they are forced to delay the operation, the ailments are usually more serious than they would have been had the operation been performed earlier. Then, too, overweight women have much more difficult pregnancies than their slimmer friends have. And in many cases their excess fat endangers the life of the unborn child. The added weight of the baby plus their own extra weight cause the function of the respiratory and other systems to be over-worked and thus affect the health of the baby.

It is clear that overweight people have reason to be less jolly than their slimmer friends. Perhaps their happy nature is mere appearance—an attempt to forget their problems.

1. Appeal to authority. We often rely on the work of others, experts, as evidence to support our arguments. This is called appeal to authority, and is useful in many cases but can be fallacious when

1. We quote the expert outside his/her field. To offer Defense Secretary Casper Weinberger's reading of the trade deficit problem as a part of our argument or in support of it would be to commit an appeal to authority fallacy.
2. We accept an expert's opinion rather than his arguments. Opinion is less reliable than fact.
3. We accept the view of the majority, using the crowd as authority. This is also known as the democratic fallacy.
4. We accept traditional wisdom, unexamined. Senator Sam Ervin of North Carolina offers a wonderful example of this fallacy when he tells how he replied to women who were in favor of the ERA:

   I tell them, "Why ladies, any bill that lies around here for 47 years without getting any more support than this one has got in the past obviously shouldn't be passed at all. Why, I think that affords most conclusive proof that it's unworthy of consideration." As quoted in the *New York Times Magazine*, Sept. 20, 1970.

2. Provincialism. This is a tendency to allow your thoughts or perceptions to be influenced by group membership. This group may be a nation, a race, a gender, a religion or any other group. It results in we/they thinking and can be found at the core of racism, sexism and cultural prejudice.

3. Irrelevant Reason. This fallacy is sometimes known as a *non sequitur* (does not follow) and describes arguments whose conclusions do not follow from their premises because the premises are irrelevant to the conclusion.

My physics professor is pretty, so I'll do okay in physics.

4. Slippery slope. This fallacy suggests that once a particular mistake is made, it will lead to a worse mistake which will in turn lead to an even worse one and so on. The fallacious argument holds that once the first step is taken, the slide down to whatever horror awaits us at the bottom of the slope is inevitable. The domino theory is a good example of this fallacy.

Once Vietnam falls Communist, the rest of Asia will follow, just as would a line of dominoes.

5. Ad hominem argument. This is an attack on the person rather than the person's ideas. When such an attack is irrelevant, it is fallacious.

Don't listen to John's argument on marketing strategy. Why, he doesn't even attend church on Sunday.

6. Hasty conclusion. Here the problem is that insufficient evidence is given, so that the argument is not fully supported.

Last night once again, vandals stole grave markers from our cemetery. This goes to prove how dangerous are the times.

7. Faulty analogy. Analogies are helpful comparisons because they explain an unknown in terms of a known. But make certain that the comparisons the analogy makes hold and are true. Going back to our domino theory example which suggest that if Vietnam falls to Communism, then the other nations of Asia will in turn fall, we have to ask:

1. Are the properties of dominoes similar to the properties of nations? and
2. How exactly do they differ and is this a problem for our analogy?

8. Oversimplification. Oversimplification is a bit like hasty conclusion, but oversimplification is concerned with arguing cause. In oversimplification, we label one thing the cause of something else based on insufficient incomplete evidence.

Poverty causes crime.

Poverty may well be a contributing cause of crime, but we all can come up with a counter example to the generalization, an instance of poverty in which no crime occurs. Suggesting that poverty causes crime oversimplifies the causal relationship.

A special kind of oversimplification is known by the Latin phrase *post hoc ergo propter hoc* (after this, therefore because of this). In this fallacy, we argue that A precedes B, so therefore, A causes B.

You wear your special blue suit and win the lottery that same day. To suggest that wearing the blue suit had anything to do with winning the lottery would be to suggest a causal relationship based on sequence, a *post hoc* fallacy.

Simple temporal sequence does not indicate cause.

When you write an argumentative essay, be certain to analyze your reasoning and review it for possible fallacies while your work is at the outline stage. Although this process may feel cumbersome at first, largely because we're not used to paying such particular attention to ideas and their relationships, after a while you will become adept at pointing out premises, spotting unstated or oversimplified ones, and recognizing fallacies.

Let's examine several fallacious reasoning examples in order to spot fallacies.

Example 1

How to Do the Telemark

To begin the Telemark, advance one ski into a snowplow well ahead of your body and steer it diagonally across the tip of the trailing ski. Although you steer with the front ski—and may apply more weight to it on packed slopes to bring the ski around quickly—your weight should fall evenly on both skis. The rear ski carves through the snow. The front knee, bent and driven forcefully into the turn, acts a moving fulcrum.

In Telemarking, the lead ski is like the front wheel of a bicycle; you turn the forward ski slightly in the direction you want to go. On a bike, your body weight is supported by both wheels, and the rear wheel follows virtually the same path as the front wheels. In Telemarking, again, weight both skis. Steer with the front-ski, carve with the rear, and imagine both skis working together as one ski to leave a continuous C-shaped pattern in the snow.

It helps many first-time Telemarkers to think of the forward knee leading the turn. On a gentle slope, to get a feeling for how the turn works, sink down and drive one knee and ski forward. This sounds confusing, but the knee of the forward leg should be over the ball of the foot and the knee of the trailing leg directly below your hip. Don't be tentative—drive that knee forward!

The problem here is the analogy (see p. 150) drawn between telemarking (a skiing technique) and bicycling. What are the similar properties? Are these outweighed by their differences?

Example 2

High School Social Clubs

There are several reasons why social clubs in high school ought to be abolished. In my high school, which I won't name, there were three classes of students: the bookworm, the boys who played sports, and the ones in social clubs.

The kids in the social clubs were the rich kids in school. Not real rich, but they had the money when we had a dance or a big party. They thought they were above the rest of the school because they belonged to the club and got to do things they kept secret, that is they thought they were secret. And so they spent all their time with themselves and didn't make good grades or have the fun of playing on any of the teams. And they spent so much time running around they didn't do their school work.

The athletes didn't have much time for school work either because they were always playing some sport in season. Our school was pretty small and so the same boys played on all the teams. But the athletes were not like the kids in the social clubs. They were making some contribution to the school when they played.

The bookworms didn't have time for athletics or running around. All they did was spend their time in the library or studying or working in the laboratory doing experiments. They were too interested in grades. That is the trouble with grades. Students get too involved in studying and miss getting a well rounded education.

But the worst thing about the social club was they were undemocratic and made people snobs. Like I said before, they thought they were above the rest of the students. Some kids who didn't think this way before they got in a social club started thinking it before long or got out of the club. This sort of thing doesn't belong in a democratic country. Some of the mothers and dads got mad about the way the kids in the club acted toward their kids. And there was talk of doing away with the clubs. They were still going strong last year and I guess they will this year too. One of these days some of those kids will see they are wrong. Some of them did last year and quit the club when they couldn't run around with some of their friends especially girls that were not in clubs.

This student essay, which incidentally, earned a grade of D, has several serious problems, but the major one is that it commits the *post hoc* fallacy (see p. 150).

Example 3

Let's Abolish Television

Let's abolish television because it may be a bad influence and may become a bad habit. Both adults and children may be influenced by the undesirable programs and commercials on television everyday.

While watching television we tend to forget about our homework and chores so they go undone. As a young child we sometimes deliberately stretch the truth to our parents about our homework in order to be permitted to watch a program we wish to see. We have stayed up half of the night to watch television and the next day we wake up tired, cranky, and unable to do our school work properly.

Many young people in trouble with the law may attribute their troubles to the bad influence of some television programs and commercials. There are many crime stories, murder mysteries, and horror movies on television. In almost all of these programs someone is either beat up or shot to death. These programs tend to give young people ideas and create poor illusions. Some people lose themselves in a western or murder mystery, to them it is no longer a story but something very real.

There are very few family programs on television. Most programs neglect to show any family love or concern. Instead they show hatred and killing. A few family programs that deal with family relations are "The Andy Griffith Show," "Hazel," and "The Dick Van Dyke" show. Unfortunately the undesirable programs far out number the family programs.

Some programs seem to suggest that the producer considers his audience uneducated or not very intelligent. There is no challenge for the audience of a show such as the "Red Skelton Show." It requires very little thought from its audience. It almost treats them as if they were not intelligent. With programs like this, television becomes a waste of time.

Commercials often have a bad influence on children because they advertise cigarettes and alcoholic beverages which are harmful for children. This type of commercial is so prevalent that it not at all unusual for a very small child to know all the words to such a commercial. Children's show commercials are different. They tempt children with such items as soda pop, bubble gum, tricks and the like as prizes included in certain foods. Then the children nag their parents to buy the product with the prize.

Until television programs have become more educational or portray a wholesome experience, it should be wise to abolish television.

This student essay earned a C grade, and one of its most basic problems is that it commits the fallacies of over-simplification (see p. 150) (TV causes us to forget our homework and chores) and hasty conclusion (that TV may be a bad influence leads to its abolition).

PERSUASION

We have been speaking about argumentation as if it were a wholly rational process. A moment's thought about particular cases in which we've been swayed will indicate that emotional appeal is often a factor in successfully convincing our reader to agree with our position. Establishing a common ground with our audience and appealing to their emotions may help, and this art is known as persuasion. Be careful because with persuasion comes the danger of provincialism. Prime Minister Nakasone encountered this problem:

> In the Fall of 1986 when in attempting to introduce an emotional element into Japan's argument on the world trade debate, he forgot who his audience was and explained American trade problems as a result of American mixed ethnic population. Nakasone-san was guilty of provincialism. His comments so provoked the American public that many of us responded emotionally. The force of Nakasone-san's rational argument, which had to do with the benefits of an homogeneous society, were completely overshadowed by American emotional response. His appeal overwhelmed reason, and the rational part of his argument was weakened. This is another danger of persuasion—it may weaken the rational argument.

1. Returning to our family vacation discussion, what emotional appeal might you use to persuade your family that a Maine vacation plan is best?
2. What combination of reason and persuasion would be most effective? Would you use the same combination in convincing your boss that you should have your vacation in late August?
3. Outline an argument, pro and con, on a controversial issue. Now review your argument for fallacies.
4. Choose one of the example essays and rewrite it, improving the reasoning and adding persuasion.

In a recent book, *No Contest: The Case Against Competition*, Alfie Kohn argues that competition is dysfunctional. The following adaptation summarizes his argument. When you review the article, note that it uses classification as a basic structure to outline the arguments, the four myths, and that the examples use narrative description, dynamic description, comparison and contrast, and cause and effect.

NO CONTEST
A case against competition

The tension between you and your spouse at breakfast this morning was part of a running argument about who is giving more in the relationship. A few hours later at the office you eye a colleague warily, wondering whether she will snatch that promotion from under your nose. Playing tennis after work, you are again amazed at how unrecognizable your closest friend seems on the court, because he will do anything to win. At home you find your child in tears: this afternoon at school she was eliminated from a spelling bee in the first round. That night on the evening news you hear about a medical researcher who admitted to fabricating his data so he could stay ahead.

Because these events take place in different arenas of our lives, it is easy to overlook their common denominator: competition. All reflect our culture's obsession with winning. Competition is so pervasive, in fact—infecting the workplace and the classroom, the playing field and the family—that many of us take it for granted, failing to notice its destructive consequences.

Competition can be defined as "mutually exclusive goal attainment": my success requires your failure; our fates are negatively linked. Put differently, two or more individuals are trying to achieve a goal that cannot be attained by both or all of them. The all-too-familiar pressure to be number one grows out of this arrangement. We have become accustomed to living with it and quick to defend it. We have been trained, in effect, not only to compete, but to believe there is value in doing so.

I have spent the last few years examining the arguments used to support competition and sorting through the evidence from various disciplines. My research has convinced me that these arguments are really myths—that competition is neither necessary nor desirable. In the order of their popularity, here are the four central myths of competition and what the research actually shows.

Myth 1: Competition Is Inevitable

As with a range of other unsavory behaviors, we are fond of casually attributing competition to something called "human nature." Since this account is so popular, you might expect that there is considerable evidence to support it. In fact, it is difficult to find a single serious defense of the claim—let alone any hard data to back it up. It is not difficult at all, however, to come up with reasons to *doubt* that competition is inevitable.

We in the United States often assume that our desperate quest to triumph over others is universal. But half a century ago Margaret Mead and her colleagues found that competition was virtually unknown to the

Zuni and Iroquois in North America and to the Bathonga of South Africa. Since then, cross-cultural observers have confirmed that our society is the exception rather than the rule. From the Inuit of Canada to the Tangu of New Guinea, from kibbutzniks in Israel to farmers in Mexico, cooperation is prized and competition generally avoided.

Working with seven- to nine-year-olds, psychologists Spencer Kagan and Millard Madsen found that Mexican children quickly figured out how to cooperate in an experimental game, while those from the United States could not. In fact, 78 percent of the Anglo-American children took another child's toy away "for apparently no other reason than to prevent the other child from having it." Mexican children did so only half as often.

Such findings strongly suggest that competition is a matter of social training and culture rather than a built-in feature of our nature. Further evidence comes from classroom experiments in which children have been successfully taught to cooperate. Gerald Sagotsky and his colleagues at Adelphi University, for example, trained 118 pairs of first-through third-grade students to work together instead of competing at a variety of tasks. Seven weeks later a new experimenter introduced a new game to these children and found that the lesson had stuck with them. Other researchers have shown that children taught to play cooperative games will continue to do so on their own time. And children and adults alike express a strong preference for the cooperative approach once they see firsthand what it is like to learn or work or play in an environment that does not require winners and losers.

Myth 2: Competition Keeps Productivity High and Is Necessary for Excellence

It is widely assumed that competition boosts achievement and brings out the best in us—that without it life would be "a bland experience" and we would become "a waveless sea of nonachievers," as Spiro Agnew once put it. Many people who make such claims, however, confuse success with competition—even though the two concepts are quite different. I can succeed in knitting a scarf or writing a book without ever worrying whether it is better than yours. Or I can work *with* you—say, to write a report or build a house.

Which method is more productive—competition or cooperation? The answer will take many by surprise. David and Roger Johnson, brothers who are educators at the University of Minnesota, recently analyzed 122 studies of classroom achievement conducted from 1924 to 1980. Sixty-five found that cooperation promotes higher achievement than competition, eight found the reverse, and thirty-six found no significant difference. One after another, researchers across the country have come to the same conclusion: Children do not learn better when education is transformed into a competitive struggle.

In the late '70s Robert Helmreich of the University of Texas at Austin and his colleagues decided to see whether this was also true in the "real world." They gave personality tests to 103 male scientists and found that those whose work was cited most often by their colleagues (a reasonable measure of achievement) were those who enjoyed challenging tasks but were not personally competitive. To make sure this surprising result wasn't a fluke, Helmreich conducted similar studies on businessmen, academic psychologists, undergraduates, pilots, and airline-reservation agents. Each time he found the same thing: a significant negative correlation between competitiveness and achievement.

On reflection, these results—and similar findings from scores of other studies in the workplace and the classroom—make perfect sense. First of all, trying to do well and trying to beat others really are two different things. A child sits in class, waving her arm wildly to attract the teacher's attention. When she is finally called on, she seems befuddled and asks, "Um, what was the question again?" Her mind is on edging out her classmates, not on the subject matter. These two goals often pull in opposite directions.

Furthermore, competition is highly stressful; the possibility of failure creates agitation if not outright anxiety, and this interferes with performance. Competition also makes it difficult to share our skills, experiences, and resources—as we can with cooperation.

All of this should lead us to ask hard questions not only about how we grade—or degrade—students and organize our offices, but also about the adversarial model on which our legal system is based and, indeed, about an economic system rooted in competition.

Myth 3: Recreation Requires Competition

It is remarkable, when you stop to think about it, that the American way to have a good time is to play (or watch) highly structured games in which one individual or team must triumph over another. Grim, determined athletes memorize plays and practice to the point of exhaustion in order to beat an opposing team—this is often as close as our culture gets to a spirit of play.

Children, too, are pitted against one another as they conduct serious business on Little League fields. Sports psychologist Terry Orlick observed that such activities often leave their mark on young participants. "For many children," he wrote, "competitive sports operate as a failure factory that not only effectively eliminates the 'bad ones' but also turns off many of the 'good ones'. . . . In North America it is not uncommon to lose from 80 to 90 percent of our registered organized-sports participants by fifteen years of age." Research in nonrecreational settings clearly shows that those who are not successful in initial competitions continue to perform poorly and drop out when given the chance.

Even the youngest children get the message, as is obvious from the game of musical chairs, an American classic. *X* number of players scramble for *X*-minus-one chairs when the music stops. Each round eliminates one player and one chair until finally a single triumphant winner emerges. Everyone else has lost and been excluded from play for varying lengths of time. This is our idea of how children should have fun.

Reflecting on the game, Orlick came up with an alternative: what if the players instead tried to squeeze onto fewer and fewer chairs until finally a group of giggling kids was crowded on a single chair? Thus is born a new game—one without winners and losers. The larger point is this: All games simply require achieving a goal by overcoming some obstacle. Nowhere is it written that the obstacle must be other people; it can be a time limit or something intrinsic to the task itself—so that no win-lose framework is required. We can even set up playful tasks so everyone works together to achieve a goal—in which case opponents become partners.

Myth 4: Competition Builds Character

Some people defend striving against others as a way to become "stronger." Learning how to win and lose is supposed to toughen us and give us confidence. Yet most of us sense intuitively that the consequences of struggling to be number one are generally unhealthy. As the anthropologist Jules Henry put it, "a competitive culture endures by tearing people down."

To a large extent, we compete to reassure ourselves that we are capable and basically good. Tragically, though, competing does nothing to strengthen the shaky self-esteem that gave rise to it. The potential for humiliation, for being exposed as inadequate, is present in every competitive encounter.

Trying to outperform others is damaging—first of all, because most of us lose most of the time. Even winning doesn't help, because self-esteem is made to depend on the outcome of a contest, whereas psychological health implies an *unconditional* sense of trust in oneself. Moreover, victory is never permanent. King of the Mountain is more than a child's game; it is the prototype for all competition, since winning promptly establishes one as the target for one's rivals. In any case, the euphoria of victory fades quickly. Both winners and losers find they need more, much like someone who has developed a tolerance to a drug.

Two sports psychologists, Bruce Ogilvie and Thomas Tutko, after studying some fifteen thousand athletes, could find no support for the belief that sport builds character. "Indeed, there is evidence that athletic competition limits growth in some areas," they concluded after recording depression, extreme stress, and relatively shallow relationships in competitors. Many players "with immense character strengths" avoid competitive sports, they found. Other research has found that competition leads people to look outside themselves for evidence of their self-worth. Cooperativeness, on the other hand, has been linked to emotional maturity and strong personal identity.

Perhaps the most disturbing feature of competition is the way it poisons our personal relationships. In the workplace, you may be friendly with your colleagues, but there is a guardedness, a part of the self held in reserve because you may be rivals tomorrow. Competition disrupts families, making the quest for approval a race and turning love into a kind of trophy. On the playing field it is difficult to maintain positive feelings about someone who is trying to make you lose. And in our schools students are taught to regard each other not as potential collaborators, but rather as opponents, rivals, obstacles to their own success. Small wonder that the hostility inherent in competition often erupts into outright aggression.

Ridding ourselves of the ill effects of rivalry is not an easy task. It is not enough to get rid of "excessive competition"—cheating and Vince Lombardi-style fanaticism—because the trouble lies at the very heart of competition itself. Instead of perpetuating an arrangement that allows one person to succeed only at the price of another's failure, we must choose a radically new vision for our society, one grounded in cooperative work and play.

But first we must leave the myths about competition behind us. Then we can work to change the institutions that define us as opponents and devise healthier, more productive alternatives.

Alfie Kohn
From *The New Age Journal*, October, 1986

1. Criticize Kohn's reasoning in this article. Do you find any fallacies?
2. Write an argumentative essay in response to Kohn's assertion, taking a clear stand in favor or opposed to it.
3. How does he use persuasion? Is he successful?

THE OTHER SIDE OF ISLAM

A gun, a beard and a chador do not make a good Muslim

The extreme and often violent Muslim groups that crop up in the world's trouble spots give an incorrect impression of Islam to the West. They worry the majority of traditional Muslims just as much. The few and simple essentials of Islam, says our Islam correspondent, are being obscured by views and actions that are not reflected in the Koran.

One way of putting it is to say that the militant Muslims insist on observances that in many cases are non-Islamic. The militantly Muslim male, for instance, is expected to wear a beard, whether it be the luxuriant growth of Ayatollah Khomeini or the chic, slim-line variety favoured by Saudi Arabia's Sheikh Yamani. Yet there is nothing in the Koran about beards. Of course, in almost all major religions a link seems to have been accepted between hairiness and holiness: only Buddhism has preferred the shaven face. In Islam one explanation offered for not shaving is that it is an imitation of Muhammed, who was bearded. But to imitate the personal characteristics of the Prophet, rather than his spiritual qualities, is a first step towards a Muhammedolatry which he would have been the first to condemn.

For militant Muslim males the most Islamic garb is supposed to be the long flowing robe, which is why it is worn by Islam's men of religion, the *ulema*, and by many over-zealous western converts, along with the skull cap and turban. The Koran says nothing about the male dress. It is simply an imitation of Arab practice, because Muhammed was an Arab. But the message of Muhammed is that Islam is a universal faith, valid for all humanity. So anything a believer may do to suggest that Islam has merely a regional character is anti-Islamic.

So too with women's clothing. There has been endless controversy over the interpretation, or rather the misinterpretation, of the verse in the Koran (XXIV, 31) which refers to feminine dress and behaviour:

> And tell the believing women to lower their gaze and be modest, and to display of their adornment only that which is apparent, and to draw their veils over their bosoms.

This cannot, by any canon of reason or commonsense, be interpreted to require the wearing of the tentlike *chador* or the *hijab*, the head-scarf. It was from the Persians that the Arabs borrowed these female fashions, as well as the idea of purdah, or the seclusion of women.

Another practice that also denies Islam's universality is the taking of Arab names by Muslims of all races, especially by converts. This custom is favoured by converts to other faiths, too, who are given Christian, Hindu or even Tibetan Buddhist personal names. The custom is, of course, non-Islamic. There are millions of Indonesian, Turkish and subcontinental Muslims with non-Arab names.

It may be said that these are non-essentials. But even some Koranic injunctions have been interpreted by the new enthusiasts in a non-Islamic way. No sooner had Muslim militants taken control last year of the towns of Tyre and Tripoli in Lebanon than it was decreed, "for the greater glory of Islam", that the weekly day of rest was to be changed from the Christian Sunday to the Muslim Friday. In fact the Koran rejects sabbatarianism and merely says that the midday prayer on Friday has a special communal significance and that work should stop for the time necessary to make attendance at prayer possible.

The Lebanese militants interpreted the Koran correctly in banning the public consumption of alcohol (its semi-clandestine sale is still allowed because Lebanon is a multi-religious state). This is certainly a Koranic injunction. There is no getting round it: a Muslim must be a teetotaller. Equally Koranic are the prohibitions of usury, gambling, eating pork and the making of images. The last of these vetoes is blatantly violated by those two most Islamic states, Iran and Saudi Arabia, with their stamps, official portraits and posters depicting their rulers.

The self-consciously Muslim governments are also most zealous in enforcing the severe seventh-century Arabian punishments for the Koranic crimes of theft, brigandage, adultery and apostasy, although in the Koran there is constant stress on the virtues of repentance and forgiveness, for God is "the compassionate, the merciful". It is the severing of the hands of thieves that, more than anything else, has made militant Islam appear cruel and anachronistic. As for the most horrific of the so-called canonical punishments, the stoning of adulterers, this is not even mentioned in the Koran.

There are perfectly sincere ways of mitigating the punishments: *Ijtihad*, or independent judgment, applied to *maslaha*, that which is beneficial, permits judges to choose the interpretation most conducive to human welfare. Using these principles, it became possible for reformers to argue that it would be just to cut off a thief's hand only in a society in which he did not have to steal in order to live. Similarly, it is surely not beneficial for the emotional health of a society for crowds to gloat over gory public choppings, whippings or beheadings.

There is a surprising degree of flexibility in Islam's system of moral judgments. The system is not one of black and white, of simple right and wrong. By Islamic custom, there are five categories of actions: the obligatory, the approved, the neutral, the disapproved and the prohibited. Doubtless the militant Muslims would not accept these realistic gradations. In all religions the zealots, those harking back to what they consider a state of past purity, seem to find it necessary to buttress their renewal of faith with negative proscriptions. Hence, perhaps, the importance given by Christian fundamentalists to such proscriptions.

For the Muslim the one and only source of guidance is the revelation of the Koran, and it is noteworthy that the legal provisions it lays down are only about a tenth of the whole. As well as the Koran there is the Hadith, the traditions of the acts and the non-revealed sayings of the Prophet, which were manufactured by the hundred thousand. Even after severe sifting, the "authoritative" collections of Hadith made by scholars contain several thousand examples, of which perhaps a few score may be accepted as authentic. In any case, authentic or not, no Hadith has scriptural sanction, which is why one Hadith has Muhammed saying, "Take from me only the Koran".

Five pillars of Islam

What, according to the Koran, are the essentials of Islamic belief and behaviour? There are five pillars of Islam. First is the affirmation of the faith, the *shehadah*, in the words, "There is no God but God and Muhammed is his prophet". Then there are the five daily prayers, and the fasting during daylight hours during the month of Ramadan. Numbers four and five are the Haj pilgrimage to the shrine of the Kaaba in Mecca and to the valley of Arafat outside Mecca, and the payment of the tax called *zakat*. Of these the *shehadah* is essential, for without making that affirmation no person can be a Muslim. But having made that affirmation, nobody can say, and only God can know, whether a person is or is not a Muslim.

Many Muslim reformers, looking for the inward spirituality of the faith, have said that the only permanent and indispensable factors in Islamic belief are the *shehadah*, the daily prayers and the Ramadam fast. Not the robes, not the turban or the veil, not the beard, not the Arab names, not the cruel punishments. Only those actions that are a product of a believer's direct, face-to-face relationship with the one and only God are essential: those that refer to relationships between people are not. In a revealing and damning statement of the militants' upside-down view, the Muslim zealots in Egypt denounced those for whom "prayer, the fast and the pilgrimage are all there is to Islam". They claimed it must also include the application of *sharia* Islamic law on divorce, alcohol, criminal punishments and so on.

In the Prophet's lifetime only three prayers a day were stipulated, a number later increased to five. Today three prayers a day is considered incomplete but acceptable. And while Muhammed gave importance to communal prayers in the mosque, especially those at midday on Friday, he said that the most valuable prayers were those made in the privacy of a room and in the believer's heart.

The true observance of the Ramadan fast, the third pillar, as a solemn reminder of the deprived lives of the poor and hungry, is very difficult nowadays. Children, travellers and the physically ailing are exempted from the fast. Many of those who do observe it overcompensate for the deprivation of the daylight hours by indulgence during the hours of darkness, if they can afford to.

Ramadan has become a time of jollification, with children permitted to stay up until all hours, joining "the fasters" in enjoying special Ramadan dishes, especially sweet preparations. The less fortunate, who do not need to be reminded of the deprivation of the poor, lose weight during Ramadan and become testy and short-tempered: the more fortunate "fasters" suffer from sleepiness and even a gain in weight. Ramadan is not the time to try to get any serious work done in Muslim countries.

Pilgrims all

The Haj, the fourth pillar, is much more truly observed. The pilgrimage should be undertaken only by those who can afford it and whose domestic obligations have been fulfilled. The Haj, which this writer has been privileged to witness, is essentially Islamic in two ways.

It is visible proof of the existence of the Muslim *umma*, the community of the faithful, which is now worldwide. It is visible proof, too, that membership of the *umma* of Islam cuts across the barriers of race and colour. Above all, during the Haj there is a renewal of the inward spirituality of the pilgrim's faith in a way that is singularly free, open and spontaneous. This is expressed in the pilgrim's cry, "*Labayk, allahuma, labayk*", "Here I am, O Lord, here I am". The most important ritual, the half-day of individual prayer and meditation during "the standing at Arafat", facing the rocky knoll of that name from where Muhammed preached his last sermon, emphasises the direct, face-to-face, relationship of the Muslim with God. The fifth pillar, the payment of *zakat*, a form of property tax, was firmly insisted on by the Prophet.

The components of the essential core of Islam—the Koran and the five pillars—are thus few. They could quite easily dominate the spiritual life of the believers. But do they? Because the Koran is the word of God, and was revealed in an Arabic of miraculous splendour, there has been a strong sentiment against translating it into other languages. This, plus the fact that the majority of the world's 1 billion

Muslims are illiterate, means that most Muslims cannot be really familiar with their holy text, though Koranic recitations on radio and television have helped to fill this gap in knowledge. The five daily prayers, spaced out through the day and night, are too onerous a duty for most Muslims.

However, because Muslims can, and do, pray anywhere, on a roadside, in a factory or an aeroplane, prayer comes easily to them. The turning towards Mecca for the prayer, and the knowledge that every praying Muslim turns in that direction, is a constant and powerful reminder of the unity of the *umma*.

There must be very few Muslims who, at some time in their lives, have not observed, with whatever limitations, the Ramadan fast. There must be just as few, even the most sceptical, who have not wished to perform the Haj: and, as the growing numbers of pilgrims indicate, 2m at last count, more and more Muslims are making the pilgrimage. While the average Muslim, in a personal way, is charitable enough, he does not pay *zakat* if he can possibly help it. Which is why President Zia ul Haq's government in Pakistan, in correct Islamic fashion, imposed it compulsorily and deducts it at source. Of all the Muslim governments, only Iran's and Pakistan's do this.

Revival, not militancy?

Some non-Muslim scholars, especially anthropologists, observing how the core of Islam has been coated by layers of local custom, belief and superstition, have argued that there is no such thing as Islam, or at least no one Islam but rather many Islams. But even if there is such a thing as Moroccan Islam or Indonesian Islam, there is also, underlying them, a common Islamic foundation provided by such events as the daily prayers, the Haj and the strong sense of solidarity in and with the Muslim *umma*.

Nevertheless, because the spiritual core of Islam is so stripped down, with the believer face-to-face with a God who is transcendental, this became a factor of weakness as well as of strength. The weakness arises because of the all-too-human need for a mediator between the human and the divine. Islam is almost too severely monotheistic. The Shias have accepted the mediating Imam, which the Sunnis, 90% of all Muslims, do not. But even the Sunnis have had to accept mediatory practices such as the worship of saints and membership of *tarikas*, or religious brotherhoods. Some of these Sufi are mystical; others are more mundane, and resemble Masonic lodges or even Rotary clubs.

Though the brotherhoods are omnipresent across the Islamic world, they are also Islam's best-kept secret. This back-sliding from Koranic Islam is, in practice, an inescapable and essential part of day-to-day popular Islam. Fortunately, in Islam today, besides the militants with their insistence on non-essentials, there are revivalists trying to produce good Muslims by emphasising the inward spiritual qualities of the faith.

The Tabligh movement, easily the largest and single most important group in the Islamic world, began in India but now has a global following. Its guiding principles are the profession of faith, knowledge and remembrance of God, kindness and respect for fellow-Muslims, sincerity of intention, and giving time and energy to spreading the faith. So long as such movements exist, and attract millions of Muslims, essential Islam remains alive and well.

From *The Economist*
February 15, 1986

1. "The Other Side of Islam" is presented as a counter-argument, almost a rebuttal, to a largely unexplored position. What is the "Other Side" other to?
2. Comment on the method of development in this essay.
3. Does the author use persuasive techniques? Are they successful?

Cross-discipline Essay Questions

1. International trade flows should be bilaterally reciprocal. In an essay, argue this assertion, agreeing or disagreeing.
2. Cultural style follows economic change. Do you agree with this assertion? Explain.
3. Good technical writing and good poetry are surprisingly similar. Given this assertion to be true, construct an argument for a new approach to the training of technical writers.
4. Marketing is mostly a waste of money, and inevitably it is the consumer's money which is wasted. Agree or disagree with this assertion, supporting your argument with what you have learned about marketing this term.
5. Euthanasia is a personal right. It should be protected, not obstructed, by the justice system.

A Student Example •

Nearly every student has, at least once, thrown out a perfectly good beginning paper either because of anxiety that somehow this work will never meet the instructor's standards or because the writer doesn't quite know how to rewrite and repair a flawed essay. How to revise and salvage a good start is a technique that everyone needs to learn.

The first step is to correct all the technical aspects of composition in the rewriting of the essay: grammar, punctuation, organization, and style. Such a revision may not be enough to change a "C" essay into an "A" but, of course, no essay is going to be acceptable without this vital step.

When you read this first draft of a student's essay, notice that although there are many real problems within it, the central idea is good. Like many essays, this composition is worth saving, but it needs *lots* of repair work before it will earn the grade that the topic could merit..

Human Greed

My visit to the Skeleton Cave will remain in my memory as an unforgettable experience. This sublime creation of nature possessed a delicate beauty. It also had irreparable damage, caused by man's greed.

The Skeleton Cave is located on the east coast of Spain a few minutes from the Mediterranean. The Cave is situated at the foot of a mountain named after it. The majestic entrance dominates the scene. It has multicolored petreous formations protruding in all directions except on the side where the cafe is located. This cafe is the first scar left by man in this inspiring sanctuary of beauty. It looks more like a hotdog stand in front of Buckingham palace.

Inside the Cave there are a souvenir shop and a small teller where the attendant sits. The attendant calls the attention of the tourists to pay the entrance fee. Once the fee is paid, the tourists pass through a set of curtains that are high enough to prevent them from having free looks at the inside. To the right of the curtains is the Skeleton. These fossilized bone fragments gave the name to the Cave. They look more like the ashtray of a southern fried chicken restaurant, since there is no way of telling fossils from cigarette butts.

A few yard inside the Cave all there was to be found was a poorly illuminated passage with some urine smelling rocks. The smell forced the tourists to reach for their handkerchiefs, if they could be found in the dark.

After the passage there was a gigantic room, where nature really excelled in the art of shaping and coloring rocks. In the same room man excelled in the art of spoiling nature with badly arranged lights and the mixture of smells from food preparations in the cafe, and from urine in the passage behind.

To the right of the room was what appeared to be the continuation of the

Cave. But the owner decided not to develop it any more. He installed heavy iron bars to block the access to the rest of the Cave.

The Cave has multicolored stones that give you the feeling of being in an immense gem. To see the light playing with the polished surfaces as it strikes them in different angles, makes you wonder about the spark of life itself. But to see the human greed and corruption inflicted in the Cave, makes you realize that it was not developed for the purpose of sharing that beauty, but for the purpose of making a profit. This act has ruined in a few years the millenial work of art of nature.

How to Revise "Human Greed"

First, read the essay to form your own opinions of it; then very carefully read through the two annotated versions that follow. Note what the instructor marked when grading the first effort, and then note the annotations on the first revision of the essay.

Then, ask yourself the following questions:

1. Is there a blocking-out pattern for "Human Greed" as it now stands? If you decide that the essay in its present form does not have any blocking-out structure to support it, create your own.
2. How would you develop the controlling idea in "Human Greed?"
3. Which cause and effect pattern would you employ to tighten the structure of the essay?
4. What dynamic details does the student use to create a sense of movement or action?
5. What details create static description in this essay?
6. Do you feel that the beginning and the ending are satisfactory? How would you introduce this subject? How would you conclude it?

Your investigation of how this paper was revised and changed will serve as a valuable guideline to help you learn how to revise your own work.

Instructor's First Comments

Human Greed

Indicate contrast — join sentences for fluency.

My visit to the Skeleton Cave will remain in my memory as an unforgettable

but had..

experience. This sublime creation of nature possessed a delicate beauty, ~~it also had~~

Contrast needs emphasis here, since whole essay hangs on this one idea

caused it

irreparable damage, ~~caused by~~ man's greed.

, walk? ride?

The Skeleton Cave is located on the east coast of Spain;a few minutes from the

Mediterranean. The Cave is ~~situated at~~ at the foot of a mountain named after it. The majestic entrance dominates the scene. It has multicolored petreous formations protruding in all directions except on the side where the cafe is located. This cafe is the first scar left by man in this inspiring sanctuary of beauty. It looks more like a hotdog stand in front of Buckingham palace.

Inside the Cave ~~there are a~~ souvenir shop ~~and~~ a small teller where the attendant sits. The attendant calls the attention of the tourists ~~to~~ pay the entrance fee. Once the fee is ~~paid,~~ the tourists pass through a set of curtains that are high enough to prevent them from having free looks at the inside. To the right of the curtains is the Skeleton. ~~These~~ fossilized bone fragments gave the name to the Cave. They look more like the ashtray of a southern fried chicken restaurant, since ~~there is no way of telling fossils from cigarette butts.~~

A few yard inside the Cave ~~all there was to be found was a~~ poorly illuminated passage with ~~some urine~~ smelling rocks. The smell forced the tourists to reach for their handkerchiefs, if they could be found in the dark.

After the passage ~~there was~~ a gigantic room, where nature really excelled in the art of shaping and coloring rocks. In the same room man excelled in the art of spoiling nature, ~~with~~ badly arranged lights and the mixture of smells from food preparations in the cafe, and from urine in the passage behind.

To the right of the room was what appeared to be the continuation of the Cave. But the owner decided not to develop it any more. He installed heavy iron bars to block the access to the rest of the Cave.

The Cave has multicolored stones that give you the feeling of being in an immense gem. To see the light playing with the polished surfaces as it strikes them in different angles, makes you wonder about the spark of life itself. But to see the human greed and corruption inflicted on the Cave, makes you realize that it was not developed for the purpose of sharing that beauty, but for the purpose of making a profit. This act has ruined in a few years the millenial work of art of nature.

• Instructor's Second Comments

After the student's English instructor marked this essay, this student revised and rewrote the essay using the suggestions and ideas that the instructor had given him. This new version was also graded and returned so that the student could see both progress and where polishing was still necessary.

Human Greed

My visit to Skelton Cave will be forever etched in my memory. Nature's sublime creation of this cave with its delicate and unusual beauty has been, however, sadly damaged by man's greed.

Skeleton Cave, on the east coast of Spain only a few minutes walk from the Mediterranean, lies at the foot of a glorious mountain named for the cave. Enormous, protruding multicolored rock formations form a majestic entrance to the cave and dominate the entire scene. Regrettably, the exterior of this awe-inspiring natural wonder is marred by a tawdry little cafe that seems as inconsistent with the natural beauty of the scene as would be a hotdog stand in front of Buckingham Palace.

Barely inside the cave is a sleazy little souvenir shop where the attendant hawkes his wares and like the carnival huckster cries out for tourists to pay their money and visit the cave. After paying an extortionate entance fee, the traveller is finally allowed to enter beyond the heavy striped curtains and pass through into the cave itself.

The skelton at the right of the curtained doorway is a collection of fossilized bone fragments and is the original source of the name of the cave. Unfortunately, like everything else about this cave, the bones, once a focal point of interest for a visitor, now seem more like the contents of an ashtray from a southern fried chicken truckstop. The priceless fossils are mixed with cigarette butts and gum wrappers.

As the tourists stumble along a poorly lighted passage toward the main cave, the stench of urine makes the visitors gag and fumble for their handkerchiefs to stifle their gorge that rises from their throats in response to the reeking aroma.

A gigantic room opens off the passage; here nature has excelled in the artistry of shaping and coloring rocks. Man, too, has excelled here, but in the art of spoiling beauty. Badly arranged and inadequate lighting prevents the tourists from seeing the glories of the cave, and nauseous smells of stale food preparation and urine make the air noxious and the atmosphere unbearable.

When the light strikes the gleaming multicolored stones of the inner room of Skeleton Cave, visitors often feel as if they are standing within the heart of a gem itself. The splendor of the light playing on the polished surfaces of the rocks may tempt the visitors to draw parallels between these beams of light and the spark of life. Unfortunately, all metaphysics is dimmed and dulled by the revolting evidences of man's vandalism. Perhaps materialism is the true skelton in this cave.

• The Finished Version

Finally after much rewriting, polishing, and reworking, the student turned in this finished version. Like so many things in life, the old cliche—"anything worth doing is worth doing well"—holds true. Good luck with your own writing and revisions!

Human Greed

Skeleton Cave is a sad reminder of man's greed. My memories of that sublime creation are haunted by the damages of grasping and destructive commercialism that human beings have inflicted on the cave's delicate and unusual beauty.

Skeleton Cave, on the east coast of Spain only a few minutes' walk from the Mediterranean, lies at the foot of a glorious mountain named for the cave itself. Enormous, protruding multicolored rock formations form a majestic entrance to the cave and dominate the entire scene. Sadly, the exterior of this awe-inspiring natural wonder is marred by a tawdry little cafe that seems as inconsistent with the natural beauty of the scene as would be a hotdog stand in front of Buckingham Palace.

Barely inside the cave is a sleazy little souvenir shop where the attendant hawks his wares and, like the carnival huckster, cries out for tourists to pay their money and to visit the cave. After paying an extortionate entrance fee, the traveller is finally allowed to enter beyond the heavy striped curtains and pass through into the cave itself.

The skeleton at the right of the curtained doorway, the original source of the name of the cave, is just a collection of fossilized bone fragments. Unfortunately, like everything else about this cave, the bones, once a focal point of interest for a visitor, now seem more like the contents of an ashtray from a southern fried chicken truckstop. The priceless fossils are intermixed with cigarette butts and gum wrappers.

As the tourists stumble along a poorly lighted passage toward the main cave, the stench of urine makes the visitors gag and fumble for their handkerchiefs to stifle their gorge that rises from their throats in response to the reeking aroma.

A gigantic room opens off the passage; here nature has excelled in the artistry of shaping and coloring rocks. Man, too, has excelled here, but in the art of spoiling beauty. Badly arranged and inadequate lighting prevents the tourists from seeing the glories of the cave, and nauseous smells of stale food preparation and urine make the air noxious and the atmosphere unbearable.

At intervals, when the light strikes the gleaming, multicolored stones of the inner room of Skeleton Cave, visitors feel as if they are somehow standing within the heart of a gem itself. The splendor of the light playing on the polished surfaces of the rocks may tempt the visitors to draw parallels between these beams of light and the spark of life. Unfortunately, all metaphysical wonderings are dimmed and dulled by the revolting evidences of man's vandalism. Perhaps materialism is the true skeleton in this cave.